Methods and Procedures for the Verification and Validation of Artificial Neural Networks

Methods and Procedures for the Verification and Validation of Artificial Neural Networks

edited by

Brian J. Taylor
Institute for Scientific Research, Inc.
Fairmont, WV, USA

 Springer

Brian J. Taylor
Institute for Scientific Research, Inc.
320 Adams Street
Fairmont, WV 26555-2720
USA
btaylor@isr.us

*METHODS AND PROCEDURES FOR THE VERIFICATION AND
VALIDATION OF ARTIFICIAL NEURAL NETWORKS*
Edited by Brian J. Taylor
Institute for Scientific Research, Inc.

ISBN-13: 978-1-4419-3935-7

e-ISBN-13: 978-0-387-29485-8

Printed on acid-free paper.

Printed in the United States of America.

springeronline.com

Contents

vi

Contributing Authors

Brian J. Taylor
Marjorie A. Darrah
Laura L. Pullum
Kareem Ammar
James T. Smith
Spiro T. Skias
Institute for Scientific Research, Inc., Fairmont, WV

Bojan Cukic
Sampath K. Yerramala
Martin Mladenovski
Lane Dept. of CSEE, West Virginia University, Morgantown, WV

Edgar J. Fuller
Dept. of Mathematics, West Virginia University, Morgantown, WV

Preface

Artificial neural networks are a form of artificial intelligence that have the capability of learning, growing, and adapting within dynamic environments. With the ability to learn and adapt, artificial neural networks introduce new potential solutions and approaches to some of the more challenging problems that the United States faces as it pursues the vision of space exploration. For instance, one of the areas of potential problems is in air and ground vehicle control. To be successful on manned missions to Mars and the Moon, intelligent adaptive systems, such as neural networks, may be needed to assist in crew operations to accommodate an ever changing environment. The major obstacle to deploying such highly complex systems is the verification and validation of these systems.

The need is being recognized by organizations such as NASA, that the supporting function of verification and validation must be brought to bear for neural network systems to gain the necessary acceptance within their respective problem domains. As the facility responsible for assuring software safety, reliability, and quality of programs and missions, the NASA Independent Verification and Validation (IV&V) Facility will be increasingly challenged to certify and evaluate software systems that contain neural network technologies. The NASA IV&V Facility has recognized the need and importance of neural network technology as it is becoming more feasible for use in future space applications. To address this need, the NASA IV&V Facility sponsored the Institute for Scientific Research, Inc. (ISR) under Research Grant NAG5-12069 through the NASA Goddard Space Flight Center, to research and develop methodologies for the independent verification and validation of artificial neural networks.

This book is a result of three years of research conducted for the NASA IV&V Facility and examines some of the more promising methods and procedures for the verification and validation of artificial neural networks and adaptive systems. This book does not endorse artificial neural networks as the perfect solution, but instead disseminates the methods and procedures for verifying and validating these highly complex systems so that they can be used in safety-critical and mission-critical applications. The methods and procedures presented in this book were chosen because of their applicability, technology maturity level, technical feasibility, and usability in the verification and validation of neural networks.

The NASA IV&V Facility is working to be at the forefront of software safety and assurance for major NASA programs. This book is an excellent tool for preparing NASA IV&V and other V&V practitioners to assure neural network software systems for future NASA missions.

Mr. Nelson Keeler

Director, NASA Independent Verification and Validation Facility

Acknowledgments

The research described in this book was sponsored by NASA Goddard Flight Research Center through the NASA Independent Verification & Validation (IV&V) Facility, under Research Grant NAG5-12069. The NASA IV&V Facility greatly contributed to the successful completion of this project. Special thanks should be given to Markland Benson, Christina Moats, Ken McGill, and Nelson Keeler for their support, technical direction, and suggestions throughout the project.

Special mention should be given to NASA Dryden Flight Research Center and NASA Ames Research Center whose previous and ongoing research in this area has been a motivating influence on this work.

Acknowledgment

Chapter 1

BACKGROUND OF THE VERIFICATION AND VALIDATION OF NEURAL NETWORKS

Spiro T. Skias
Institute for Scientific Research, Inc.

1. INTRODUCTION

This book is an introduction to the methods and procedures that have proven to be successful for the verification and validation (V&V) of artificial neural networks used in safety-critical or mission-critical applications. Although the methods and procedures discussed are oriented toward artificial neural networks, some of them have also shown to be usable for V&V of generic adaptive artificial intelligent systems. Throughout this book, an example of a safety-critical and mission-critical intelligent flight control system is used to demonstrate the applicability of the presented methods and procedures. This chapter provides a brief introduction to artificial neural networks, verification and validation, and an overview of the Intelligent Flight Control Systems (IFCS) project, which was used as the test scenario for the methods and procedures in this book.

1.1 What are Artificial Neural Networks?

An *artificial neural network*, or simply *neural network*, is a type of artificial intelligence (computer system) that attempts to mimic the way the human brain processes and stores information. It works by creating connections between mathematical processing elements, called *neurons*. Knowledge is encoded into the network through the strength of the connections between different neurons, called *weights*, and by creating groups, or *layers*, of neurons that work in parallel. The system learns through a process of determining the number of neurons or *nodes* and adjusting the weights for the connections based upon training data. In supervised learning, the training data is composed of input-output pairs. A neural network tries to find a function which, when given the inputs, produces the outputs. Through repeated application of training data, the network then approximates a function for that input domain. There are two main types of neural networks, *fixed* (non-adaptive), and *dynamic* (adaptive).

Fixed neural networks, sometimes referred to as Pre-Trained Neural Networks (PTNN), are those that have undergone training and then become set. The internal structure of the network remains unchanged during operation. After training is complete, all weights, connections, and node configurations remain the same, and the network reduces to a repeatable function. A common use of a fixed neural network might be a classification system to identify malformed products on a manufacturing line where the definition of an undesirable characteristic would not change and the network would be expected to perform the same classification repeatedly.

Dynamic neural networks, sometimes referred to as Online Learning Neural Networks (OLNN), are never fixed in that the system continues to develop throughout its life. An OLNN is continuously adapting to current data, changing its internal structure of neurons and weights. OLNNs are employed in situations where a system must learn new information while in use. This is useful where unforeseen scenarios occur, such as aircraft failures, or when input domains change over time, such as stock market analysis.

1.2   Historical Highlights of Artificial Neural Network Development

The origin of artificial neural networks stems from research of the human brain. The basic component of the brain, the neuron, was discovered in 1836. In addition to a nucleus, the neuron cell has two specialized appendages: dendrites, which receive impulses from other neurons, and an axon to carry signals to other neurons. The gap between dendrites and axons is called a synapse as shown in Fig. 1-1.

Functionally, the neuron acts as a multi-input/single-output unit. A single neuron can have several neighbors connect to it and bring in electrical signals across the synapses and through the dendrites while it alone can connect to one other neuron via the axon. Within the brain, all of the neurons connect to one other via, and work together in, what can be considered a network of neural cells.

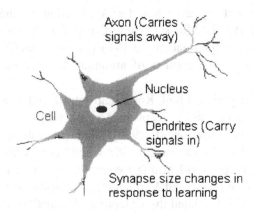

Axon (Carries signals away)

Nucleus

Cell

Dendrites (Carry signals in)

Synapse size changes in response to learning

Figure 1-1. Diagram of a Biological Neuron

The neuron performs a summation of the electrical signals arriving at its dendrites. This summation is compared against a threshold to determine if the neuron shall excite (referred to as firing), resulting in a generation of a signal to the dendrite of another neuron. In the late 19th century, input signals into a neuron were found to be subject to attenuation in the synapses, meaning the synapses helped to control the strength of the electrical signal passed into the neuron.

The modern era of neural network research and development began with the classic work of W.S. McCulloch, a psychiatrist and neuroanatomist, and W. Pitts, a mathematical prodigy, associated with the University of Chicago. With their classic 1943 paper, "A Logical Calculus of the Ideas Immanent in Nervous Activity," they united the fields of neurophysiology and mathematical logic [McCulloch 1943]. In particular, they showed that a model of a biological neural network could, in principle, calculate any computable function.

In 1949, Donald Hebb, a psychologist at McGill University in Canada, published a novel postulate of neural learning: the effectiveness of a synapse to transfer a signal between two neurons is increased by repeated activation across that synapse [Hebb 1949]. This theory, also known as "Hebb's Rule," explained the physiological concept of synaptic modification, the increase or decrease of a neuron's response to electrical stimulus. This corresponds to the use of weighted connections between the neurons of an artificial neural network and gave rise to the use of techniques in adjusting these weights during learning.

Hebb's work influenced Marvin Minsky, who would later go on to found the MIT Artificial Intelligence Laboratory in 1959. While a student at Princeton in 1954, Minsky developed his thesis on "Theory of Neural-

Analog Reinforcement Systems and Its Application to the Brain-Model Problem" [Minsky 1954]. Minsky's book *Computation: Finite and Infinite Machines* [Minsky 1967] extended the 1943 results of McCulloch and Pitts by explaining them in the context of automata theory and the theory of computation.

During this same period, Frank Rosenblatt introduced as a new approach to pattern recognition, the perceptron, culminating in his perceptron convergence theorem [Rosenblatt 1960]. The perceptron represented a significant step over previous attempts at artificial neural networks because it introduced the idea of auto-learning frequently occurring patterns. In the same year, Bernard Widrow and Marcian Hoff introduced the least mean-square algorithm and formulated the ADaptive LINear Element (ADALINE) [Widrow 1960]. The ADALINE network used weighting on the inputs into a neuron for pattern classification; it also could take continuous data instead of the predominantly binary inputs used by other networks, including the perceptron.

But even with these new emerging network architectures, the research field was about to collapse. In their book "Perceptrons" [Minsky 1969], Minsky and Seymour Papert mathematically demonstrated some fundamental limitations on single-layer networks like the perceptron. They also expressed their doubt that multi-layer versions could overcome them. These limitations deflated the hype surrounding the great potential of neural network technology and led to the decline of continued funding for neural network research across the next couple decades (i.e. the Dark Ages. in Fig. 2-1).

Even though interest in neural networks waned, there were several researchers still working actively in the field. In the 1970s, von der Malsburg [von der Malsburg 1973] introduced the Self-Organizing Map (SOM). Later, with D.J. Willshaw [Willshaw 1976], he further developed an association of SOMs with topologically ordered maps in the brain. Then in 1980, Grossburg built upon this with a new principle of self-organization known as adaptive resonance theory (ART), which basically involves a bottom-up recognition layer and a top-down generative layer [Grossburg 1980]. Later, in 1982, Tuevo Kohonen introduced the development of SOMs based on one- or two-dimensional lattice structures [Kohonen 1982].

In 1982, J.J. Hopfield introduced the use of an energy function in formulating a new way of understanding the computation performed by recurrent networks with symmetric synaptic connections [Hopfield 1982]. This new perspective, based on energy principles, resulted in attracted many researchers from other scientific disciplines, such as physics, to explore and contribute to the field of neural networks. The Hopfield paper also was the first to explicitly make the case for storing information in dynamically stable networks.

In 1983, Kirkpatrick, Gelatt, and Vecchi [Kirkpatrick 1983] introduced a new principle for solving combinatorial optimization problems called simulated annealing, which is rooted in statistical mechanics. Building upon this approach, Ackley, Hinton, and Sejnowski [Ackley 1985] developed a stochastic machine known as the Boltzmann machine, which was the first successful realization of a multilayer neural network. This work with the Boltzmann machine provided the foundation for the linking of neural networks to belief networks [Pearl 1988] and, in particular, for the development of sigmoid belief networks by Neal [Neal 1992].

In 1986, D.E. Rumelhart and J.L. McClellan, in their monumental two-volume work *Parallel Distributed Processing: Explorations in the Microstructure of Cognition* [Rumelhart 1986], introduced the back-propagation algorithm, which has emerged as the most widely used learning algorithm for training multilayer perceptrons.

In 1988, D.S. Broomhead and D. Lowe introduced an alternative to multilayer perceptrons with their layered feed-forward networks based on radial basis functions (RBF). This work has led to significant efforts to link the design of neural networks to the areas of numerical analysis methods and linear adaptive filters [Broomhead 1988].

For a more comprehensive historical analysis of significant achievements in the field of neural networks, the reader is referred to the "Historical Notes" section at the end of Chapter 1 in Simon Haykin's *Neural Networks: A Comprehensive Foundation* [Haykin 1999].

1.3   Neural Network Applications

NASA [DFRC 2004], the Department of Defense (DoD) [Johnson 2002], the Department of Energy (DOE) [Basher 2003], the Federal Aviation Administration (FAA) [Steck 2003], the Food and Drug Administration (FDA) [Rodvold 2001], and private companies such as Goodrich Aerospace [6] are currently considering approving neural networks for use in mission- and safety-critical systems. These agencies are encountering neural networks being utilized in applications such as flight control systems, medical devices, and process management systems. These high assurance neural network applications require rigorous verification and validation techniques. Given that traditional techniques are not entirely suitable for the V&V of neural networks, new and practical techniques and supporting tools must be developed.

One application of particular interest is the Intelligent Aircraft. There are several organizations investigating the use of neural networks in aircraft, though the majority of this work remains in the realms of research and experimental aircraft. The trend for this type of technology has been to start within research, apply the concepts to military vehicles, and then finally transition the use of new technology to commercial aircraft. An excellent example of this trend is the Intelligent Flight Control Systems (IFCS) Project being conducted at the NASA Dryden Flight Research Center (DFRC).

1.3.1   Intelligent Flight Control Systems

The IFCS Project is a collaborative effort among the NASA DFRC, the NASA Ames Research Center (ARC), Boeing Phantom Works, ISR, and West Virginia University (WVU).

The goal of the IFCS Project is to develop and flight-demonstrate a flight control concept that can efficiently identify aircraft stability and control characteristics using neural networks, and utilize this information to optimize aircraft performance in both normal and simulated failure conditions. A secondary goal is to develop the processes to verify and validate neural networks for use in flight-critical applications. The flight project results will be utilized in an overall strategy aimed at advancing neural network flight control technology to new aerospace systems designs including civil and military aircraft, reusable launch vehicles, uninhabited vehicles, and space vehicles.

The intelligent flight control system was first tested in flight on the NASA F-15 Advanced Control Technology for Integrated Vehicles (ACTIVE) aircraft. This aircraft, shown in Fig. 1-2, has been highly modified from a standard F-15 configuration to include canard control surfaces, thrust vectoring nozzles, and a digital fly-by-wire flight control system. The use of canard surfaces, along with simulated *stuck* stabilator deflections allows the IFCS program to simulate different actuator failures during flight.

Two types of neural networks make up the components to the first generation (GEN1) intelligent flight control scheme. A pre-trained neural network component provides the baseline approximation of the stability and control derivatives of the aircraft. This neural network is composed of 34 separate multilayer perceptrons, with some of the networks' outputs combined to form the derivatives. The networks were trained with two different training techniques: a modification of Active Selection and the Levenberg-Marquardt algorithm. The second neural network integrated into the GEN1 intelligent flight control system is a highly advanced neural network called a Dynamic Cell Structure (DCS). The DCS is a member of a group of neural networks known as self-organizing maps (SOMs). The DCS algorithm, implemented in the GEN1 system by NASA ARC Jorgensen

[1997], was originally developed by Bruske and Sommer [1994] and is a derivative of work by Fritzke [1994] combined with competitive Hebbian learning by Martinez [1993].

Figure 1-2. NASA IFCS Project F-15 ACTIVE Aircraft

Flight tests of the online learning network will demonstrate a flight control mode for a damaged fighter or transport aircraft that can return the aircraft safely to base.

Since ensuring pilot and aircraft safety along with overall mission success is a success criterion for this program, each of the participating organizations contributed toward the development of a V&V guide [Mackall 2002], "Verification and Validation of Neural Networks for Aerospace Systems." This guide was written to assist NASA DFRC in the development of research experiments that use neural networks. It is a first approach toward extending existing V&V standards to cover fixed and adaptive neural networks.

1.4   Verification and Validation

Before software finds its way into safety-critical applications, users of these systems must be assured of highly reliable operation. In non-critical systems, failure may result in loss of work, profits, or mere inconvenience. In systems where high reliability is a requirement, failures can result in massive destruction of loss of human life.

One industry with a high reliability/low failure requirement is aviation. Civilian airliners require highly reliable systems to transport millions of passengers daily. The Federal Aviation Administration, the ruling authority in the U.S., has mandated a failure rate of less than 10-9/hour as the acceptable occurrence of failures within aircraft systems. This means that for every billion hours (roughly 114,000 years) of operation, only one failure should occur.

Other industries with high demand for reliability have adopted similar guidelines for acceptable failure rates. Requirements for monitoring systems for nuclear power plants are 10^{-4} failures per hour of operation. The telephone industry commonly cites a limit of 10^{-5} failures per hour (Customers expect flawless operation from their telephone service provider, so the failure rate is set even higher than the nuclear power industry guidelines). Phone service should not be interrupted more than two minutes per year, though experience says this is difficult to achieve.

One way to assess the correctness and reliability of a software project is to utilize the practices of verification and validation. V&V methods attempt to answer two questions concerning the entire software lifecycle of a project:

Verification: Is the product being built right?
Validation: Is the right product being built?

Verification looks at the end result of the software development process and evaluates the correctness of the software. It seeks to answer questions concerning the adequacy of the processes that went into the system development. Verification also analyzes the outcome of tests conducted on the system that result in metrics that measure the system's expected reliability.

Validation examines the system from a different perspective. Given the original intended uses and needs for the system, and all of the changes and modifications made to those specifications during the software development, does the end product still fulfill those requirements? Validation seeks to ensure that all requirements are met throughout the development of the system. These can include statements on system reliability, failure rates, and other issues important in safety-critical systems.

The software lifecycle can be separated into several stages: concept, requirements, design, implementation, testing, operation, and maintenance. Due to the visibility of the results from testing, a common misconception is that V&V occurs only during the testing. However, to be adequate in any kind of system development each stage must contain its own assurance practices.

The Institute of Electrical and Electronics Engineers published IEEE Standard 1012-1998 (and 1012a-1998) to provide a V&V template for software developers. The IEEE Standard for Software Verification and

Validation can be used across all processes, activities, and tasks of the software lifecycle. The standard identifies key activities that can be conducted within each stage, such as documentation and assessments of risks, hazards, and requirements traceability from stage to stage.

Current V&V techniques, including those described within the IEEE standard, are not well equipped to handle adaptive systems like neural networks. The use of neural networks, especially within safety-critical systems, has been increasing over the past 15 years because they prove very useful in systems that contain ill-defined non-linear functions.

Instead of being programmed and designed in a traditional sense, neural networks are "taught" using a learning algorithm and a set of training data. Because of their adaptation, neural networks are considered a "black box". Its response may not be predictable or well defined within all regions of the input space.

Of particular concern is the trustworthiness and acceptability of dynamic neural networks that continue to adapt or evolve after the system is deployed. While some OLNNs may be given a priori knowledge of their input domain, the adaptation that they undergo offers no guarantee that the system is stable or continues to meet the original objectives.

The V&V technique commonly applied to neural networks is brute force testing. This is accomplished by the repeated application of training data, followed by an application of testing data to determine whether the neural network is acceptable. Some systems may undergo intensive simulations at the component level and perhaps at the system level as well. However, these may be no better than "best guesses" toward a system analysis.

In assessing a safety-critical neural network system, a V&V expert must know what to look for with a neural network and how to analyze the results. Many questions face the analyst regarding the network's implementation:

- Has the network learned the correct data, or has it learned something else that correlates closely to the data?
- Has the network converged to the global minimum or a local minimum?
- How will the network handle situations when data is presented to it outside of the training set or unique from previous training data?
- Is there a quantifiable metric to describe the network's "memory" or data retention?
- Is the network making use of the right set of input parameters for the problem domain?

One oft-cited story [Skapura 1996] recounts a neural network pattern recognition system that was being developed for the army to identify the presence of enemy tanks. Once trained, the system appeared to work perfectly, able to identify tanks in the testing samples and in a completely separate data set. When taken to the field, however, the system failed. After analysis, it was discovered that the system was actually identifying qualities of the pictures it was being presented with: every photo in the test set that had a tank hidden within it was taken on a cloudy day; coincidentally, every photo without a tank was taken on a clear day. The system had learned to identify cloudy skies and not tanks. This bias had been undetected.

It is stories like this that push the software industry to establish V&V for neural network processes. As the development of neural networks is often considered more of an art form than a science, so too might it be said about V&V of neural networks. Like the IEEE standard, developers need well-defined practices that they can use in their own systems.

2.   SUMMARY

This book is an introduction to the methods and procedures that have proven to be successful for the V&V of artificial neural networks used in safety-critical or mission-critical applications.

There are two types of neural networks discussed in this book, fixed (non-adaptive) and dynamic (adaptive). Fixed neural networks are trained before deployment and do not change. Dynamic neural networks learn during deployment.

Artificial neural networks stem from research of the human brain. Neural networks are made up of neurons (or nodes), connections, weights, and layers. The first development of experimental artificial neural networks dates back to 1943 with research conducted by W.S. McCulloch. Since then, neural networks have made their way into safety-critical and mission-critical applications, such as intelligent flight control.

V&V is the formal process by which to test and examine a system for dependability, reliability, and assurance. Verification tries to answer the question "Is the product being built right?" Validation tries to answer the question "Is the right product being built?"

The methods and procedures presented in this book have been evaluated on a real-world intelligent flight control application for the IFCS project at NASA DFRC. The IFCS project uses adaptive neural networks to control and stabilize an F-15 research aircraft in catastrophic conditions for pilot assistance.

REFERENCES

Ackley, D.H., G.E. Hinton, and T.J. Sejnowski. 1985. A Learning Algorithm for Boltzmann Machines. *Cognitive Science* 9:147-169.

Basher, H. and J. S. Neal. 2003. Autonomous Control of Nuclear Power Plants. Report ORNL/TM-2003/252. Prepared by Oak Ridge National Laboratory for U.S. Department of Energy.

Broomhead, D.S. and D. Lowe. 1988. Multivariable Functional Interpolation and Adaptive Networks. *Complex Systems* 2:321-355.

Bruske, Jorg and Gerald Sommer. 1994. Dynamic Cell Structures. *In Proceedings of Neural Information Processing Systems (NIPS)*, 497-504.

Dryden Flight Research Center. 2004. Intelligent Flight Control System Project Summary. http://www.nasa.gov/centers/dryden/news/FactSheets/FS-076-DFRC.html

Fritzke, B. 1994. Growing Cell-Structures – a Self-Organizing Network for Unsupervised and Supervised Learning. *Neural Networks.* 7(9): 1441-1460.

Grossburg, S. 1980. How does a brain build a cognitive code? Psychological Review, 87:1-5.

Haykin, S.. 1999. Neural Networks: A Comprehensive Foundation. Second edition. New York: MacMillan Publishing.

Hebb, D.O. 1949. The Organization of Behavior: A Neurophysiological Theory. New York: Wiley.

Hopfield, J.J. 1982. Neural Networks and Physical Systems with Emergent Collective Computational Abilities. *In Proceedings of the National Academy of Sciences.* 81:3088-3092.

Johnson, E.N. and Kannan, S.K. 2002. Adaptive Flight Control for an Autonomous Unmanned Helicopter. *Proceedings of the AIAA Guidance, Navigation, and Control Conference.*

Jorgensen, Charles C. 1997. Direct Adaptive Aircraft Control Using Dynamic Cell Structure Neural Networks. NASA Technical Memorandum 112198, NASA Ames Research Center.

Kirkpatrick, S., C.D. Gelatt, and M.P. Vecchi. 1983. Optimization of simulated annealing. Science, 220:671-680.

Kohonen, T. 1982. Self-Organized Formation of Topologically Correct Feature Maps. *Biological Cybernetics.* 43:49-59.

Mackall, Dale; Stacy Nelson; and Johann Schumman. 2002. Verification and Validation of Neural Networks for Aerospace Systems. NASA Dryden Flight Research Center and NASA Ames Research Center. June 12.

Martinetz, T. M. 1993. Competitive Hebbian Learning Rule Forms Perfectly Topology Preserving Maps. *In Proceedings of International Conference on Artificial Neural Networks (ICANN)* 427-434. Amsterdam: Springer.

McCulloch, W.S. and W. Pitts. 1943. A logical calculus of the ideas immanent in nervous activity. Bulletin of Mathematical Biophysics 5:115-133.

Minsky, M.L. 1954. Theory of neural-analog reinforcement systems and its application to the brain-model problem. Ph.D. thesis, Princeton University, Princeton, NJ.

Minsky, M.L. 1967. Computation: Finite and Infinite Machines. Englewood Cliffs, NJ: Prentice-Hall.

Minsky, M.L., and S.A. Papert. 1969. Perceptrons. Cambridge, MA: MIT Press.

Neal, R.M. 1992. Connectionist learning of belief networks. *Artificial Intelligence* 56:71-113.

Pearl, J. 1988. Probabilistic reasoning in intelligent systems. San Mateo, CA: Morgan-Kaufmann.

Rodvold, David M. 2001. Validation and Regulation of Medical Neural Networks. *Molecular Urology* 5 (4):141-145.

Rosenblatt, F. 1960. On the convergence of reinforcement procedures in simple perceptrons. Cornell Aeronautical Laboratory Report, VG-1196-G-4, Buffalo, NY.

Rumelhart, D.E. and J.L. McClelland, eds., 1986, Parallel Distributed Processing: Explorations in the Microstructure of Cognition, Vol. 1 & 2, Cambridge, MA: MIT Press.

Skapura, David M. and Peter S Gordon. 1996. Building Neural Networks. Addison-Wesley.

von der Malsburg, C. 1973. Self-organization of Orientation Sensitive Cells in the Striate Cortex. *Kybernetik* 14:85-100.

Steck, James E., Kamran Rokhsaz, U. J. Pesonen, Sam Bruner, and Noel Duerksen. 2003. Simulation and Flight Test Assessment of Safety Benefits and Certification Aspects of Advanced Flight Control Systems. Report DOT/FAA/AR-03/51 prepared for the Department of Transportation, Federal Aviation Administration.

Widrow, B. and M.E. Hoff, Jr. 1960. Adaptive Switching Circuits. IRE WESCON Convention Record. 96-104.

Willshaw, D.J. and C. von der Malsburg. 1976. How Patterned Neural Connections Can be Set up by Self-Organization. *In Proceedings of the Royal Society of London Series B* 194:431-445.

Chapter 2

AUGMENTATION OF CURRENT VERIFICATION AND VALIDATION PRACTICES

Kareem Ammar, Laura Pullum, Brian J. Taylor
Institute for Scientific Research, Inc.

1.   INTRODUCTION

Many agencies, including the NASA IV&V Facility use the IEEE Standard for Software Verification and Validation (IEEE 1012-1998) [IEEE 1998] as a basis for verification and validation (V&V) activities. Standards like IEEE 1012-1998 are sufficient for traditional software development, but are inadequate for adaptive systems that can change their implementation and behavior over time. Faults may manifest themselves because of autonomous changes and this may introduce problems that were not present during design or testing.

Given the fault handling and other capabilities of neural networks, their use in the control systems of advanced avionics, aeronautics and other safety- and mission-critical systems is seriously being pursued. Along with the capabilities come challenges in the verification and validation (V&V) of these systems, as well as the need for V&V practitioner guidance. Neural networks that continue to learn while the system is in operation require additional steps for proper software assurance.

This chapter highlights research that was performed to determine the gaps in the traditional standards and guidelines for performing V&V when applying them to adaptive neural network systems. Previous work in the area of guidance for the V&V of neural network systems consisted primarily of efforts by NASA Ames Research Center and NASA Dryden Flight Research Center [Mackall 2002, 2003]. The NASA reports provide valuable inputs into what should be done to verify and validate adaptive aerospace systems. The authors of these reports align their guidance with the ISO/IEC

12207 [IEEE/EIA 1998], a standard that addresses the implementation of general software lifecycle processes, and offer guidance specific to adaptive aerospace systems.

Based on the research described in this chapter, the Institute for Scientific Research, Inc. (ISR) has developed a comprehensive guidance document [ISR 2005] aligned with the IEEE 1012-1998 to assist the V&V practitioner in evaluating general neural network systems. The goal of the guidance document is to provide relevant and applicable guidance for the V&V practitioner when faced with an adaptive system with a neural network component. This chapter will discuss the approach to the research, gaps found in the V&V standards when faced with a neural network system to V&V, and several augmentations to V&V processes to satisfy these gaps. Specifically, V&V methods are described in this chapter that address adaptive system requirements, neural network software requirements, neural network design, enhanced configuration management, modified lifecycle models, and neural network testing.

1.1   Combining Previous Research and Standards

In order to identify what needed to be done to augment current practices to accommodate the V&V of neural networks, current standards and practices were examined. The documents examined during the research for this chapter included: IEEE 1012-1998, the IEEE ISO/IEC 12207, the NASA Ames and Dryden reports, and a sample software verification and validation plan (SVVP). (Note that before the release of this book the IEEE 1012 – 2004 became available. The guidance document produced from this research remains applicable to the majority of this updated standard.)

The first step in the research approach was to create a mapping between the ISO/IEC 12207 to IEEE 1012-1998. This bi-directional mapping allowed for gap analysis to be preformed with all available information.

The guidance developed by NASA Ames and NASA Dryden, though fairly top-level, provided an initial input into this effort. The NASA reports were aligned with ISO/IEC 12207 standard and so the mapping of ISO/IEC 12207 to IEEE 1012-1998 helped to map the Ames and Dryden guidance to IEEE 1012-1998. Also, in this step the sample Software Verification and Validation Plan was examined. The SVVP of the Airborne Research Test System II (ARTS II) of the Intelligent Flight Control System (IFCS) [Casdorph 2000, ISR 2003] provided insights into one implementation of a V&V plan for a neural network system. The IFCS was an excellent case study as it utilized safety- and mission-critical online adaptive neural networks. This text contains several examples from the IFCS Program to illustrate augmented V&V methods.

These mappings were then combined to determine the coverage of the V&V of neural networks problem space and to form a framework for the general V&V guidance document. The guidance document is the final product of the ISR's research initiative. The steps of this research plan, including intermediate and final results, are illustrated in Fig. 2-1.

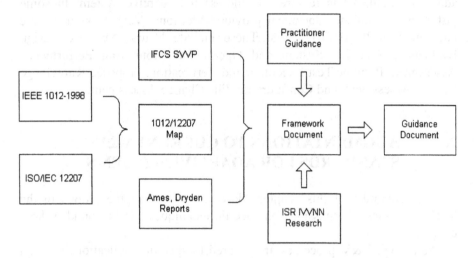

Figure 2-1. Research Plan – Interim and Final Results

1.2 Guidance for the Independent Verification and Validation of Neural Networks

The guidance document, *Guidance for the Independent Verification and Validation of Neural Networks* [ISR 2005], outlines general augmentations to lifecycle processes to assist the V&V practitioner. The guidance document provides a detailed listing of all IEEE 1012-1998 V&V tasking and provides augmentations for the V&V neural networks for every task. The guidance document also introduces novel V&V tasks when augmentations to IEEE 1012-1998 tasks are not sufficient. Finally, the guidance provides supporting examples from IFCS. In summary, the guidance document provides assistance to the V&V practitioner in designing V&V methodologies for neural networks.

The guidance document is generally aligned with the IEEE 1012-1998 in terms of section enumeration. The alignment provides the V&V practitioner the ability to quickly reference information on specific areas of interest. The document is organized into five sections. Section 1 is the overview of the document. Section 2 contains the important references for the document. Section 3 contains definitions, abbreviations, and conventions. Section 4 provides a summarized list of areas of consideration for neural network/adaptive systems. Section 5 provides detailed guidance for all lifecycle processes, activities and tasks related neural network and adaptive systems.

For a few tasks, no significant the guidance was needed. For many tasks, additional guidance is required to address the adaptive system. In some instances the guidance document provided additional V&V tasks that were not found in IEEE 1012-1998. These include Neural Network Design Evaluation, Adaptive System and Operational Monitoring Performance Assessment, Periodic Test Execution and Verification, Proposed Knowledge Change Assessment, and Configuration File Change Assessment.

2.   AUGMENTATIONS TO CURRENT V&V STANDARDS FOR ADAPTIVE SYSTEMS

The remainder of this chapter addresses several augmentations to the V&V processes. Discussions on specific techniques can be found in later chapters.

As a note, V&V processes are tailored to specific applications through the selection of software integrity levels to plan for appropriate V&V tasking. The additional methods outlined in this chapter are not intended to replace existing processes, but are designed to provide suggestions to the V&V practitioner to augment an established V&V process to address specific characteristics of neural networks. Use of the following techniques should be based upon assigned software integrity levels, and thus the safety- and mission-criticality level of the system. This section does not try to identify at what level these techniques should be employed. V&V practitioners should also be aware that many of these techniques mentioned here still maturing, and the cost associated with developing the technique to a technology readiness level usable by the project could highly influence how quickly the project might adopt the technique.

2.1   Enhanced Configuration Management for Neural Networks

Typically, configuration management identifies configuration items, implements version control upon baselined configuration items, and describes processes to establish new baselines. A configuration item is usually software, documentation, or data. In IEEE 1012-1998, configuration management assessment of a project is conducted by determining the completeness and adequacy of documentation produced that describe the configuration management process. Since adaptive systems have an added component of knowledge that is not present in conventional software, the configuration management processes must describe the methods neural networks use to obtain knowledge as well as the neural network knowledge itself.

The neural network design is often an iterative process. The process cycles through the steps of design-train-test multiple times. The neural network undergoes changes as it attempts to learn what the system designers intend. If this process is not tracked via configuration management, the project may lose the ability to repeat the design. Neural network validation techniques such as cross validation or bootstrapping should also be tracked through configuration management.

Neural network developers can also choose to modify the structure of the neural network. Based upon the evaluation of neural network performance, a designer might want to change the architecture, add additional neurons and neuron layers to the architecture, or change the algorithms the network uses to learn or grow. Alterations in structure, function, and architecture must be captured through configuration management.

Pre-trained neural networks rely on training sets to learn. After using a set of training data, the network begins to adjust internal parameters as it migrates to learning the features of the training data. The V&V practitioner should ensure that these training sets are tracked through configuration management. It is equally important to track the order and frequency in which training sets are applied to a neural network. Capturing the neural network during training is also useful. The partial learning in the neural networks allows for an evaluation of how the network is changing, and allows for developers to revert to an earlier state if the current neural network is lacking in performance.

The considerations outlined for pre-trained neural networks can be applied to online adaptive neural networks. Online adaptive neural networks are usually initialized with parameters that control variants such as learning rate and initial weight values. This configuration data should be under stringent version control, since slight alterations in parameters may considerably alter the way the neural network learns and performs.

2.2   Adaptive System Requirements V&V

The V&V practitioner evaluates the system requirements early in the lifecycle. The system requirements are validated to ensure they can be satisfied by the defined technologies, methods and algorithms defined for the project, and the system requirements verified for their consistency to the needs of the user.

The feasibility of the requirements determines if the defined technologies can fulfill the requirements adequately and efficiently. In order to evaluate if any specifications requiring the use of an adaptive system can meet the overall system requirements, the practitioner must first evaluate whether an adaptive system or a neural network is appropriate. There are numerous types of neural networks. Neural networks may be either supervised or unsupervised. They may have feed-forward architecture or feedback architecture. Different neural networks are applied to different problem domains. While no complete taxonomy exists that defines appropriate neural network architecture selection, there are general guidelines. These guidelines are described in Chapter 4.

To establish consistency with the needs of the recipient of the system, the needs must be clearly documented. For an adaptive system, the user needs should be represented as goals depicting system behavior and characteristics from a very high level of abstraction. The high-level goals are first stated in early documents and are then traceable through systems requirements and software requirements. To ensure complete coverage of user needs, system and software requirements are traced to high-level goals.

High-level goals of an adaptive can be difficult to write very early in the lifecycle. They should address two aspects of the system:

- How the adaptive system acquires knowledge and acts on that knowledge. (Control)
- What knowledge the adaptive system should acquire. (Knowledge)

Table 2-1 provides an example of high-level goals for an online adaptive neural network used in an intelligent flight control application. The table also shows traceability to system requirements. From high-level goals the developer will be able to understand the nature of the system. Once high-level goals are established for a project, consistency of the system requirements to the user needs can then be easily established.

2.3   Neural Network Software Requirements V&V

Neural networks are based on statistics and mathematics. Requirements describing neural networks should be written in formal mathematical notation to describe the functionality of the neural network and intended knowledge. The V&V practitioner will need to make sure software requirements are readable and it may be necessary to provide appendices to software requirement documentation that includes a brief mathematical background explaining some of the specifications.

Table 2-1. Example of Adaptive System High-Level Goals

High-Level Goal	Classification	Software Requirement ID	Software Requirement Description
The IFCS system shall include a safety monitor that safely limits the online learning neural network commands	Control	1.1.1.1[01]	The system shall[01] include a safety monitor that safely limits the online neural network commands and outputs or reverts to the conventional (non-research) flight control system in the case of a command that could damage the vehicle, precipitate departure from controlled flight, or injure or incapacitate the pilot.
		1.1.1.1[02]	The safety monitor shall[02] limit the authority of the experimental control laws to ensure that the control commands remain within the allowed loads limits of the NASA vehicle.
The IFCS system shall use an online learning neural network to adjust the feedback errors to achieve desired system behavior in the presence of off nominal behavior or failures.	Knowledge	2.2.2.2[01]	The system shall[01] use an online learning neural network to adjust the feedback errors to achieve desired system behavior in the presence of off nominal behavior or failures.
		2.2.2.2[02]	When the neural network is off, the adjustment to the feedback shall[02] be zero, and the adaptation shall be disabled.

The notion of *control* requirements and *knowledge* requirements discussed within Section 2.2 is used in the next two section to further explore neural network requirement analysis.

2.3.1   Neural Network Control Requirements

The following paragraphs outline some of the more common areas that the V&V practitioner may address when assessing completeness of the software control requirements specifications for an adaptive system or a neural network.

The convergence time and precision of a neural network should be outlined in the software requirements. Convergence refers to a global minimization of the neural network error. The developers should be able to prove that the adaptive system can converge within a specified amount of time. This is a necessity for safety-critical systems that adapt in real time.

Many neural networks increase the amount of memory use when running in real-time. The increase in memory use may be attributed to an increase in the number of nodes that account for new operational conditions or an increase in connections or associations between nodes. The software requirements should specify the precise conditions under which a neural network will be allowed to grow and constraints on the growth such as maximum memory size.

In a safety- or mission-critical system, developers should use operational monitors or run-time monitors to periodically check the conformance of the adaptive system to the requirements. If an operational monitor is used, then high-level descriptions of operational monitors must be included in the requirements specifications. Different types of operational monitoring approaches are discussed in Chapter 10.

Input and output requirements for neural networks are crucial since input data has the greatest influence on adaptation. Requirements that describe input scaling, gains, and limits are common for neural networks. The V&V practitioner should also verify the input and output data and the amount of acceptable error.

The learning algorithm used within the neural network should also be defined with the requirements. A learning algorithm is used to adapt the neural network based on an update law. The V&V practitioner should verify the description of the learning algorithm. Examples of learning algorithms include calculating the mean squared error between the desired output and the actual outputs, Newton methods, and Levenberg-Marquardt [Bishop 1996].

2.3.2   Neural Network Knowledge Requirements

With an adaptive neural network system the states of neural network are unknown prior to operation. One of the motivations for employing an adaptive control system is the versatility to react to unknown operating conditions. Requirements related to what the neural network must and must not know are important in determining valid operation of the system. However, specifics of neural network knowledge are difficult to establish before the input domain is clearly understood and a preliminary neural network is constructed. As a result, software requirements should depict general knowledge of an adaptive neural network.

A neural network is initialized before it begins to learn upon input data. This method should be captured in the software requirements. Neural networks may be initialized from a data file, software module, or another software system. Purely adaptive online neural networks are initialized by randomizing the weights, or by setting the weight values to some constant.

For fixed neural networks or neural networks with knowledge prior to deployment, the requirements should specify the type of training data used. The requirements should depict the source of the training data, data ranges and attributes, and metrics of expected performance of the neural network upon the training data.

Software requirements specifications should impose limitations on neural network knowledge. These requirements should set specific knowledge limits or describe undesirable behavior. Software requirements may describe what the adaptive system shall not do as well as what the adaptive system must do.

A method to developing requirements depicting neural network knowledge is to describe the knowledge in the form of rules. Initially, domain experts can compose symbolic knowledge from the target problem domain. Neural network developers may then transform this knowledge into rules that is used in rule extraction and rule insertion techniques. Information attained from these processes can provide a sufficient level of detail for neural network knowledge requirements. A more detailed explanation of rule extraction is provided in Chapter 8.

2.4 Neural Network Design V&V

After the neural network is designed to some desirable state, the V&V practitioner must evaluate the design based on the criteria of correctness, consistency, completeness, accuracy, readability, and testability. Although these criteria may seem identical to traditional software design evaluation outlined by IEEE 1012-1998, the methods for evaluating a neural network system vary greatly from the methods used for traditional software. Consequently, a new task needs to be considered to describe methods to V&V the neural network design.

In evaluating the neural network design, the V&V practitioner must focus on areas such as neural network structure, neural network performance criteria, training and testing data, training processes, and operational monitors. Each of these areas should be described in sufficient detail in design documentation. Because of the extra significance given to the neural network design, it is recommended that the project team develop a special appendix to the software design document for the neural network. Another option is the creation of a stand-alone neural network design document.

Many people of varied backgrounds participate in a project, so the documented design should contain enough information to convey the purpose, rationale, mathematics, and development of the neural network that anyone not familiar with neural networks in general would be able to understand it. Essential information would include a summary of all terms used for the specific neural network, as well as visualization techniques to aid understand such as diagrams or flowcharts.

Many of the ideas discussed in this section should appear in the documentation. There should be sections describing the functions that comprise the neural network, how the neural network is to learn and grow, and specific design details for input pre-processing, output post-processing.

Based upon the system design, there may be other considerations for inclusion into the design. Some systems may require that the neural network perform data recording for later analysis. Others might make use of multiple neural networks in a form of N-version programming for neural networks. All of these specifics should be present in the documentation.

Neural networks have several design elements that must be evaluated for correctness. These include the neural network structure that is composed of the specific neural network architecture and the internal neural network parameters. Design documentation should include a clear description of the neural network nodes, the connection matrix between the nodes, weights, activation functions, growth functions, learning functions, hidden layers, inputs, and outputs.

While some of these elements can number into the hundreds and thousands, each individual element need not be documented. Instead, the focus should be on descriptive qualities like the number of nodes, the number of connections per node, what mathematical functions occur for each node, etc.

Neural network architectures such as multilayer perceptron, self-organizing map, radial basis function, recurrent, and Hopfield are used in very different problem domains. V&V must validate that the selection processes for the neural network architecture is based upon solid theoretical or empirical evidence. The selection process may also be based upon comparison studies, recommendation from experts in the field, or past experiences within a similar problem domain. V&V should ensure that the reasons are clearly expressed within concept documentation.

Neural network designs must have sufficient acceptance and rejection criteria well documented. System testers need to have metrics to determine the acceptability of the system. These criteria should describe specific knowledge, stability, and performance constraints. Other possible performance criteria may include necessary operating frequencies (i.e., the neural network must produce an output at a rate of 40Hz), and acceptable variance qualities of the output signal.

V&V must evaluate the accuracy of the neural network design by ensuring that the training set conforms to system accuracy requirements and physical laws and that the knowledge acquisition has adequate precision for system requirements. Training and testing data need to be considered as design elements. Analysis on this data should address if this data is appropriate for the intended usage of the system and if it is precise enough for expected results. The origins of the training and testing data should be evaluated to remove any possible problems from corrupt data collection, inappropriate sources of data collection, and problems associated with combining previous separate data sets into a single larger set.

The training process itself must undergo evaluation for correctness. The training process should be clearly documented and describe why it is appropriate for meeting the project needs. This includes identification of relevant training data sets, justification for the choice of the data sets, and consideration of the correct data formats for the training data. If multiple data sets are used, and certain data sets are emphasized during training more than others, this should also show up in the documentation with justification. A description of configuration management as used on the training process should also be present. Information here can include the training data configuration items that were use, the procedures employed for applying the training data configuration items, and identification and tracking of evaluation metrics used throughout the process.

If the system makes use of operational monitors (see Chapter 10), their design needs to be a part of the documentation. The project can decide to include these within the neural network documents, to make the operational monitor design a separate document, or to include it within the overall software design document. Operational monitor design can influence the neural network design and vice versa, the neural network design can influence the operational monitor design. Because of this, the design documentation needs to contain detailed information on the performance and interface of any operational monitors in order to minimize problems during integration with the neural network.

2.5   Modified Lifecycle for Developing Neural Networks

The neural network development lifecycle is different from traditional lifecycle models. It does not follow the basic waterfall methodology nor does it follow a pure spiral lifecycle model. Instead neural network development utilizes parts of both methodologies. The V&V practitioner should understand the details of the neural network lifecycle model used and ensure conformance of development activities to the model. The following sections discuss three distinct models for neural network development.

2.5.1   Common Neural Network Development Model

A common method for development of a neural network is an iterative cycle that is performed until the neural network has been proven adequate by some quantifiable measure. The stages in this process are the design, training, and testing of the neural network.

During the design stage, the neural network developer chooses the architecture, and the initial number of neurons and layers. The developer then establishes a connection matrix between all neurons, selects the learning algorithm and possible growing algorithms, and determines the initial values for internal parameters including weights and constants controlling the algorithms. Subsequent passes through the design stage may involve major overhauls of the design or may simply fine-tune neural network parameters.

During the training stage, training data is used by the neural network to learn. Depending on the nature of the problem, the neural network may be designed to approximate a function describing the training data, or may learn relationships between input and output data within the training set for classification. Training sets can be significant in size with several thousand training examples. After each example, the learning algorithm continues to adjust the network structure. The goal of the training stage is that after training the neural network to some state, the internal neural network parameters are developed enough to satisfy designated requirements and objectives

After completing a pass through the training data, a separate set of data called the testing data is used. This set of data has similar properties to the training data, but with examples the neural network has never seen. By using new data, the performance of the network can be measured without influence of examples that were used for training. Results from testing may indicate that another pass through the design-train-test cycle is necessary. Usually, the neural network developers have some target metric value they wish to achieve such as a 95% classification accuracy rate on new data. Until the metric values are met, the design-train-test cycle is iterated.

2.5.2   Rodvold's Neural Network Development Model

Rodvold [1999] identified that many current neural network development processes tend to be developed through empirical processes rather than through precise construction and training methods. To rectify this problem,

Rodvold constructed the nested loop model for neural network development. The model was constructed from common neural network development processes, and contains elements from both the waterfall lifecycle development model and the spiral lifecycle development model. Rodvold's model, shown in Fig. 2-2, is composed of five steps.

Step 1: Develop a set of neural network requirements, goals, and constraints into a document labeled Network Performance Specification.

Step 2: Assemble the data that will be used for training the neural network including data sources, original format of data, and modifications performed on the data. This step results in the Data Analysis Document.

Step 3: Training and testing loops are an iterative process in which the neural network architecture is developed and trained. The first loop, Variations of Artificial Neural Network (ANN) Topologies, involves changing the neural network architectural parameters. The middle loop, Variations of ANN Paradigms, involves modifications to the type of neural network used. The outer loop, Selection and Combination of ANN Input Neurons, concerns altering neural network inputs. All design and training from this step is documented in the Network Training Summary.

Step 4: Network deployment is completed through commercial tools, automatic code generation provided by commercial tools, or by saving raw neural network data to file with code to load and execute the neural network. The deployment of the neural network is documented in the Network Integration Document.

Step 5: Independent testing and verification produces the Network Test Plan and the Data Analysis Document. This step also involves creating the Network Test Report, which summarizes of all tests performed.

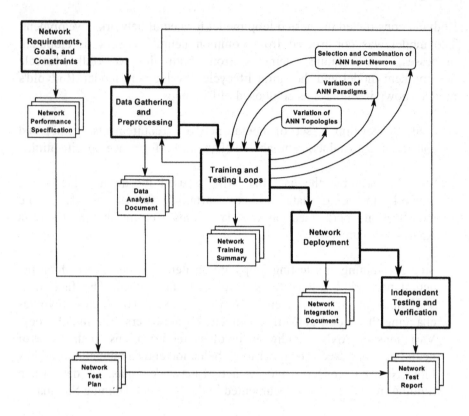

Figure 2-2. Critical Neural Network Development Process Model [Rodvold 2001]

2.5.3   Kurd's Neural Network Development Model

A major problem for the V&V practitioner, when faced with a safety-critical neural network, is the inability to effectively perform white-box analysis. The Safety Lifecycle [Kurd 2003] is a process for developing neural networks considering the safety criteria that must be enforced to justify safety operation of a neural network. This model ties hazard analysis into the development of the neural network's knowledge and specifically addresses neural networks developed for safety-critical applications. Fig. 2-3 illustrates the development and safety lifecycles. There are three levels in the diagram:

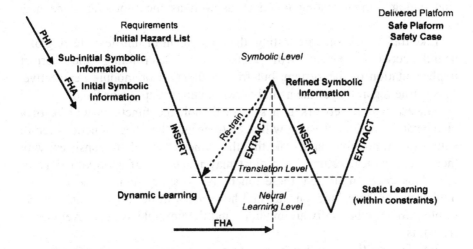

Figure 2-3. Safety Lifecycle for Hybrid Neural Networks [Kurd 2003]

The Symbolic Level is associated with the symbolic knowledge representations. The Translation Level is where the symbolic knowledge is modified into knowledge that is represented through rules for rule extraction and insertion. The Neural Learning Level trains the neural network through empirical data formulated from knowledge from the translation level.

Brief descriptions of the stages in the development model which traverse the above levels are as follows:

- Determine neural network requirements and goals,
- Collect symbolic sub-initial knowledge from domain experts,
- Compose initial knowledge for the neural network from sub-initial knowledge,
- Train the neural network on empirical data produced from the initial knowledge,
- Extract knowledge from neural network and refine this knowledge, and
- Train the neural network with a new refined knowledge set.

2.6 Neural Network Testing

Testing of an online learning neural network is difficult. Formal method testing techniques such as model checking and theorem proving are not practical given the characteristics of many neural networks. Theorem proving is too difficult in complex problem domains. For online adaptive neural networks, model checking would be inadequate since the neural network is non-deterministic at run-time. Instead the system tester is left to augmenting normal testing practices as well as incorporating some new ones.

Like traditional software testing, the component or unit-level testing of a neural network system will focus upon determining the correct implementation of the system, but from a function or module perspective. This is true regardless of the neural network being adaptive or fixed.

Since a neural network is a statistical tool, the functions will be of a mathematical nature. Testing will need to ensure that these functions return values for all possible inputs and that the values returned are consistent with their mathematical nature. A project may make use of approximations or table lookups to implement these functions. Testing should concentrate on how accurate these functions are and how errors in the implementation can ripple through other software modules and the possible system level effects from this.

Interface testing, another aspect to testing that exists for non-adaptive software, can require more concern for adaptive software. Neural networks are very capable of performing an approximation to a solution given partially noisy and partially imprecise data. When analyzing the inputs and outputs, practitioners should inspect the pre- and post-processing of the inputs looking for poor performance or improper implementations. An example is a smoothing function that isn't smoothing the data as it was intended. Data interpolation algorithms may also contribute to generating poor data that is masked by the neural network. The system testers may know that the neural network is performing with a very minor error, but if an error in the pre-processing is corrected, the system performance could improve.

The robustness of the neural network may work as a disadvantage to the system tester. If allowed to adapt during system usage, neural networks can overcome incorrectly provided inputs. This can happen if one person or team develops a module that produces input for the neural network and another person or team develops the neural network module. If the data is switched between the module and the neural network, and the neural network adapts, it can compensate for this deficiency, possibly with only a minor error that the team regards as negligible.

Two new aspects of testing that are normally not considered are the neural network knowledge and structure. Structure testing determines whether the design is the most optimal at learning what is intended, compared to other designs. Knowledge testing would investigate what the neural network has already learned and how well it has learned it.

Typically, when the neural network undergoes design-train-test development, the network is tested after it passes through an iteration of training. There is typically a performance metric, usually an error function, associated with how well the neural network handles the data found in the test set. Over time, this error metric should decrease towards zero representing the neural network has learned the exact function it is to perform.

System testers may want to make sure these iterative testing stages are tracked and the error values recorded. By looking at these error values over time, it can provide evidence that the neural network design is improving and is better than any of the previous other states the design was in. The tester may not actually be responsible for conducting this kind of test, they just make sure the results are collected and analyzed.

Since structure testing is testing if the current design is better than previous designs, the results do not need to prove that the current design is the best possible design achievable. It only needs to prove that the design is better than it was previously. While it would be very useful to know that the current design is the absolute best, trying to show this through testing would be impractical.

Knowledge testing is perhaps the hardest area for neural network analysis because it involves evaluating whether the neural network is learning what the designers want it to learn. This goes beyond the use of a performance metric like the error function mentioned before. An error metric only tests for one particular input set; it does not reflect how the neural network would perform for a larger set of inputs.

Testing knowledge may require the use of rule extraction techniques to translate the network knowledge into a set of symbolic rules. The rules present a more tangible representation; they can be individually tested, used within existing testing tools, and can facilitate other analysis methods. Further discussion of this approach can be found in Chapter 8.

Another method for testing knowledge, though limited and often times impractical, is to use a brute force approach that tests the neural network for a very large set of possible inputs. By looking at the performance over a greater range, some sense of how the neural network will perform for an input domain can be gathered. This kind of testing may also fall into reliability assessment or sensitivity analysis where minute differences within the input domain are studied to determine if the neural network could behave erroneously. The tester may need to rely upon test data generation techniques to assist with this kind of evaluation. Consult Chapter 9 for further details.

3.   SUMMARY

This chapter has revealed several gaps in current V&V practices for adaptive systems, and has shown augmentations to traditional V&V processes to satisfy these gaps. Through the mapping of software V&V standards, process guidance, previous research, and IFCS documentation, a guidance document was formulated to augment current V&V practices to accommodate the characteristics of neural networks or adaptive systems. The guidance document [ISR 2005] embodies a comprehensive methodology for the V&V of neural networks and gives the V&V practitioner direction on how to augment established V&V processes to address neural networks or adaptive components within a system.

REFERENCES

Bishop, C. M. 1996. *Neural Networks for Pattern Recognition*. Oxford University Press, Oxford, England.

Casdorph, Van; Brian Taylor; et al. 2000. Software Verification and Validation Plan for the Airborne Research Test System II, Intelligent Flight Control Program. Institute for Scientific Research, Inc. IFC-SVVP-F001-UNCLASS-120100, Dec. 1.

IEEE Std 1012-1998. 1998. *IEEE Standard for Software Verification and Validation*. New York, NY.

IEEE/EIA 12207.2-1997. 1998. *IEEE/EIA Guide, Industry Implementation of International Standard ISO/IEC 12207:1995, (ISO/IEC 12207) Standard for Information Technology – Software Lifecycle Processes - Implementation Considerations*. New York, NY.

Institute for Scientific Research, Inc. (ISR). 2001. DCS Design Report for the Intelligent Flight Control Program. IFC-DCSR-D003-UNCLASS-010401.

Institute for Scientific Research, Inc. (ISR). 2003. Software Verification and Validation Plan for the Airborne Research Test System II of the Intelligent Flight Control Program. IFC-SVVP-F002-UNCLASS-050903.

Institute for Scientific Research, Inc. (ISR). 2005. Guidance for the Independent Verification and Validation of Neural Networks. IVVNN-GUIDANCE-D001-UNCLASS-072505.

Kurd, Zeshan, and Tim Kelley. 2003. Safety Lifecycle for Developing Safety Critical Artificial Neural Networks. *In Proceedings of 22nd International Conference on Computer Safety, Reliability, and Security (SAFECOMP'03)* 23-26 September 2003.

Mackall, Dale; Stacy Nelson; and Johann Schumman. 2002. Verification and Validation of Neural Networks for Aerospace Systems. NASA Dryden Flight Research Center and NASA Ames Research Center. June 12.

Mackall, Dale; Brian Taylor; et al. 2003. Verification and Validation of Adaptive Neural Networks for Aerospace Systems, Version 1.2 (Draft without Appendices). NASA Dryden Flight Research Center and NASA Ames Research Center. March 31.

Pullum, Laura L. 2003. Draft Guidance for the Independent Verification and Validation of Neural Networks. Institute for Scientific Research, Inc. IVVNN-GUIDE-D001-UNCLASS-101603. October.

Rodvold, D.M. 1999. A Software Development Process Model for Artificial Neural Networks in Critical Applications. *In Proceedings of the 1999 International Conference on Neural Networks (IJCNN'99)*. Washington D.C.

Rodvold, DM. 2001. Validation and Regulation of Medical Neural Networks. *Molecular Urology* 5(4): 141-145.

Chapter 3

RISK AND HAZARD ANALYSIS FOR NEURAL NETWORK SYSTEMS

Laura Pullum, Brian J. Taylor
Institute for Scientific Research, Inc.

1.   INTRODUCTION

The *IEEE Standard for Software Verification and Validation* [IEEE 1998] includes activities for risk and hazard analyses. The standard is intended to be general in nature and apply to all types of software. However, specific guidance for risk and hazard analysis related to the special characteristics of neural network software is required, and is not presently available. Smidts [2001], Chillarege [1992], and others provide general frameworks and taxonomies for software probabilistic risk assessment. These, too, apply in general to software, but are not specific, nor applicable in some instances, to neural networks. The goal of the research described in this chapter is to provide a suggested research path for risk assessment for neural network systems and an example failure modes and effects analysis (FMEA) for practitioner use. In the following sections, we present the results for the risk assessment of neural network systems (Section 2.0) and neural network FMEA research (Section 3.0).

2.   NEURAL NETWORK RISK ASSESSMENT

The processes, activities, and tasks in the IEEE verification and validation (V&V) standard that are related to risk and hazard analyses are listed in Fig. 3-1 and Fig. 3-2. We note the required activities, and what is recommended by our research and by the Ames/Dryden V&V guidance documents [Mackall 2002, 2003] in the paragraphs below.

Process: Development	
Activity: Concept V&V	
Hazard Analysis Tasks	Analyze potential hazards to and from the conceptual system. The analysis shall 1) identify potential system hazards; 2) assess severity of each hazard; 3) assess probability of each hazard; and 4) identify mitigation strategies for each hazard.
Risk Analysis Tasks	Identify the technical and management risks. Provide recommendations to eliminate, reduce, or mitigate the risks.
Activity: Requirements V&V	
Hazard Analysis Tasks	Determine software contributions to system hazards. The hazard analysis shall a) identify the software requirements that contribute to each system hazard; and b) validate that the software addresses, controls, or mitigates each hazard.
Risk Analysis Tasks	Review and update risk analysis using prior task reports. Provide recommendations to eliminate, reduce, or mitigate the risks.
Activity: Design V&V	
Hazard Analysis Tasks	Verify that logic design and associated data elements correctly implement the critical requirements and introduce no new hazards. Update the hazard analysis.
Risk Analysis Tasks	Review and update risk analysis using prior task reports. Provide recommendations to eliminate, reduce, or mitigate the risks.
Activity: Implementation V&V	
Hazard Analysis Tasks	Verify that the implementation and associated data elements correctly implement the critical requirements and introduce no new hazards. Update hazard analysis.
Risk Analysis Tasks	Review and update risk analysis using prior task reports. Provide recommendations to eliminate, reduce or mitigate the risks.
Activity: Test V&V	
Hazard Analysis Tasks	Verify that test instrumentation does not introduce new hazards. Update the hazard analysis.
Risk Analysis Tasks	Review and update risk analysis using prior task reports. Provide recommendations to eliminate, reduce, or mitigate the risks.
Activity: Installation and Checkout V&V	
Hazard Analysis Tasks	Verify that the installation procedures and installation environment does not introduce new hazards. Update the hazard analysis.
Risk Analysis Tasks	Review and update risk analysis using prior task reports. Provide recommendations to eliminate, reduce, or mitigate the risks.

Figure 3-1. IEEE Std. 1012 Hazard and Risk Analyses Tasks (Part 1)

Process: Operation	
Activity: Operation V&V	
Hazard Analysis Tasks	Verify that the operating procedures and operational environment does not introduce new hazards. Update the hazard analysis.
Risk Analysis Tasks	Review and update risk analysis using prior task reports. Provide recommendations to eliminate, reduce, or mitigate the risks.
Process: Maintenance	
Activity: Maintenance V&V	
Hazard Analysis Tasks	Verify that software modifications correctly implement the critical requirements and introduce no new hazards. Update the hazard analysis.
Risk Analysis Tasks	Review and update risk analysis using prior task reports. Provide recommendations to eliminate, reduce, or mitigate the risks.

Figure 3-2. IEEE Std. 1012 Hazard and Risk Analyses Tasks (Part 2)

2.1   Concept V&V Hazard and Risk Analysis Tasks

During the Concept V&V activity, the scope of hazard and risk analysis tasks is typically at the conceptual system level.

A preliminary hazard analysis can be conducted by use of hazards and operability studies (HAZOPS). Given a neural network system that adapts during operation, then the following potential hazards should be considered for the HAZOPS:

1. The neural network does not adapt.
2. The neural network adapts, but is unable to reach convergence.
3. The neural network adapts and converges, but converges to an incorrect output.
4. The neural network converges to a correct state, but cannot do so in the required time.
5. The neural network grows beyond available system resources during adaptation.

Identification of technical and management risks at the conceptual system level is a task that is essentially unaltered by whether or not neural networks are used. In addition, recommendations for risk elimination, reduction and mitigation are on the system level and black box "non-view" into the neural network operations and risks would produce similar strategies for a system with or without neural networks.

In terms of assessing management risk, the practitioner should look at project team member expertise with neural network development. Teams who have never developed neural networks will face schedule and budget risks. They may not have enough experience to know how to efficiently design the neural network and may spend extra resources developing the network and identifying effective ways of testing and validating the neural network system.

From the technical risk standpoint, the analysis needs to concentrate on the justification for the use of a neural network solution. Questions that investigate technical risk may ask if a neural network system is an appropriate solution given the problem being solved, if the neural networks should be online adaptive or not, and what types of built in safety the system will need.

2.2   Requirements V&V Hazard and Risk Analysis Tasks

At the requirements stage, hazard and risk analyses for systems employing neural networks start to differ from that for systems employing more conventional software. There will be requirements specifically addressing the neural network component(s) and these requirements can be used, as with non-neural network software requirements, to support the hazard and risk analysis tasks during this stage. Better means of specifying neural network requirements will aid in determining their contribution to system hazards and in validating the control or mitigation of each hazard. At this stage, a top-level fault model of the neural network can be initiated. The fault model is used to provide a foundation for risk assessment methods such as HAZOPS, FMEA, and fault tree analysis (FTA). Refer to Section 3.0 for additional information.

Risk identification for neural network systems during the requirements stage can be more difficult than the same identification conducted for traditional software systems. Examples of areas of risk that can be considered during this stage include:

1. Risks introduced by the specification and collection of training and testing data

Risks from the specification of training and testing data for neural network development can fall into either technical or management risks. For management risks, there may be concerns associated with the time it will take to collect these data sets and the ability of the project to track and identify the data sets once collected.

A technical risk associated with the training data is the lack of a sufficiently large and rich enough set of data to allow for proper knowledge acquisition. In other words, the neural network will not be able to approximate the desired function well. The project team may need to consider means of increasing the size of the dataset such as test data generation.

The normal training-testing approach to neural network systems may leave an inadequate size of testing data, especially in the case of safety- and mission-critical systems. Typically, the entire available data set is split into 75% training and 25% testing data. That limit on the testing set may not allow proper system evaluation. Activities like reliability assessment and robustness analysis may require on the order of tens of thousands of test cases. If the project does not prepare for some of these concerns in their specifications of testing data, associated risks need to be documented.

2. Risks introduced by specification of neural network performance

If neural network performance requirements are incorrectly stated or are too difficult to obtain, a project may spend a longer time developing the neural network to meet the performance criteria. A result is that schedules slip and budgets overrun. Possible ways to mitigate this risk are the use of reliable neural network training tools, inclusion of knowledgeable neural network developers on the team, and the establishment of well-defined performance criteria.

2.3   Design V&V Hazard and Risk Analysis Tasks

At the design stage, hazard analysis tasks include verifying that logic design and associated data elements correctly implement the critical requirements and introduce no new hazards. Risk analysis tasks at this stage include providing recommendations to eliminate, reduce, or mitigate the risks. Details can now be added to the neural network fault model and subsequently more detailed FMEA and FTA can be performed. Additional research and example analyses of FMEA and FTA for neural networks are required. This chapter provides an example FMEA for the Intelligent Flight Control System (IFCS) next generation (GEN2). Refer to Section 3.0 for additional information. Lyapunov stability analysis can be used to prove convergence (see Chapter 5) and safety monitors can be used to reduce or mitigate risks related to the use of neural networks in real-time safety critical systems. Both Ames/Dryden guidance documents [Mackall 2002, 2003] provide recommendations for the design V&V stage, although no specific recommendations are made for hazard or risk analysis.

Neural networks undergo a design-train-test development that may be iterated any number of times. For the Design V&V stage, hazard analysis should only be concerned with the design aspect of the development. This includes the design of the neural network architecture, size, intended use, collection of training-testing data, etc. The train-test aspects are better considered under Implementation V&V Hazard and Risk Analysis Tasks in Section 2.4.

Hazards introduced due to the design of the neural network include:

- Training data set does not model intended goals.
- The collection of training and test data sets is not tracked under configuration management and is not described in design documentation.
- Lack of adequate testing data to achieve component-level project-specific certification standards.
- Neural network architecture is not completely specified.
- The implementation of the network prior to training is incorrect (initial number of neurons, connection matrices, growing/learning functions, or activation functions contain errors).
- Inappropriate growing/learning algorithm is selected, causing sub-optimal knowledge acquisition.

Some of the management risks that could be encountered during the design phase include cost impact associated with the need to purchase neural network development environments or specialized testing tools and suites. There could also be schedule risks due to the project teams lack of experience with developing neural network solutions.

Technical risks include insufficient training and testing data. With insufficient training data, the project may not be able to generalize or specialize the neural network learning. With insufficient testing data, the project may lack the ability to prove correctness, safety and reliability of the neural network. Both training and testing data must represent the entire data domain, rather than just a few constrained examples. Especially in the case of safety- and mission-critical applications, the ability to demonstrate the performance of the neural network algorithm throughout the application domain is necessary for system acceptance.

Another technical risk arises due to the proper selection of the neural network base architecture, given the problem being solved. Selecting an appropriate neural network algorithm impacts the feasibility of system design and implementation. The process of selection is not well documented in the literature.

Projects may be tempted to ignore software engineering best practices because they don't easily apply to the neural network. It has often been said of neural network development that design is more of an art than a science. If the development team does not take all the necessary precautions such as controlling the training data, recording design and training procedures, then it is possible that the end result, no matter how appropriate a solution, will be an unexplainable and unlikely to be repeated should it become necessary.

2.4 Implementation V&V Hazard and Risk Analysis Tasks

At the implementation stage, hazard analysis tasks include verifying that the implementation and associated data elements correctly implement the critical requirements and introduce no new hazards. Risk analysis tasks at this stage include providing recommendations to eliminate, reduce or mitigate the risks. Risk assessment models, such as the fault model, FMEA, hazard analysis, and FTA, can be updated per implementation details. Sensitivity analysis and fault injection may be useful tools to examine the performance of risk mitigation techniques. Both Ames/Dryden guidance documents [Mackall 2002, 2003] provide recommendations for the implementation V&V stage, although no specific recommendations are made for hazard or risk analysis.

During the implementation phase, hazard analysis should focus on those hazards affected or introduced through the learning of the training data by the neural network. The actual design of the neural network was dealt with in the design stage. Here, the focus needs to be on the knowledge and how well the knowledge was acquired. Some examples of hazards include:

- Through learning and/or growing, the neural network structure exceeds the computational limitations of the system.
- Neural network takes too long to adapt to new stimuli.
- The neural network never reaches a point of stability. The neural network performance oscillates around the designated success criteria metric but never achieves the intended metric.
- Neural network is over-generalized and cannot provide a suitable solution to the specific problem.
- Neural network is too specialized and cannot provide a general solution for the problem domain.
- Observable behavior of the neural network is not predictable or repeatable.

A management risk associated with the implementation stage is the potential loss of time due to a poor understanding of effective training strategies. If the neural network learning never converges, the project team may spend too much time trying to achieve a desired performance measure and never come close. Another management risk is the loss of version control of the neural network training process, leaving the project unable to repeat a training process or later inspect it when looking for problems.

Technical risks include a lack of sufficient training or testing data, especially to meet the needs of rigorous testing and reliability assessment. Another possible technical risk occurs when the neural network designers have trained a neural network to meet performance criteria, but they fail to adequately test the neural network across the entire operational profile. In this case, the network may seem to be performing correctly, but in certain situations that are not considered, the network actually performs quite poorly.

2.5   Test V&V Hazard and Risk Analysis Tasks

At the test stage, hazard analysis tasks include verifying that test instrumentation does not introduce new hazards. Risk analysis tasks at this stage include providing recommendations to eliminate, reduce, or mitigate the risks. Fault injection testing may be used to examine the performance of risk mitigation techniques. Faults to inject may be found in the fault model details. This may also be called FMEA testing and is suggested in the Ames/Dryden guidance documents [Mackall 2002, 2003].

During the testing stage, the risks and hazards usually relate to accepting a neural network system inappropriately. This could occur through the use of testing techniques or simulations that fail to adequately exercise the neural network. Other examples include:

- Failure to examine the training data for completeness and correctness.
- Failure to review input selection (ensuring the input choices are correct, based upon an acceptable technique like principal component analysis, etc.).
- Failure to review input preprocessing and output post-processing for correctness.
- The test procedures described in the test plans do not properly assess neural network performance criteria such as stability and convergence.
- For software-in-the-loop simulations (SILS), the test cases do not accurately reflect how the adaptive component performs within the entire system.
- For hardware-in-the-loop simulations (HILS), near-identical versions of the hardware do not accurately reflect performance of the true hardware.

The most significant technical risk during testing, especially for that of an adaptive neural network system with high integrity levels, is a catastrophic failure of an accepted system. Management risks can be associated with the loss of effectiveness due to the unavailability of proper testing tools and simulations and the time it takes to utilize the testing tools and simulations that are available.

2.6   Installation and Checkout V&V Hazard and Risk Analysis Tasks

At the installation and checkout stage, hazard analysis must consider the contributions to system hazards introduced from incompleteness and incompatibility.

If the neural network system requires some environment in which to operate, a potential hazard is the lack of delivery of this environment with the installation package. Another possible area of omission is the failure to deliver checkcases that will exercise the system after installation to make sure that the installation did not introduce any kind of error. If the system makes use of real-time operational monitors, the monitors need to be a part of the complete package as well.

Incompatibility can be introduced when the target environment is not similar to the development environment. The interface between modules providing input or accepting output from the neural network may be different. Computer hardware attributes like processor size and speed may be different, introducing performance issues. There may be multiple threads running on the same board as the neural network software, competing for resources and impeding the network's operation.

In general, the risks encountered during the installation and checkout phase are based on whether or not the system operates properly. Other risks must be of concern in this phase especially when the neural network is part of a safety-critical system with the potential to terminate the mission or harm humans. In such a system, a minor incident can put humans at risk and escalate into budget cuts, schedule extensions, program delays and even the cancellation of a program.

2.7   Operation V&V Hazard and Risk Analysis Tasks

At the operation stage, hazard analysis tasks include verifying that the operating procedures and operational environment does not introduce new hazards. Risk analysis tasks during this stage include providing recommendations to eliminate, reduce, or mitigate the risks. It is highly recommended that V&V evaluate the use of operational monitors (see Chapter 10), stability and convergence analysis (see Chapter 5), and risk assessment techniques (used throughout the lifecycle) (see Section 3.0) prior to the system under development reaching the Operation V&V phase.

With a neural network system that continues to learn and adapt during system operation, hazard analysis is more significant than that of traditional software. The reason is that it is often assumed with traditional software, any hazards that might be identified already exist prior to the system being deployed. However, with an adaptive system, new hazards can be introduced based upon what data comes into the system and thus how the system learns. Example of hazards include:

- Operating procedures are inconsistent with the user documentation or with system requirements.
- Operating conditions differ from those intended by system developers.
- Input data is received from a source that was not originally intended.
- Computational resource limits are approached or exceeded (as may happen with growing neural networks that add more neurons and connections over time).
- Operational monitors function inappropriately as either too restrictive or not restrictive enough.

The technical risks encountered during the Operation phase are similar to those in the Installation and Checkout phase. The system either does not operate or operates improperly which is directly related to risks of adverse impacts on schedule and budget.

The use of operational monitors may be a part of a wider risk mitigation strategy. If so, the specifics of their usage within mitigation should be well defined. This may include contingency planning when operational monitors indicate system performance problems.

2.8   Maintenance V&V Hazard and Risk Analysis Tasks

At the Maintenance stage, hazard analysis tasks include verifying that software modifications correctly implement the critical requirements and introduce no new hazards. Based upon what is carried out during maintenance, updating the hazard analysis is recommended. For example, if the design is unaltered but the neural network knowledge is changed through re-training, the hazard analysis should consider the suggestions found within the Implementation V&V Hazard Analysis section, but it need not reconsider the Design V&V suggestions. Likewise, risk analysis tasks at this stage include providing recommendations to eliminate, reduce, or mitigate risks based upon what was modified.

3. FAILURE MODES AND EFFECTS ANALYSIS FOR NEURAL NETWORKS

To study risk assessment for neural networks, we must resolve the issue of how a neural network becomes defective and the nature of the defects. This is included in a fault model. The next issue is applying the fault model to the various tools used in risk assessment – namely FMEA, FTA, and HAZOPs. The research reported in this section developed a fault model for the multi-layer perceptron (MLP) neural network and examined the use of that fault model to enable FMEA.

3.1 Fault Model

A fault model describes the types of faults a system can develop, including where and how those faults occur in the system. The MLP neural network architecture is considered for examination because of its use in the IFCS [Rumelhart 1986]. An abstract model for the MLP neural network is illustrated in Fig. 3-3. It provides a graphical representation of, as well as the operation and training equations governing, the system.

From this abstract definition of the neural network, we examine the entities in the model for possible fault locations. Both training and operation phases are considered in the discussion below of the entities and potential fault locations. The following information is derived from Bolt's work on neural network fault tolerance [Bolt 1992].

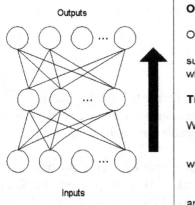

Operation:

Output $o_i = f_i\left(\sum_j w_{ij}o_j\right)$

such that feeding units j already evaluated and where f_i is a differentiable monotonic function.

Training:

Weight change is $\Delta w_{ij} = \eta\,\delta_i o_j$

where for output units $\delta_i = (t_i - o_i)f'_i\left(\sum_k w_{ik}o_k\right)$

and for hidden units $\delta_i = f'_i\left(\sum_k w_{ik}o_k\right)\sum_l \delta_l w_{il}$

Figure 3-3. Multi-Layer Perceptron Abstract Model [Bolt 1992]

- *Weights* w_{ij} - for the operational phase (fixed values in the MLP network once training has finished) and for the training phase. For simplicity, bias values, θ_i, are viewed as weights on connections from a dummy unit that is permanently active.
- *Threshold Functions* f_i - a fault in a threshold function will alter the transformation of the activation to an output value in some manner. This will affect both training and operational phases.
- *Derivative of Threshold Functions* f_i' - this fault will affect the system only during the training phase. It is identified as a separate fault since its function is generally different to that of f_i.
- *Constant Values* - faults affecting any constant values are fixed by definition. An example during the training phase is the learning rate, η.
- *Target Values* t_i - these are not included in the constant values above since it is conceivable that a MLP network may be trained on data that is modified as time progresses, e.g., [Miikkulainen 1988].
- *Topology* - the connectivity of the neural network could easily be subject to faults in various ways, such as the loss of a connection between two units.

There are some additional entities that must be considered for inclusion in the fault model because of their functional role in MLP neural network operation, even though their lifetime is strictly limited. For example, delta values, δ_i, have to be kept at each backward pass so that errors can be evaluated at hidden units. These additional entities are noted below and are derived from Bolt [1992].

- Activation Values, a_i, where a_i is defined as

$$a_i = \sum_j w_{ij} o_j \qquad\qquad (3.1)$$

- *Delta* δ_i - faults in these are only relevant during the training phase.
- *Weight Change* Δw_{ij} - these are the alteration for the stable weight base value, and as for δ_i, faults are only applicable during the training phase.

From the fault model, it can be seen that a large number of possible fault locations exist for a MLP neural network. However, when the fault manifestations are defined, we find that many of them can be discarded from consideration.

3.2 Fault Manifestations

We have identified the entities that may be possible locations for faults using the mathematical model of the neural network. The next step is to describe the nature of the faults the entities might suffer. We use the technique for defining fault manifestations described by Bolt [1992]. First, possible faults are defined using the maximization of damage principle. This tends to lead to the development of extreme fault modes. The second step using information derived from implementation considerations is then applied to the fault modes. This has the effect of either restricting a mode's effect or ruling it out completely. A set of failure modes for the MLP neural network is defined by applying these concepts to the fault model and locations described above.

Weights w_{ij}
- $w_{ij} = 0$ causes loss of any partial information that the weight held
- $w_{ij} \rightarrow - w_{ij}$ weight is multiplied by -1; represents a unit always trying to misclassify an input

OR a saturation limit can be applied on any faulty weight by restricting weights to the range [-W, +W]. This suggests the faults:

- negative $w_{ij} \rightarrow +W$
- positive $w_{ij} \rightarrow -W$

Threshold Function
- Stuck-at-minus-one
- Stuck-at-plus-one

Derivative of Threshold Function
- Stuck-at-plus-one
- Stuck-at-zero

Learning Rate
- $\eta = 0$ typical range (0, 1]
- η = its highest possible value

Target Values
- t_i = value opposite to the fault-free value (the targets generally take only the two values at the extreme ends of the threshold function range)

<u>Topology</u>
- Loss of a connection between 2 units
- Random reconnection of a link to another unit in the network (possibly due to a short-circuit)

<u>Activation Values, a_i, and Delta, δ_l</u>
- Limit to opposite value OR
- Constrain δ_i and a_i to a limited range or randomize them

<u>Weight Change Δw_{ij}</u>
- Only needs to be considered if they are stored temporarily, then they would have similar failure modes as those for activation values and deltas

3.3   Fault Example

The next step is to use the information on failure modes above and illustrate its use in performing a failure modes and effects analysis. This requires a sample system and for these purposes, the IFCS GEN2 MLP neural network is used (Table 3-1). Note that the purpose of the IFCS neural network is to reduce system error.

When the neural network interferes with the proportional-integral derivative (PID) error compensation, the resulting system effect is poorer flying quality than with dynamic inversion alone. There are various ranges of flight quality problems based upon the Cooper/Harper handling qualities scale, e.g., 1-3 is acceptable; 4-6 there is a problem in the system and the system requires some pilot compensation; and 7-8 the pilot must provide considerable compensation to the system. If the neural network failure mode is transient, then the system effect is most likely in the 4-6 range. If the neural network failure mode is permanent, then the system effect can go to the 7-8 range. The table above notes the worst case and assumes no operational monitor or other non-PID combination for fault mitigation.

Table 3-1. FMEA for IFCS GEN2 Neural Network

Neural Network Entity	Failure Modes	Local Effect	System Effect
Weights	$w_{ij} = 0$	Incorrect error reduction	Poor handling qualities (HQ); system will compensate, but take longer to compensate than without error.
	$w_{ij} \rightarrow -w_{ij}$	Network instability; unable to converge	System instability; may lose error compensation (LEC) totally. May never regain good flying quality.
Threshold Function (sigmoidal)	Stuck-at-minus-one	Network instability; unable to converge	Poor HQ
	Stuck-at-plus-one	Network instability; unable to converge	Poor HQ
Derivative of Threshold Function	Stuck-at-plus-one	Loss of error fitting (sigmoid becomes linear)	n.a.
	Stuck-at-zero	No error compensation	Poor HQ
Learning Rate	$\eta = 0$ typical range (0, 1]	No weight change, can not accommodate system error	Poor HQ
	$\eta =$ its highest possible value	Instability, network unable to achieve local minima (most likely)	LEC
Target Values	$t_i =$ value opposite to the fault-free value (the targets generally take only the two values at the extreme ends of the threshold function range)	Network would move away from optimum error reduction, become more erroneous	LEC
Topology	Loss of a connection between 2 units	Incorrect error reduction; loss of internal knowledge	LEC, transient
	Random reconnection of a link to another unit in the network (possibly due to a short-circuit)	Incorrect error reduction; loss of internal knowledge	LEC, transient

Neural Network Entity	Failure Modes	Local Effect	System Effect
Activation Values	Limit to opposite value	Weights adjust in opposite direction giving double error	Poor HQ
Delta	Limit to opposite value	Weights change in the wrong direction	Poor HQ, transient
Weight Change	Limit to opposite value (Consider only if they are stored temporarily)	Takes longer to converge	Poor HQ

4.   SUMMARY

Guidance on risk assessment specific to the special characteristics of neural network software is required, and this is not presently available. General frameworks and taxonomies for software probabilistic risk assessment have been proposed, but they are not specific, nor applicable in some instances, to neural networks. This chapter, while limited in its applicability to every safety- and mission-critical neural network system, points out several possible risk assessment techniques as well as useful places to begin considering identification of risks and hazards.

REFERENCES

Bolt, George Ravuama. 1992. Fault Tolerance in Artificial Neural Networks – Are Neural Networks Inherently Fault Tolerant? D. Phil. Thesis, University of York. Nov.

Chillarege, R.; W. L. Kao; and R. G. Condit. 1992. Orthogonal Defect Classification – A Concept for In-Process Measurements. *IEEE Transactions on Software Engineering* SE-18:943-956.

IEEE Std 1012-1998. 1998. *IEEE Standard for Software Verification and Validation.* New York, NY.

Mackall, Dale; Stacy Nelson; and Johann Schumman. 2002. Verification and Validation of Neural Networks for Aerospace Systems. NASA Dryden Flight Research Center and NASA Ames Research Center. June 12.

Mackall, Dale; Brian Taylor; et al. 2003. Verification and Validation of Adaptive Neural Networks for Aerospace Systems, Version 1.2 (Draft without Appendices). NASA Dryden Flight Research Center and NASA Ames Research Center. March 31.

Miikkulainen, R.; and M. Dyer. 1988. Encoding Input/Output Representations in Connectionist Cognitive Systems. 1988 Connectionist Models Summer School, Carnegie-Mellon University. Morgan Kaufmann.

Rumelhart, D.E.; G.E. Hinton; and R.J. Williams. 1986. Learning Internal Representations by Error Propagation. In Parallel Distributed Processing, eds. Rumelhart, D.E.; and J.L. McClelland. pp. 318-362. MIT Press.

Smidts, Carol; Bin Li; and Ming Li. 2001 Integrating Software into Probabilistic Risk Assessment. NASA report.

Chapter 4

VALIDATION OF NEURAL NETWORKS VIA TAXONOMIC EVALUATION

Brian J. Taylor, James T. Smith
Institute for Scientific Research, Inc.

1.   INTRODUCTION

This chapter presents a taxonomic overview of neural network systems from multiple perspectives, i.e., a taxonomic view of neural network validation. Major characteristics of application problems and their neural network solutions are considered. The intent of this material is to aid the V&V practitioner with *validation*, the assessment of the appropriateness of a particular neural network-based solution for the problem being solved.

Validation of a computer system has often been summed up in the following question:

Has the right system been built?

This chapter considers that question and relates it to neural networks by phrasing the question slightly differently:

Does the system need a neural network?

In a way, the second question is a form of the first question. When considering if the right system has been built, the V&V practitioner should consider what constitutes the 'right system' and if a neural network solution is a part of that right system.

Given that a neural network solution is deemed appropriate for the project, the next question is almost as important:

Which neural network architecture is the most appropriate?

Addressing these two questions is the focus of this chapter.

Section 2.1 presents a high-level characterization of the types of problems and applications for which neural network technology may be deemed appropriate. The major characteristics of such problem domains may be divided into three categories:

1. Adaptive vs. Fixed,
2. Parallel vs. Sequential, and
3. Complete vs. Incomplete.

Section 2.2 focuses upon the relationship and comparison of neural networks to other computational models that are employed in the development of intelligent systems. General constraints or conditions that must be met to effectively use artificial neural networks are provided. A series of tables provide a summary of this comparison.

Table 4-1 [Anderson 1992] presents a high-level comparison of the neural network computational model with other prevalent computational models. Table 4-2 presents a comparison of neural networks with the other major intelligent system paradigms. Finally, Table 4-3 presents a comparison that focuses specifically on neural networks and expert systems, another widely employed computational model for the development of intelligent systems.

Section 3 outlines the more common artificial neural network architectures. They are organized in general categories based upon the type of application for which each is appropriate. Most applications of neural networks tend to fall into the following five categories:

1. Prediction,
2. Classification,
3. Data association,
4. Data conceptualization, and
5. Data filtering.

Table 4-4 summarizes the differences between these network categories and indicates which of the more common network topologies belong to which primary category. The categories support consideration of the various networks architectures in terms of how they best match these application categories. Also considered are complex systems that incorporate more than one of the above categories.

Section 4 examines some applications in which neural network systems have been used. This section provides concrete examples of the previously presented concepts and relationships among various problem domains, intelligent systems architectures, etc.

Four broad areas of application are reviewed:

1. *Pattern Recognition*, which includes vision, speech, character recognition, target discrimination and recognition.
2. *Signal Analysis*, which includes language processing, and overlaps (utilizes) pattern recognition.
3. *Robotics*, which integrates control systems, pattern recognition, and signal analysis.
4. *Expert Systems*, which includes complex analysis such as medical diagnosis or system diagnosis.

2. AUTOMATED TAXONOMIC EVALUATION OF NEURAL NETWORKS

This chapter should be seen as a concise literature survey with inclusion of the beginning of guidance for the verification and validation (V&V) practitioner. Over 50 conference publications, presentations, World Wide Web publications and journal articles were collected and analyzed for this discussion. The work by Anderson [1992] and Martinez [1989] contain very useful information. This research work can form the basis of the discussion of the two major questions:

- Does the system need a neural network?
- Which neural network architecture is the most appropriate?

2.1 High-Level Problem Characterization

The first step towards assessing the selection of a neural network for a project may reside with analyzing the problem domain of the entire system or specific system that contains the neural network component. By analyzing the type of problem being solved, a V&V practitioner can assess one of the first questions in regards to the validation of the neural network: should a neural network have been used by the project in the first place?

The major characteristics of problem domains may be divided into three categories:

1. Adaptive vs. Fixed,
2. Parallel vs. Sequential, and

3.   Complete vs. Incomplete.

The following subsections explore each of these major defining features. To facilitate evaluation of the appropriateness for a neural network solution, the practitioner may first want to study the problem area and to classify it in terms of the following features.

2.1.1   Adaptive vs. Fixed

An *adaptive* application is typically one that learns over time and thus can continue to change upon receipt of new inputs. Adaptive systems may need to accommodate dynamic operating conditions, provide capabilities to handle unforeseen events or situations, or learn a specific function that cannot be well defined by system developers. On the other hand, a *fixed* application is one where the internal mapping function that identifies a specific output with a given input does not change with time. A fixed application can be repeatable and have a well-known mathematical function to perform.

2.1.2   Parallel vs. Sequential

This application feature differentiates between applications that are naturally, and thus more efficiently, parallel and those that are more naturally sequential. At the lowest level, all applications can be performed in a parallel fashion, since all can be represented by simple mapping functions. On the other hand, any set can be well ordered and thus serialized, according to the *Well-Ordering Theorem*: [PlanetMath 2004]

If X is any set whatsoever, then there exists a well ordering of X. The well ordering theorem is equivalent to the axiom of choice.

However, either approach to a particular problem may not always lend itself to an efficient realization. Neural networks are fundamentally parallel in nature, but the cascading of impulses through a network may be viewed as sequential. Consequently, neural networks are dual-hybrids that can be viewed functional- and implementation-wise from either perspective for different purposes.

2.1.3   Complete vs. Incomplete

A given application is termed *complete* if a specific input-output mapping is required for all or nearly all of the permutations of the input variables. An example of such an application is integer multiplication where each set of integer inputs produces only one integer output. This mapping of output to input is specific for each possible combination of numbers using a well-defined procedure for producing the output.

An *incomplete* application does not have a mapping for all possible input permutations. With incomplete applications, only subsets of input permutations have specific output assignments. An example of an incomplete application is one that contains input combinations that are impossible to obtain or has input combinations that have no relevance or are known as 'don't care' states. Rule-based systems and control and decision systems can be incomplete.

The *complete-incomplete dichotomy* is not perfect. Rather, a spectrum of *hybrid* applications exist that exhibit characteristics of both complete and incomplete applications. Pattern recognition systems can be either complete or incomplete. A complete pattern recognition problem would be one that dealt with color identification given RGB values assigned into one of 255 bins. An incomplete pattern recognition problem would be one that identified only 4-door cars and ignored trucks, 2-door cars, and motorcycles.

2.1.4   Classification of Applications

Fig. 4-1 [Martinez 1989] depicts the previously discussed application domain characteristics along with an indication of the computational model currently considered most effective for that class of application. Martinez suggests that neural network models seem most appropriate for application domains that are incomplete and adaptive, with neural networks able to fit into either the parallel or sequential application.

2.1.5   V&V Practitioner Considerations on Problem Characterization

Certainly, a project may have an adequate reason for using a neural network even if it does not fit well within the incomplete-adaptive-parallel or incomplete-adaptive-sequential categories. However, a problem space that is otherwise characterized may require further explanation. At this stage of the V&V process, the goal for the practitioner should be to intercept the project that uses a neural network solution simply because it *sounds like a good idea*.

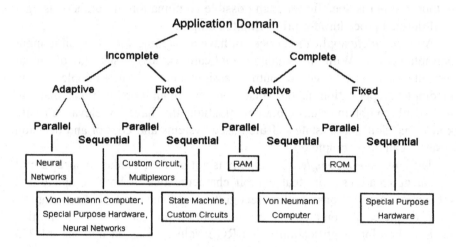

Figure 4-1. Classification of Applications [Martinez 1989]

2.1.6   Considerations of the Complete Characterization

Distinctions are necessary to describe the complete problem space: simple, moderate, and complex. A simple complete problem is one that contains a limited number of input-output matchings. A complex complete problem is one that contains, for practical purposes, an unlimited number of possible pairings. A moderate complete problem is one that falls between these two categories.

Because processing power and capabilities are always improving, clear identification of the differences between simple, moderate, and complex may be too difficult. This would be up to the practitioner who would have to judge the problem domain. Use of a neural network for a simple, possibly even moderately complete problem may be acceptable, but a different solution would be needed for a complex complete problem. Perhaps a project would be better served through use of multiple neural networks, or a combination of neural networks and other technologies, as opposed to a single neural network solution. A reduction of the complexity within the problem space through conversion to an incomplete problem might simplify the application.

2.1.7 Considerations of the Incomplete Characterization

As previously noted in Section 2.1.3, an incomplete application does not contain all possible permutations across the input space. Consequently, the amount of knowledge that a neural network needs to learn becomes smaller and thus easier to obtain. Some problems will naturally be incomplete while others might be complete problems that can be reduced to an incomplete problem.

A neural network system can be designed for *generalization*, the ability of the system to correctly or acceptably handle inputs that it has not seen previously. In an adaptive system, new input combinations may be safely incorporated into the network's knowledge provided that issues concerned with stability and convergence have been addressed in the design of the learning algorithm. For fixed applications, selection of appropriate training data and training procedures may be sufficient to ensure the network can properly, or at least adequately, handle unseen inputs. In both situations, classes of input combinations can be ignored given that the network is capable of generalization. The intention is that when novel input combinations do appear, the network is able to maintain correct operation.

Generalization may employ two different metaphors: one based on *similarity*, the other on *critical values*. The most intuitive forms of generalization follow from the incompleteness of applications. Input permutations can be deemed *similar* from different perspectives, such as hamming distance or Euclidean distance. Some neural network architectures rely upon this similarity to achieve generalization [Hinton 1984]. Hamming, or similarity, based generalization schemes set the output of a novel instance according to how closely it matches a stored *prototype* or stable state in a system. This type of generalization is employed in such approaches as Hopfield networks [Hopfield 1982], Boltzmann machines [Hinton 1984], competitive learning [Rumelhart 1986], and case-based reasoning [Hammond 1989].

Another way to reduce an input space to an incomplete application comes from observations of the behaviors of biological nervous systems. These systems often discriminate between large amounts of inputs by giving higher priority to particular nervous system inputs such as pain or discomfort. A complete system becomes an incomplete system by extracting *critical variables* from across the entire input space and ignoring the other combinations as don't care states. Approaches that seek to discover general critical features that can direct generalization of novel inputs include back-propagation [Rummelhart 1986], ID3 [Quinlan 1986], and the A^q algorithms [Michalski 1983].

2.1.8   Considerations of Adaptive vs. Fixed Applications

Classification of a problem as *fixed* does not necessarily indicate the usage of a neural network system is improper. Consider the IFCS Gen 1 system (see Foreword for full description) that made use of a fixed network, the pre-trained neural network (PTNN) system. The PTNN was chosen because the underlying mathematical function describing the relationship of stability and control derivatives with specific aircraft sensor data was not well known before hand. Yet, for a healthy aircraft under nominal conditions, this equation does not change. The network was trained on real aircraft data so that it could be used to learn the relationships, and then it was fixed and not allowed to adapt during operation. The network was a suitable solution for this fixed application.

Adaptive applications fit perfectly with the neural network solution. One of the main reasons is because artificial neural networks themselves are based upon biological neural networks that are designed for dynamic environments. If a project chooses to use a neural network within an adaptive application, a project may need no further explanation beyond describing the properties of the system that make it adaptive.

2.2   Artificial Neural Networks vs. Other Computational Models

Another way to assess the appropriateness of a neural network solution is to compare the neural network against other computing approaches, some of which may be more suitable solutions for the problem at hand. This section briefly compares the various intelligent system computational models from a variety of perspectives via a series of comparison tables.

2.2.1   Comparison of Computing Approaches

In Table 4-1 [Anderson 1992] a high-level comparison of the neural network computational model is presented along with other prevalent computational models.

Some of the characteristics in the table, such as parallel vs. sequential, were discussed in Section 2.1.2, others require some explanation. The reasoning model characteristic identifies a key difference between the traditional approach and the neural network approach. Traditional software is designed in a logical, step-by-step iterative refinement manner. While the neural network software itself exists within logical programming, its operation and adaptation place it within the realm of *statistical probability* where it reasons in a *Gestalt* fashion, operating upon geometrical similarities. While this statistical nature makes this approach useful for many applications, it also is one of the major reasons why few of those applications are safety- and mission-critical systems.

Table 4-1. Comparison of Computing Approaches [Anderson 1992]

Characteristics	Traditional Computing	Artificial Neural Networks
Processing Style	Sequential	Parallel
Reasoning Model	Logically	Gestalt
Functions via	Rules	Images
	Concepts	Pictures
	Calculations	Controls
Learning Method	by rules (didactically)	by example (socratically)
Applications	Accounting	sensor processing
	word processing	speech recognition
	math inventory	pattern recognition
	digital communications	text recognition

A consideration that a V&V practitioner may have is how a particular problem benefits from having a neural network solution as opposed to the standard form of software, and if this advantage outweighs the problems of applying the traditional approach. Traditional software is applied everywhere a problem can be broken down into a series of directions. Neural network software has only permeated the software market in areas that are too difficult to solve with logical approaches.

The V&V practitioner should be aware that scientific techniques are being developed which can transform fixed neural networks into logical programming. Much of this discussion lies within the Chapter 8 dealing with formal methods. Transformation of the network into logical programming could facilitate application of traditional V&V activities. It could also lend support for a project that wishes to make use of neural networks over a traditional system, but has too many constraints to allow the soft computing approach.

2.2.2   Comparison of Intelligent System Approaches

Table 4-2 presents a comparison of Fuzzy Systems (FS), Neural Networks (NN), Genetic Algorithms (GA), Conventional Control Theory, and Symbolic AI [Hines 2004]. The various characteristics are rated using the fuzzy terms: good (G), slightly good (SG), slightly bad (SB) and bad (B).

Table 4-2 indicates that neural networks appear to be excellent candidates for non-linear problems, especially for those domains that have some need for fault-tolerance, real-time operation, and internal knowledge representation. In terms of fault-tolerance, neural networks can be tolerant to transient bad data, adapt to accommodate true system change, and based upon the complexity of the architecture, usually have redundancy for internal knowledge because of the weights and internal connections.

Table 4-2. Comparison of Intelligent System Approaches [Hines 2004]

Intelligent Systems	FS	NN	GA	Control Theory	Symbolic AI
Mathematical Model	SG	B	B	G	SB
Knowledge Representation	B	G	SG	B	B
Learning Ability	G	B	SB	SB	G
Expert Knowledge	G	B	B	SB	G
Non-linearity	G	G	G	B	SB
Optimization Ability	B	SG	G	SB	B
Fault-Tolerance	G	G	G	B	B
Uncertainty-tolerance	G	G	G	B	B
Real-Time Operation	G	SG	SB	G	B

Since this document deals mainly with neural networks, in-depth discussions of the different forms of intelligent systems are not presented. There may even be debate regarding the ratings within Table 4-2. Still, the practitioner can use this table to begin the evaluation of whether the neural network approach would be more suitable than another soft computing solution. As a minimum, the practitioner may ask a project to discuss the alternatives and then explain why neural networks are chosen.

2.2.3   Comparisons of Expert Systems and Neural Networks

In Table 4-3 [Anderson 1992] a comparison that is specific to neural networks and expert systems is presented. Expert systems are another widely employed computational model for the development of intelligent systems.

The V&V practitioner should be aware that an adapting neural network might drift into a less than optimum state of operation. Such drifting may be in small incremental steps that are not readily detectible. Furthermore, neural networks may adapt into knowledge that upon careful examination may be considered incorrect or erroneous. On the other hand, expert systems are considered static, so insertion of new data is done with trusted knowledge, or knowledge that is considered correct for usage.

Table 4-3. Comparisons of Expert Systems and Neural Networks [Anderson 1992]

Characteristics	Von Neumann Architecture (Expert Systems)	Artificial Neural Networks
Processors	VLSI (traditional processors)	Artificial Neural Networks; variety of technologies; hardware development is on going
Processing Approach	Separate; Processes problem rule one at a one time; sequential	Separate: Multiple, simultaneously
Connections	Externally programmable	Dynamically self-programming
Self Learning	Only algorithmic parameters modified	Continuously adaptable
Fault Tolerance	None without special processors	Significant in the very nature of the interconnected neurons
Neurobiology in Design	None	Moderate
Programming	Rule based approach; complicated	Self-programming; but network must be set up properly
Ability to Be Fast	Requires big processors	Requires multiple custom-built chips

Anderson's table is not complete and some of the entries may require system-specific consideration. Anderson states that for artificial neural networks to be fast, they require multiple custom-built chips. While neural network-specific hardware does exist and can provide immense speed increases, the definition of fast may be better left to the discretion of the system designers. In the cases of some currently developed systems, *fast* has been achievable using current ruggedized[1] processors without specialization and together with existing ruggedized operating systems like VxWorks. Just as neural networks can operate fast without the necessity of custom-built processors, so too can expert systems. However, the table stands as a good beginning point for consideration. If the system undergoing evaluation has any of the above characteristics as requirements (i.e., fault tolerance), the table might aid the practitioner in evaluating the choice of using a neural network.

---

[1] Hardware hardened for safety- and mission-critical use against electromagnetic interference, extreme temperatures, vibrations, etc. and is usually one generation behind the current state of the art.

2.2.4   Artificial Neural Network Requirements vs. Other Computational Models

While the identification of a complete set of neural network requirements within this chapter is not possible, the V&V practitioner should be aware of the special requirements that neural networks have that may not exist for the other computational solutions. Each special requirement is an area where the V&V practitioner can perform some level of evaluation on the project to ensure that it has adequately addressed these needs.

- *Availability of adequate sizes of training and testing data.* All neural network development requires some amount of data to determine what the network architecture will be, to infuse the network with knowledge, to evaluate the network during training, etc. This data has to be relevant to the problem at hand. For example, F-18 flight data is probably not going to be very useful for an autonomous vehicle launched into orbit.
- *An understanding of the problem to guide neural network architecture selection.* A sufficient understanding of the problem to be addressed by the neural network must be clearly exhibited within the project documentation. As later sections of this chapter will reveal, lack of an understanding of the problem domain will leave an almost unlimited set of choices for the neural network architecture type.
- *An understanding by the neural network developers of training techniques and network parameter selection.* Lack of this understanding can lead to long development times or project delays, improper network configurations, failure to find adequate solutions, etc.
- *A mathematical neural network development environment.* The environment should be capable of allowing neural network simulation, application of the learning algorithms, evaluation of the neural network performance, the ability to save, load, and modify neural network data files, etc.
- *Careful considerations of required computing resources for the target platform.* These considerations include processor speed, memory utilization, data storage, and real-time considerations such as threaded processes, process communication, and the possible risks and hazard a real-time adaptive neural network can face.

The V&V practitioner may expand or modify the above list, but once a project has addressed these concerns, the selection of a neural network solution can be judged satisfactory.

3.   NETWORK SELECTION

Neural networks originally were designed to emulate the biological neural network. They all contain a connection of neurons and use some kind of mathematical function to adapt and to perform a recall or output when given an input stimulus. Since the first introduction, several hundred different neural network designs have been explored. Each one exhibits particular advantages given certain circumstances.

The responsibility of the neural network developer includes the selection of appropriate network architecture. The responsibility of the V&V practitioner is to ensure that selection is based upon sound mathematical principles, acceptable given the problem domain, and able to ensure correct operation for a given architecture.

New neural network architectures are continually being introduced into the research literature, and existing architectures are being employed in novel ways. Consequently, any guidance quickly can become outdated and incorrect. Generally, the suitability of a particular neural network architecture for a given application depends upon several factors, including: the number of neurons, the connection matrix between the neurons, the algorithm used for learning, and the internal transfer functions of the network.

The following sections outline some of the most common artificial neural networks. They are organized into general categories of application. These categories are not meant to be comprehensive, but to suggest which neural network architectures would be more appropriate matches to specific application domains.

Anderson [1992] offers an excellent framework for discussion of neural network architecture selection. That framework provides the basis for this section's discussion. Anderson classifies the major applications of neural networks into the five general categories:

1. Prediction,
2. Classification,
3. Data association,
4. Data conceptualization and
5. Data filtering.

Table 4-4 presents a summary of how the more common network topologies fit within the five general categories. The table is far from complete as there are too many architectures to consider, but it will hopefully serve as a basic guide to improve evaluation by the V&V practitioner.

Table 4-4. Neural Network Selection

Neural Network Type	Specific Examples	Use for Neural Network Type
Prediction	Back-propagation Delta Bar Delta Extended Delta Bar Delta Directed Random Search Higher Order Neural Networks Self-Organizing Map into Back-propagation	Use input values to predict some output (e.g. pick the best stocks in the market, predict weather, identify people with cancer risks, etc.)
Classification	Learning Vector Quantization Counter-propagation Probabilistic Neural Networks	Use input values to determine the classification (e.g. is the input the letter A, is the blob of video data a plane and what kind of plane is it)
Data Association	Hopfield Boltzmann Machine Hamming Network Bidirectional Associative Memory Spatio-temporal Pattern Recognition	Like Classification but it also recognizes data that contains errors (e.g. not only identify the characters that were scanned but identify when the scanner isn't working properly)
Data Conceptualization	Adaptive Resonance Network Self-Organizing Map	Analyze the inputs so that grouping relationships can be inferred (e.g. extract from a database the names of those most likely to buy a particular product)
Data Filtering	Recirculation	Smooth an input signal (e.g. take the noise out of a telephone signal)

Note that some neural network architectures can be employed across multiple domain classifications. For example the self-organizing map is employed both as a predictor and for data conceptualization. Omission of a particular neural network architecture from a classification is not meant to imply that architecture is unsuitable.

The dimension of the neural network selection process is further complicated by the fact that an application domain may depend upon functionality from several of the above categories. For example, a flight controller may perform data filtering and classification. How such complex systems are decomposed can greatly impact the choice of appropriate neural network architectures. Furthermore, how they interact, e.g., the output of a data filter may feed a classifier, that in turn feeds a predictor, the output of which ultimately may be fed back as part of a training update to the data filter.

A comprehensive theoretical discussion (beyond the scope of this chapter) of the various neural network computational models is found in *General purpose computation with neural networks: a survey of complexity theoretic results* by Sima and Pekka [2003]. This document, which has been updated several times since its first publishing in 1994, provides an exhaustive annotated bibliography of the major theoretical results that have been obtained in the general field of neural networks, and identifies outstanding problems and open questions that currently remain.

The following subsections describe these five general categories of application for neural networks outlined in Table 4-4.

3.1 Networks for Prediction

Prediction is a common reason for use of neural network technology. Prediction occurs because the network learns to approximate a function describing a set of data, and then given a stimulus or input, can compute values anywhere along this function. Areas where one might find predictive neural networks are in error minimization, vehicle health monitoring, and optimum decision-making. Prediction success depends on several variables, including the quality of the training data and the architecture of the neural network.

3.1.1 Feed-forward, Back-propagation

The *feed-forward* architecture [Parker 1987, Rumelhart 1986] is one of the more commonly used structures within neural network development. Applications using feed-forward architectures include image processing, prediction, signal processing, and robotics. The feed-forward architecture has been proven quite capable of approximating non-linear functions.

Fig. 4-2 shows an example diagram of the feed-forward architecture. Most of these networks contain multiple layers and are often known by another name, the multi-layer perceptron. These layers include an input layer, an output layer, and internal layers called hidden layers. While the network can contain unlimited hidden layers, research by Sima [2003] explains that no more than four layers are needed to solve complex problems. The feed-forward is named because inputs propagate from input layer to hidden layer to output layer in a forward progression. During training, back-propagation can be used to carry errors backwards through the network layers to allow for weight adjustment.

V&V Considerations

While the feed-forward architecture is widely used, there areas of concern on which a V&V practitioner should focus. First, the selection of the number of hidden layers and the number or neurons within each layer is more of an art than a science. Similarly, the V&V analysis of these choices is likewise an art form.

One approach which designers may be inclined to use is manual iterations of design choices with each next choice an attempt to improve over the previous choice. Anderson [1992] identifies three rules that can be used to guide this development.

1. The number of neurons in a hidden layer should be congruent to the complexity of the relationship between the input data and the output data. As this relationship becomes more complex, more neurons should be added.
2. Generalization of the feed-forward neural network can be achieved by adding in more hidden layers, provided that the function being learned can be separated into multiple stages. This means that if the function can be considered a combination of functions itself, then each function should have a hidden layer devoted to approximating it.
3. The number of neurons in each hidden layer is related to the amount of available training data. Eq. (4.1) is a good rule-of-thumb:

$$N_i = \frac{\text{Number of Training Data Pairs}}{(\text{Number of Input Neurons} + \text{Number of Output Neurons}) \cdot \alpha} \quad (4.1)$$

Where N_i is the number of neurons in layer i and α is a factor from one to fifty, selected based upon the noisiness of the data. Nearly noiseless data would use values between one and five, typically noisy data would use a value of ten, and data with more significant noise would use values of 25 or 50. Note that too many neurons within a hidden layer will simply cause the training set to be memorized (with worst cases being one neuron for each input-output training pair).

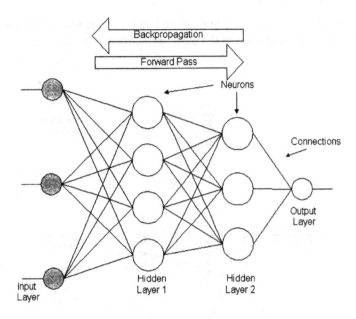

Figure 4-2. An Example Feed-forward Back-propagation Network

The above rules are not only appropriate for the use of the neural network designer, but also for the V&V practitioner. Hopefully, the neural network designer has documented these heuristics for the V&V practitioner to review.

Other problems with this architecture is the number of back-propagation training iterations that may be required due to the network attempting to generalize from too many input-output training data pairs. As characteristic of non-linear systems, network learning may converge to a local minimum, which may or may not be sufficiently near the best or acceptable solution.

3.1.2 Higher-order Neural Networks

Feed-forward neural networks are capable of handling linear separations within the input space, but are unable to generate decision regions which are concave or which are multiply connected. A neural network architecture capable of approximating higher-order functions such as polynomial equations was first proposed by Ivakhnenko [1971] which led to networks containing high-order processing units [Giles and Maxwell 1987] or *higher-order neural networks* (HONN).

A simple HONN could be thought of as describing an elliptical curve region. The HONN function that it learns can include square terms, cubic terms, and higher orders. These terms are comprised of mathematical combinations of the inputs into the network as shown in Fig. 4-3.

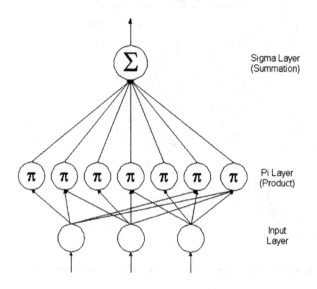

Figure 4-3. An Example Higher-Order Neural Network

The combinations of inputs can occur in any fashion, given that the inputs are only multiplied against one another. For example, with Fig. 4-3, if the three inputs are labeled A, B, and C, then possible input patterns could be: A, B, C, AB, AC, BC, AA, BB, CC, AAB, AAC, etc. The squared and cubic terms are then simply an input multiplied against itself. The polynomial equation then becomes a weighted summation of these individual input patterns. The weights are what the neural network adapts until an appropriate function for the problem is found. An example equation (4.2) is given by:

$$Output = w_1 A + w_2 B + w_3 C + w_4 AA + w_5 AB + \cdots + w_N A^N B^N C^N \quad (4.2)$$

Even more exotic components to the polynomial function can be obtained by first applying another mathematical function to the inputs. These could include functions like SIN, COS, TAN, or even LOG. An example Eq. (4.3) could then be:

$$Output = w_1 A + w_2 \sin(A) + w_3 B + w_4 \log(B) + w_5 A \sin(B) + \cdots \quad (4.3)$$

<u>V&V Considerations</u>

Higher-order neural networks can consume large amounts of computer resources if they are designed to be overly inclusive of all the possible permutations of the input space. Each neuron in the input layer can be comprised of many multiplication and division operations which when accumulated can begin to consume valuable processing time.

Additionally, HONNs of second-order or higher will contain many more weight parameters than first-order neural networks. As higher-orders are used, the explosion in the weight space creates a computational increase and this becomes another difficulty in using the HONN.

There will always be a balance between the complexity of the basis functions formed by the input layer and real-time limitations. The compensating benefit is that it is possible to arrange for the response of the neurons to be invariant to various transformations of the input, such as translations, rotations, and scalings [Bishop 1995].

3.2   Networks for Classification

Classification problems involve identification and assessment of a situation given an observation of data. Different classification problems include biometric identification, sorting out hostile targets from benign targets, and quality control.

3.2.1   Learning Vector Quantization

The *Learning Vector Quantization* (LVQ) neural network architecture was created by Kohonen [1988]. Kohonen is also the creator the Self-Organizing Map found in Section 3.4.2. The LVQ algorithm is meant for a statistical classification or recognition method by clustering the input data space into class regions.

A diagram of the LVQ network is shown in Fig. 4-4. Like most of the neural network architectures, the LVQ network contains an input layer and an output layer. Each neuron in the output layer represents an individual classification or decision. The middle layer, called a Kohonen layer, contains a number of neurons, the actual number being related to the complexity of the problem space.

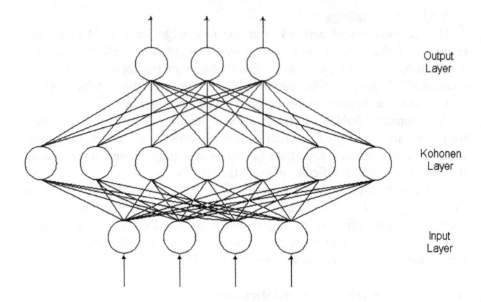

Figure 4-4. An Example Learning Vector Quantization Network

The LVQ network is designed for supervised training where the network is presented with a learning sample containing an input stimulus and a classification. Based upon the input stimulus, a neuron within the Kohonen layer is selected as the best matching unit, the closest neuron to the stimulus. A second best matching unit is also selected. A learning algorithm is then applied to the weights of the neurons to move one closer towards the training classification, and the other one away from the training classification. There are several different types of LVQ algorithms such as LVQ1, LVQ2 and LVQ3, and they each differ in how the weights are updated.

V&V Considerations

The V&V practitioner should identify if the project choosing to use an LVQ network has considered the effect of the complexity of the problem. More complex solutions will require more neurons within the Kohonen layer. Too complex of a problem could need a burdensome computational requirement. A reduction in the input space parameters through principle component analysis might solve this problem.

The project should have also considered proper selection of the particular LVQ algorithm. LVQ2 was designed for optimized classification separation but should only be used with a small value for the learning rate and a restricted number of training steps [Kohonen 1988]. LVQ1 and LVQ3 are more robust processes and can accept larger number of training steps.

3.2.2   Counter-propagation Network

The *counter-propagation network*, developed by Hecht-Nielson [1988], may be viewed as a competitive neural network that combines the functionality of a self-programming lookup table with the additional ability to interpolate between entries. The counter-propagation network tries to perform complex pattern classification but with a reduced network structure and processing time [Anderson 1992].

During the unsupervised competitive learning, the winning neurons are chosen by the Kohonen layer, which functions like a Kohonen neural network. However, not only the weights of the Kohonen layer but also the weights of the output layer are adapted in order to become closer to the output value of the presented object.

The first counter-propagation network consisted of a bi-directional mapping between the input and output layers [Chen 2001]. In essence, while data is presented to the input layer to generate a classification pattern on the output layer, the output layer in turn would accept an additional input vector and generate an output classification on the network's input layer. The counter-propagation network derives its name from this counter-posing flow of information through its structure.

An example network is shown on the next page in Fig. 4-5. The unidirectional counter-propagation network generally is implemented with three layers. The inputs must undergo a normalization to ensure the Kohonen layer can learn the correct class [Anderson 1992]. In some implementations, where the inputs have not been normalized before they enter the network, a fourth layer sometimes is incorporated. The main layers include an input buffer layer, a self-organizing Kohonen layer, and an output layer that uses the Delta Rule to modify its incoming connection weights. Sometimes this layer is called a Grossberg Outstar layer.

Hech-Neilsen's [1988] goal was to address weaknesses of the back-propagation network after which counter-propagation neural network is modeled. The back-propagation neural network is susceptible to over-fitting and the need for significant training epochs in some applications. This is particularly characteristic of situations where the relationships between inputs and outputs are subtle, and yet predictions must be accurate. Counter-propagation is an alternative technique for pattern recognition.

This approach leverages advantages of both the Kohonen unsupervised competitive learning technique, which is good in feature mapping, and the delta rule or Widrow-Hoff rule for supervised learning. The counter-propagation neural network has been demonstrated to perform better than back-propagation in some applications because of its unsupervised learning capability. The operation for the counter-propagation network is similar to that of the Learning Vector Quantization network in that the middle Kohonen layer acts as an adaptive look-up table, finding the closest fit to an input stimulus and outputting its equivalent mapping [Ellingsen 1994].

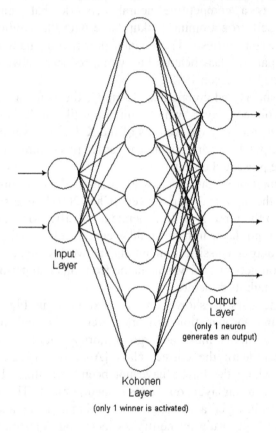

Figure 4-5. An Example Counter-propagation Network

V&V Considerations

The V&V practitioner should ensure that proper analysis has been done regarding the input layer of a counter-propagation network. The number of neurons in this layer is related to the number of independent variables that describe the input space. Presumably, the number of parameters is selected based upon some variable analysis technique such as principle component analysis. If there are too many parameters used to train the network, the network may be unable to reach an adequate generalized solution within computational time limits. If there are too few parameters then a generalized solution may not be reachable at all.

Proper scaling should be applied to the inputs to alleviate any problems from the Kohonen layer. Since this layer will likely identify winning neurons based upon a distance metric, unscaled input parameters with larger values could skew the neuron selection and decrease success.

Another consideration for the practitioner is the potential for neurons within the Kohonen layer to become over-extended and represent improper clustering on the inputs. If the learning algorithm is not set up properly, then neurons within the Kohonen layer could begin to represent several classes instead of one neuron per class. If this happens, the output from the neural network might be an erroneous mixture of multiple classes.

3.3   Networks for Data Association

Data association builds upon data classification by including one additional step. In some situations the data that comes into the system may contain errors that are more than simply noisy content. For example, the errors may be due to omissions, incorrect values, or some other defect with the data source. Data association is intended to overcome such difficulties. The strategy is for the neural network to learn a set of expected values that then constrain it to generate an acceptable (i.e., corrected) output within this questionable set. The goal is that data with imperfections can be corrected back to one of the expected outputs.

3.3.1   Hopfield Network

The *Hopfield Network*, developed by Hopfield [1982], was designed for pattern completion, auto-association, and the solving of optimization problems, such as determining the shortest path with the famous traveling salesman problem. The network is based upon energy concepts and parallels drawn from dynamical physical systems. A neuron in the Hopfield neural network changes state only if the overall *energy*, or internal weight change, of the state space is decreasing. Element state changes thus are designed to diminish the total energy level of the neural network.

Fig. 4-6 shows a basic Hopfield network where each neuron is connected to all other neurons. Originally, each processing element produced output in a binary (zero-one) format. Binary output restrictions can be relaxed with the use of a sigmoid-based transfer function.

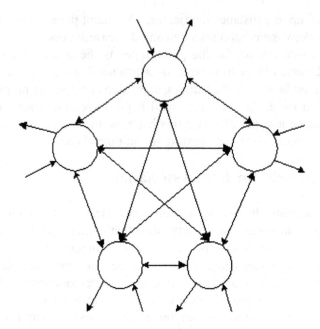

Figure 4-6. An Example Hopfield Network

<u>V&V Considerations</u>

The V&V practitioner should be cognizant of a few potential problems with the Hopfield neural network architecture:

1. The number of patterns that can be stored and accurately recalled is severely limited to approximately fifteen percent of the number of processing elements in the Hopfield layer [Anderson 1992].
2. The Hopfield network is capable of oscillations if the weights are not selected properly.
3. Stable equilibrium states can be influenced by selection of bounded activation functions and constraint conditions on the interconnection matrix.
4. The Hopfield network stability is also related to the similarity of the training patterns.

Maintaining a fifteen percent upper bound on the number of neurons and selecting highly orthogonal pattern sets can mitigate these limitations.

3.3.2   Boltzmann Machine

The *Boltzmann machine* is similar to the Hopfield network with the addition of a simulated annealing technique that searches the pattern layer's state space for a global minimum. Annealing is a concept borrowed from materials science. Under annealing, a material is heated to a very high temperature where atoms form and break bonds due to the higher energy levels. The material is then slowly cooled, coercing the atoms to form stable configurations. Similarly, the Boltzmann machine uses a simulated annealing and tends to gravitate to an improved set of values with successive data iterations through the system.

When the trained Hopfield network is presented with a partial pattern, the network will complete the missing information.

<u>V&V Considerations</u>

The previously discussed problems and limitations of the Hopfield network also apply to the Boltzmann machine. The Boltzmann machine makes uses of a *temperature* variable that is very akin to a learning rate. This variable controls the energy, or amount of internal weight change, within the network. This variable is set high initially and decreases over time. Proper selection of this variable may be an area for evaluation.

3.3.3   Hamming Network

The *Hamming Network* developed by Lippman [1987] in the mid 1980's is another version of the Hopfield neural network architecture. The difference is that a maximum likelihood classifier is added to the input layers of the network.

The Hamming distance metric, which is often used in signal processing, is the bit-by-bit distance between two binary vectors. When applied to a neural network, one binary vector is a target pattern and the second vector is a measured pattern. This measured pattern is classified to a category based upon its closeness with the learned training patterns.

A typical hamming network is shown in Fig. 4-7 on the next page. The number of network input layer nodes equals the number of separable binary features on which classification is to be based. The internal category layer is fully connected with the input layer and fully connected within that layer (all category neurons connect to one another). Each neuron within the category layer connects to only one output neuron.

The number of classifications the network is to learn also dictates the number of neurons within the category layer. This constitutes a significant specialization of the Hopfield architecture where the number of neurons in the middle layer is equal to the number of neurons in the input layer. The number of neurons in the output layer is equal to the number of neurons in the category layer.

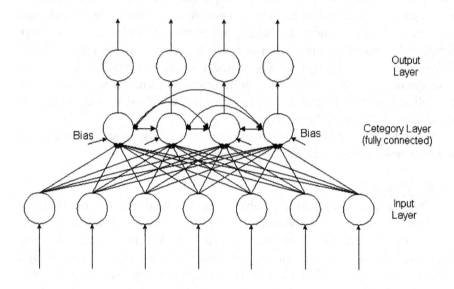

Figure 4-7. An Example Hamming Network

The neurons in the output layer compete with one another to determine which neuron activates, and thus performs the classification.

<u>V&V Considerations</u>
The Hamming network has some improvements over the Hopfield neural network:

1. The Hamming network makes use of fewer category layer neurons because of its specialization,
2. The Hamming network is a little more insensitive to randomness, and
3. The Hamming network is both faster and more accurate than the Hopfield network [Anderson 1992].

However, the Hamming network, like the Boltzmann machine still shares the same disadvantages as those identified with the Hopfield neural network.

3.3.4   Bi-directional Associative Memory

The *bi-directional associative memory* (BAM) model developed by Kosko [1987] is another generalization of the Hopfield model. An example of a BAM neural network is diagrammed in Fig. 4-8.

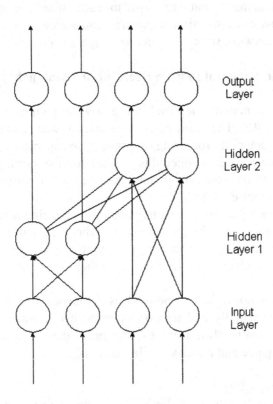

Figure 4-8. An Example Bi-directional Associative Memory

The BAM is capable of recalling one piece of information when given another piece. For example, the network might recall a person's face when given their voice signature. The advantage to using a BAM neural network is that if the input information is noisy or otherwise partially missing/corrupted, the BAM might be able to correct the input information and retrieve the associated information.

The name bi-directional comes from the manner in which information is recalled from the network. Information passes into the BAM through the input layer, is processed in a hidden layer, these inputs can be passed into a second layer, and then back again from the second layer into the first. This continues until there are no further changes in the weights of the units within the two layers.

V&V Considerations

As with the Hopfield network, the BAM network can incorrectly determine a pattern when input information which complements the specific pattern is given to the network. The BAM network can also suffer from *crosstalk* when patterns that are close to each other are applied to the network. In this case, the similar patterns can create an erroneous stable state within the network stabilizing on meaningless vectors [Freeman 1991].

3.3.5   Spatio-temporal Pattern Recognition (Avalanche)

The Avalanche network depicted in Fig. 4-9 on the next page is a result of Grossberg [1970]. The purpose for development was driven by efforts to account for the temporal processing of information capable by the biological brain. Hecht-Nielsen later applied this network to time-varying signals such as radar applications, resulting in the spatio-temporal pattern recognition network [Hecht-Nielsen 1986].

Spatio-temporal patterns are patterns that are changing across space and time. An example would be human speech where the voice of the human speaker changes based upon what they are saying and how they are saying it. Other signals can change across time including sonar patterns and video imagery.

The *spatio-temporal pattern* network is comprised of a Kohonen layer that can extract spatially and temporally correlated features. Subsequent layers of the network then learn to categorize these features making it possible to recognize and classify similar patterns.

V&V Considerations

Guidance for this network is limited, but several factors will need to be addressed by a project wishing to use a spatio-temporal approach:

1. The number of patterns that must be learned and how this affects the number of neurons within the network's Kohonen layer
2. Application of different forms of training (learning single temporal sequences vs. learning multiple temporal sequences
3. Specific approaches to the design of a spatio-temporal structure as there are many different variants
4. Computational resource requirements.

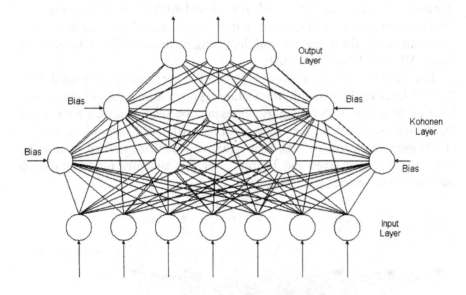

Figure 4-9. An Example Spatio-temporal Pattern Network

3.4   Networks for Data Conceptualization

Data conceptualization is a data mining technique. It doesn't have any strong definitions of data description, or how the data is related to one another. Instead the neural network develops a functional understanding of how pieces of data are related. Clustering similar data into meaningful groups that are connected via some previously undefined characteristic would be one form of data conceptualization.

3.4.1   Adaptive Resonance Theory Network

A problem with the back-propagation approach to neural network learning is that when the environment of the network changes, to accommodate this change the neural network must undergo retraining. To learn new patterns, the network might just be trained on the most recent patterns in its environment. This would result in the newest patterns being best remembered and the older patterns slowly being forgotten. Another approach might be to retrain the network upon all the patterns at once, but this is computational expensive and not practical for most situations.

The Adaptive Resonance Theory (ART) network, developed by Grossberg [1976] is an attempt to solve this issue. The basic premise with the ART approach is that learning can be incremental with new learning adding to existing learning rather than overwriting it. Two ART neural network architectures have been developed: ART-1 and ART-2. ART-1 works with binary patterns while ART-2 is for continuous patterns. There are also many other variants of the neural network including inclusion of fuzzy logic in the Fuzzy ART and Fuzzy ARTMAP.

The ART network is a recurrent network where inputs are passed from the first layer of the network, the feature representation field, to the second layer of the network, the category representation field, and then back to the feature representation field as shown in Fig. 4-10. ART networks make use of unsupervised learning. The term adaptive resonance is used to describe when the category layer and feature layer are mutually reinforcing each other and have reached a stable state.

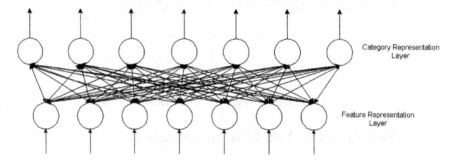

Figure 4-10. An Example ART Neural Network

V&V Considerations

The V&V practitioner must consider the effects of noisy data on the ART network as noise can cause the network to become confused when trying to match a pattern it has already learned. A vigilance parameter is used to control how the network reacts to difference within the pattern classes. High vigilance causes the network to be aware of small differences while low vigilance causes the network to only be aware of large differences. If the vigilance parameter is not set optimally, then the network may be overcome by noise or it could misidentify patterns.

The ART-1 has a limitation in its ability to be robust [Paul 2003]. Within ART-1 a single neuron within the category representation layer handles a complete pattern classification. This can be considered a limit on the network's fault tolerance, as there is no secondary storage in neighboring neurons.

3.4.2   Self-organizing Map

Neural networks known as *self-organized feature maps* or *self-organizing maps* (SOMs) are designed as topology representing networks whose roles are to learn the topology of an input space with perfect preservation. In this sense, they learn the function that describes a map of the input space.

Developed by Kohonen [1988] the SOM belongs to a class of networks known as competitive neural networks. Unlike the feed-forward neural networks, competitive neural networks operate under a *winner-take-all* learning algorithm. When the network receives an input stimulus, it searches throughout the network structure looking for a neuron that is closest to this input. This neuron is known as the *best matching unit* (BMU) and the network will adjust this unit, and its neighborhood comprised of neurons connected to the BMU. In this way, the input space becomes compressed by being represented by neurons spatially.

An example of an SOM is seen in Fig. 4-11. SOMs make use of unsupervised learning because they do not require a specific output during adaptation. Because of this, SOMs are very good at data compression and identifying underlying clusters of data in an input space.

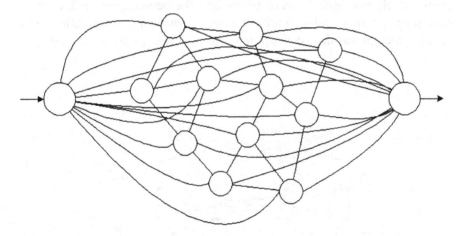

Figure 4-11. An Example SOM Network

<u>V&V Considerations</u>
There are different forms of the SOM architecture, but they all share some common considerations that the V&V practitioner may want to be aware of. First, these networks are usually designed to grow by adding new neurons into the network over time. This can lead to a network expand in size beyond its computational capabilities, both in regards to memory utilization and processor time requirements.

There are usually several variables which control the learning and growing of the SOM. Determination of an optimum set of controlling parameters can take a significant amount of study. A project may want to perform experiments to guide selection of learning rates, forgetting constants, and error thresholds.

3.5   Networks for Data Filtering

Data filtering problems require that two or more pieces of information be separated from a single source. Removal of noise from a transmitted message requires filtering. Error in a system could be thought of as noise and a neural network solution may try to remove the error by correcting or compensating for it from another piece of information.

3.5.1   Recirculation Neural Networks

Hinton [1988] gives two criticisms against back-propagation neural networks: (1) they require the selection of desired outputs for supervised training and (2) their very nature of passing back errors along the same paths, which propagate forward inputs into the network, make developing back-propagation neural networks in hardware difficult. The solution to the second problem was the *Recirculation neural network*, shown in Fig. 4-12.

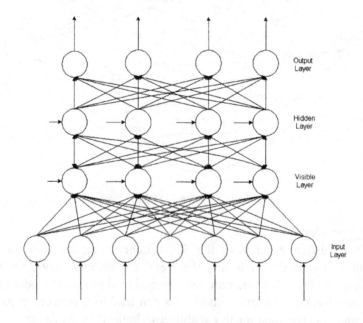

Figure 4-12. An Example Recirculation Network

The recirculation network contains a visible layer and a hidden layer. Hinton [1988] described the process by which additional visible-hidden layer combinations can occur where the hidden layer of a lower layer forms the visible layer of a higher layer so the neural network can scale. The visible and hidden neurons are fully connected. In order to facilitate the network's implementation into hardware, the same group of neurons used for the visible neurons are used for the output neurons. The weight update on the visible neurons is then done in a feed-forward progression based on the calculations of the hidden layer. The data from the visible layer is recirculated back to the same neurons (now within the output layer) giving rise to the name of this network architecture.

The hidden layer learns to represent the data passed on by the visible layer. For applications that want to compress these representations, fewer neurons in the hidden layer than in the visible layer can be used [Anderson 1992]. Because the network can perform compression, the network can be thought of as acting like a low bandpass filter with a transition point given by the number of neurons within the hidden layer.

V&V Considerations
Limited literature has been found regarding use of the recirculation neural network since its inception in 1988, leaving this architecture as young and perhaps not well explored. Any project that makes use of this neural network type will need to ensure that assumptions taken in [Hinton 1988] are reasonable. The main assumption is that the recirculation network can perform back-propagation given a linear functional constrain for neurons in the visible layer, the weight matrix between the visible and hidden neurons is the symmetrical, and the visible neurons have a high regression. Hinton [1988] found that the network performs a back-propagation-like learning when the visible neurons are non-linear, but this evidence was somewhat more difficult to explain.

3.6   Others

The five general categories of application are not the only areas where neural networks are used. Because neural networks can be trained to minimize an error function, they can be used in optimization scenarios where the error is simply a cost function that the system developers want to improve. Neural networks have also been used in sensor failure detection, identification, and accommodation problems to improve the fault-tolerance of aircraft. Neural networks can also be combined with genetic algorithms, expert systems, and fuzzy logic to create sophisticated complex solutions. It could be argued, however, that the V&V practitioner could decompose any neural network solution into one of the five basic classes.

4.   HOW ARTIFICIAL NEURAL NETWORKS ARE BEING USED

Many of the problem domains in which neural networks are being employed involve applications where answers are by their nature *nebulous*— or at least, are not 100 percent certain. Neural network solutions are being employed because they perform better than alternative computational models, rather than because they yield *perfect* solutions.

Loan approval is an example where neural networks have been shown to produce better results than existing technologies, yet they still are not 100% accurate. Banks have long used experts to identify the likelihood of a successful loan payback from a borrowing entity. Sometimes this knowledge has even been transformed into an expert system, but still lending institutions look for an improved accuracy in predicting bad loans. Predictions that are 90% accurate would be an improvement over other current selection processes. Kemsely [1992] discusses how neural network solutions improved bad loan prediction and how neural network improvements have led to their adoption by credit card companies as a part of an application screening process.

To provide the V&V practitioner some familiarity with neural network uses, four broad application areas are reviewed:

1. *Pattern recognition*, which includes vision, speech, character recognition, and target discrimination and recognition.
2. *Signal Analysis*, which includes language processing, and overlaps pattern recognition.
3. *Robotics*, which integrates control systems, pattern recognition, and signal analysis.
4. *Expert Systems*, which includes complex analysis such as medical diagnosis or system diagnosis.

The choice of example applications considered here is intended to complement Section 3 that analyzed the major characteristics and potential limitations of the prevalent neural network architectures and learning methods, and the major characteristics of problem domains to which neural network solutions could be deemed appropriate. The above broad areas are not disjoint. Each is complex, and necessarily draws upon the other problem domains.

4.1   Pattern Recognition

Pattern recognition includes such areas as vision, speech, and character recognition, as well as target discrimination and recognition.

The V&V practitioner may see neural networks being used for pattern recognition activities.   One example comes from the JFK airport where neural networks were used to detect bombs by recognizing a pattern from the data generated by gamma ray sensors. In this case the neural network was trained to identify small variances that it associated with the presence of a bomb.

A second example is that of a trained back-propagation neural network that was used to provide a probability that a patient in a hospital was experiencing an actual heart attack. The neural network was trained upon data collected from emergency rooms. From this data the network discerns patterns to assist doctors in identifying the real attacks from the false alarms.

4.1.1   Quality Control

Quality control within manufacturing is concerned with ensuring that the product on the assembly line meets a desired specification.   This specification can be written to describe a product's shape, size, color, texture, etc. Neural networks can be trained to recognize good examples and through pattern recognition can detect when a product fails to match the example.

Neural network quality control systems never tire and can be easily deployed and produce consistent measurements.   These systems are excellent candidates to replace the human inspector, who can become distracted or overwhelmed to perform the same job.

4.1.2   Character Recognition

Having computers capable of reading human written language can improve the human-computer interface that will lead to more ubiquitous computing solutions. One of the ways that can accomplish this is through character recognition systems that make use of neural network technology.

Character recognition can be used as part of a paper document scanning technology known as optical character recognition. In this technology, paper documents are first scanned, converted into some intermediary computer readable form, and then processed by neural networks looking for alphabetical patterns to identify what letter or number is represented. These systems can be quite complicated given that every human has a distinguishing writing style that can vary from very neat to very sloppy.

Another area where neural networks can be used within character recognition is in direct human-to-computer interfaces such as the notepad or palm computing devices that have recently begun being sold. These devices translate the written input in real-time with the added advantage of instant feedback to allow the user to correct improper conversions.

Anderson [1992] cites several more examples including a credit card reader with a 98–99% accuracy, systems which can read cursive, and neural networks that have been developed to interpret Asian language characters. These characters can be much more difficult than the roman-based languages because they use far more intricate combinations of brush strokes.

4.1.3   Language Processing

Like character recognition, language processing also has a generally fixed set of patterns that can be interpreted and converted by neural network systems. Instead of the patterns being made up of images representing characters or words, language is made up of phonetic patterns that comprise letters, syllables, and words.

Language processing has matured to a point where it is somewhat common. More recently, neural networks are found in interactive voice response systems where many speakers use a reduced subset of language, namely, the digits "1" through "0," the English alphabet and place names (e.g. proper names of states and major cities). Word processing applications can perform speech-to-text conversions to provide highly useful digital dictation applications. One of the hopes behind development of neural networks that are able to translate speech is to bridge the gap between humans and computers even more by providing a direct voice-to-command interface. With this technology pilots can communicate orders to their vehicle or ground control can describe commands to robotic satellites.

4.2   Signal Processing

Signal processing is an application area that will be discussed separate from pattern recognition, even though the two share computational similarities. For this discussion the difference will be based upon the transformation of the raw signal data. Signal processing applications do something to transform this data and then make a decision, prediction, etc. while pattern recognition systems can perform an action on the raw data without transformation.

Signal analysis encompasses applications that can collect and analyze sensor data, sometimes for feedback into the system or for decision-making purposes. Kemsley [1992] identifies a signal processing application for *signal recognition and classification* where target recognition occurs through interpretation of a reflected signal such as radar. More recently, neural nets have used to recognize a person by the gait of their walking.

A likely area for neural networks with signal processing is in noise reduction. An adaptive neural network could learn the underlying behavior describing the noise function, and then remove this function from the data signal.

Another application area for neural networks with regards to signal processing is that of data compression. Some neural network data compression techniques train the network on raw data in an unsupervised manner – without guidance, allowing the network to figure out how best to perform the compression. Data sets can experience dimension reduction and via internal data clustering, groups of similar data can be represented by fewer pieces of data. The DCS network within the IFCS system can be thought of as performing data compressions as it associates stability and control derivatives into clustered regions of the flight envelope.

Data compression is not without some drawbacks. Reducing a ten-dimensional data set to seven dimensions can save on data storage, but when the data is decompressed to the original higher dimension, some of the information is lost. The advantage in using a neural network approach is that if the underlying compression mechanism isn't well known, the neural network is able to implement an approach through adaptation.

Gelenbe [2004] discusses the use of neural networks for the compression/decompression of image data used within videoconferencing, HDTV, and videophones. Gelenbe suggests that the popularity of employing neural networks in image compression is primarily due to their learning nature. Carrato [1992] provides an example where a feed-forward neural network model was able to achieve a 16:1 compression ratio on several images.

The V&V practitioner may see projects that employ neural networks in the areas of noise reduction and data compression, especially when considering that future space missions will utilize a wide array of instrumentation each with increasing precision. NASA may use neural networks for noise reduction of telemetry data, satellite data feeds, or transmissions that have traveled long distances through deep space. As the precision increases and the size of the data collected grows, the neural network data compression techniques might offset some of the associated problems.

4.3   Robotics

Robotics is another area in which a V&V practitioner likely will see extensive use of neural network technology. Robotics integrates several complex functions including: control systems, pattern recognition, and signal analysis. Robotics also utilizes many different intelligent system technologies where specific forms of intelligent software are employed to solve very specific problems, yet the component systems are expected to work together as a whole. Neural networks often are employed because of their capabilities to adapt to new situations, to obtain and maintain knowledge, and to generalize beyond their original training.

Beyond the complex realm of autonomous systems, neural networks are being deployed in a wide range of servo-control applications. These range from sophisticated aerospace applications such as the IFCS, to various mobility support systems such as anti-lock breaking systems in automobiles, to thermostats that adapt to environmental conditions.

Neural networks are not only embedded in many robotics systems in manufacturing, they are often involved in other areas of process control, for example, shop floor planning [Jain 1998] and diagnosis [Zhang 1995].

4.3.1   Autonomous Vehicles

The name of the research and production field that uses robotic vehicle technology is *autonomous vehicles*. Two areas within autonomous vehicles are robotic ground vehicles and unmanned-aerial (and aquatic) vehicles (UAV).

The Defense Advanced Research Projects Agency (DARPA) recently sponsored a robotic competition called the *Grand Challenge* [DARPA 2003] to promote the development of autonomous vehicle technologies. Contest entrants had to design a vehicle that could traverse a desert route in less than ten hours, with no human interface or control, deciding its own navigation, and handle varying terrain conditions and obstacles. Thirteen entries were allowed to compete in the race, but ultimately none of them managed to succeed. Still, the possibilities of employing unmanned robots for combat or reconnaissance maintains a worthy goal and DARPA plans to host the competition again next year.

NASA has a particular interest in developing autonomous robotic exploration because of the time-delays that can be experienced by ground control as they manually direct a rover or satellite to perform complex functions. Good example cases where robotic vehicle technology could have been employed are the recent NASA Mars rovers, Spirit and Opportunity. The planet-to-planet time delay between Earth and Mars is around 12 minutes. The time delay situation is even worse as the mission extends to the outer planets. Very likely robotic exploration will be an area where the V&V practitioner will see neural networks being employed.

The development of UAVs will become one of the major areas to employ neural network technology. Primarily, this is because the technology has matured sufficiently that companies like Boeing now are prepared to include neural network technology in their military development. The success of the US Air Force unmanned reconnaissance aircraft, the Globalhawk, further encourages development in this area.

4.3.2   Manipulator Trajectory Control

Kemsely [1992] reports on neural networks being used in the area of robotic manipulator trajectory control. The design of a robot's kinematics is very difficult and time consuming. If neural networks are used, they may save valuable development time and solve the problem on their own because of adaptability and generalization.

Consider a NASA rover with an instrument arm that extends to collect data from its environment. As that arm moves, an algorithm controls where it can move, how fast it can move, and knows how it can move at the next step. If the manipulator should somehow become changed due to collision, vibration, internal damage, or even software failure, the algorithm has to be changed to accommodate this. Trying to account for all the possibilities of failure can very nearly, if not completely, make traditional algorithm development impossible. Adaptable intelligent systems could re-learn the functionality on their own.

In addition to failure, another dynamic consideration for manipulator control is obstacle avoidance. Instead of the changes in the system due to a failure, the system has to be able to change behavior given differing environmental conditions or objects. Much like the failure scenario, having an adaptable algorithm can alleviate much of the complexity of designing a control algorithm that accounts for every possible scenario.

4.3.3   Intelligent Flight Control

Intelligent flight control is listed under robotics because in most of these systems, the neural networks act autonomously to change the behavior of the aircraft. NASA has been studying intelligent flight control for at least the past ten years. These systems can vary in the degree of control the neural network is given within the system.

The IFCS Gen 1 system used two different neural networks. As this was one of the first flight-tested neural network flight control systems, strong limitations were placed upon the neural networks within the system. The PTNN was fixed and did not adapt during system operation. Instead of computing aircraft gains and feeding them directly into surface controls, the PTNN only provided data to other parts of the flight controller that then carried out their own computations. The DCS only augmented the knowledge of the PTNN. It too was limited in its effect on the system.

The second generation allowed the neural network more control within the system. The job of the online adaptive component was to improve error tracking and provide direct feedback into a dynamic inversion module. This dynamic inversion module computed the aircraft controls and the neural networks were a more integral part of that computation than they were for the first generation.

Subsequent generations will probably make the neural network modules even more integral to the system. Their continued use and rise in importance within intelligent flight control is tied directly to the success of the V&V practitioner to certify the system. These neural network solutions will not fade away because the research conducted by NASA has shown that great improvements can be made to a flight control system through adaptation to accommodate failure or damage.

4.4   Expert Systems

Expert Systems are generally thought of as being symbolic, rule-based systems. However, neural networks also can be trained to perform expert tasks—tasks that have been viewed as requiring some level of expertise, or knowledge (knowledge-based systems). Of course, the manner in which the expertise is encoded in a neural network is radically different than a set of human-readable rules. Their use includes such complex analysis as required for medical diagnosis, system diagnosis, and financial analysis.

Sometimes the required knowledge is not explicitly documented, or even consciously known, but must be extracted from actual data. This is the realm of data mining [Müller 2000]. In contrast to the prior discussion of pattern recognition, where at least the pattern to be recognized is known, data mining is focused on identifying previously unrecognized patterns.

Group Method of Data Handling theory and its applications is one example of efforts at the propagation of inductive self-organizing methods to the solution of complex practical problems [Madala 1994].

4.4.1   Diagnosis

One such diagnostic application is a diagnosis system that can detect engine misfire simply from the noise. Kemsley [1992] discusses the system developed by Odin Corp., which works to detect misfires on engines that run upwards of 10,000 rpms. The benefit is that misfires are thought to be a leading cause of pollution and detection and accommodation of misfires could reduce the problem.

A most likely area involving diagnosis that the V&V practitioner will encounter is in the area of intelligent vehicle health monitoring. Systems that are expected to operate for long periods of time without human interaction will require this technology in order to detect failures in the system and make corrections. Expected benefits are for satellites, remote robotic exploration, and even military and commercial aircraft that can diagnose an impending problem and report it immediately to the pilot.

Another field within neural network diagnosis is the recognition of patterns within the sensor data of the medical industry [Lisboa 1999]. A neural network is now being used in the scanning of PAP smears. This network attempts to do a better job at reading the smears than can the average lab technician. Missed diagnosis in this industry can be a serious problem. In many cases, a professional must perceive patterns from noise, such as identifying a fracture from an X-ray or cancer from an X-ray "shadow." Neural networks promise, particularly when faster hardware becomes available, help in many areas of the medical profession where data is hard to read.

In some situations, the diagnosis system is merely used for filtering out false-positives rather than being the upfront evaluation. This is because the system is considered more trustable when it isn't making a life-or-death diagnosis. The V&V practitioner may encounter this technology as it moves into the realm of first stage detection.

4.4.2 Financial

While it is unlikely that a V&V practitioner will see neural networks projects within the realm of financial analysis, this commercial area does deserve some recognition. As mentioned during the introduction to this section, lending institutions are making use of neural networks to identify expected success/failure of possible loans. Telemarketers also make use of similar technology by applying data mining techniques to their databases to identify combinations for higher positive responses to their product. This includes identifying households with larger families, identifying better times to call a household, and extracting information on household purchasing habits, all much to the chagrin to the American public.

Neural networks are also used in making decisions within the financial market such as stock trading and currency trading. By analyzing the trends of a particular stock or currency, and learning the behavior of the item over time and against multiple variables, one can improve the decision making process of selecting highs and lows. Anderson [1992] reports that the Daiwa Research Institute developed a neural network stock system which scored up to 20% better than the Nikkei average and can boost successful hit rates by as much as 70 – 80%.

4.5   Mission-critical and Safety-critical Applications

Many more examples could be provided. Neural networks are being more frequently developed and deployed in applications that would be termed *mission critical* or *safety critical*. While much concern still exists regarding the employment of neural networks in such areas, the research to address this need is making considerable progress. The following is a list of recent survey papers covering various application areas where neural network solutions now are finding ever-widening acceptance:

- Neural networks as data mining tools in drug design [Gasteiger 2003]
- An introduction to bio-inspired artificial neural network architectures [Fasel 2003]
- Nonlinear image processing using artificial neural networks [De Ridder 2003]
- Logistic regression and artificial neural network classification models: a methodology review [Dreiseitl 2002]
- Evaluation of inherent performance of intelligent medical decision support systems: utilizing neural networks as an example [Smith 2003]
- Image processing with neural networks - a review [Egmont-Petersen 2002]
- Neural networks as an intelligence amplification tool: A review of applications [Poulton 2002]
- A review of evidence of health benefit from artificial neural networks in medical intervention [Lisboa 2002]
- Neural-network models of learning and memory: leading questions and an emerging framework [Carpenter 2001]
- A brief overview and introduction to artificial neural networks [Buscema 2002]

Some of these papers not only discuss the employment of neural networks in a particular application domain, but also consider the V&V implications that their use raises for that application domain [Smith 2003; Lisboa 2002].

5.   SUMMARY

The purpose of the material in this chapter is to aid the V&V practitioner with the *validation*, of a proposed or implemented neural network-based system.   Validation involves the assessment of the appropriateness of a particular neural network-based solution for the problem being solved

This chapter has presented a taxonomic overview of neural network systems from multiple perspectives.   Major characteristics of applications and their solution via neural networks have been presented.

At the highest level, the issue addressed here is whether any neural network architecture could be an appropriate choice for the problem being solved.   Given that a particular neural network model should be able to solve the problem, the next major concern is to focus upon the supporting requirements that should be addressed, e.g., the particular neural network architecture.

REFERENCES

Anderson, Dave and George McNeil. 1992. *Artificial Neural Networks Technology.* Data & Analysis Center for Software, Contract Number F30602-89-C-0082, August 20.

Bishop, C.M.   1995.   *Neural Networks for Pattern Recognition.*   Oxford, NY: Oxford University Press, England.

Buscema M. 2002. A Brief Overview and Introduction to Artificial Neural Networks. *SUBSTANCE USE & MISUSE* 37 (8-10): 1093-1148.

Carpenter, G.A. 2002. Neural-Network Models Of Learning and Memory: Leading Questions And An Emerging Framework. *Trends in Cognitive Sciences.* 5 (3): 114-118 MAR 2001.

Carrato, S. 1992. Neural Networks For Image Compression.   In Gelenbe, E. (ed.) *Neural Networks: Advances and Applications 2,* Elsevier North-Holland: 177-198.

Chen, Hong. 2001. Neural Networks for Digit Recognition: A Comparison Between Counter-propagation and Back-propagation.   Masters thesis, Computer Science Department, Rochester Institute of Technology.

Cukic, Bojan, Brian J. Taylor, and Harhsinder Singh. 2002. Automated Generation of Test Trajectories for Embedded Flight Control Systems. *International Journal of Software Engineering and Knowledge Engineering* 12(2):175-200.

DARPA. 2003. http://www.darpa.mil/grandchallenge/.

De Ridder, D., R.P.W. Duin, M. Egmont-Petersen, L.J. Van Vliet, and P.W. Verbeek. 2003. Nonlinear Image Processing Using Artificial Neural Networks. *Advances in Imaging and Electron Physics* 126: 351-450.

Dreiseitl, S. and L. Ohno-Machado. 2002. Logistic Regression and Artificial Neural Network Classification Models: A Methodology Review. *Journal of Biomedical Informatics* 35 (5-6): 352-359.

DeTienne, K.B., D.H. DeTienne, and S.A. Joshi. 2003. Neural Networks as Statistical Tools For Business Researchers. *Organizational Research Methods* 6 (2): 236-265.

Egmont-Petersen, M., D. de Ridder, and H. Handels. 2002. Image Processing with Neural Networks - a Review. *Pattern Recognition* 35 (10): 2279-2301.

Ellingsen, B.K. 1994. A Comparative Analysis of Backpropagation and Counterpropagation Neural Networks. *Neural Network World* 4(6):719-734.

Fasel, B. An Introduction to Bio-inspired Artificial Neural Network Architectures. *Acta Neurologica Belgica*103 (1):6-12.

Freeman, James A., and D. Skapura. 1991. *Neural Networks: Algorithms, Applications, and Programming Techniques (Computation and Neural Systems Series).* Addison-Wesley Pub Co.

Gasteiger J., A. Teckentrup, L. Terfloth, and S. Spycher. 2003. Neural networks as Data Mining Tools in Drug Design. *Journal of Physical Organic Chemistry16* (4):232-245.

Gelenbe, Erol, M. Sungur, and C. Cramer. 2004. Learning Random Networks for Compression of Still and Moving Images. [cited 6 May 2004]. Available from World Wide Web: (http://www.ee.duke.edu/~cec/research/neuralcompression/JPL/paper.html).

Giles, C. L. and T. Maxwell. 1987. Learning, Invariance, and Generalization in High Order Neural Networks. *Applied Optics* 26(23)4972.

Grossberg, Stephen. 1970. Some Networks That Can Learn, Remember, and Reproduce any Number of Complicated Space-Time Patterns, II. *Studies in Applied Mathematics* 49.

Grossberg, Stephen. 1976. Adaptive Pattern Classification and Universal Recoding: I. Parallel Development and coding of Neural Feature Detectors. *Biological Cybernetics* 23.

Hammond, K. 1989. In *Inside Case-Based Reasoning*, Eds C.K. Riesbeck & R.C. Shank, Hillsdale, NJ, Erlbaum.

Hecht-Nielsen, Robert. 1986. Nearest Matched Filter Classification of Spatio-temporal Patterns. Special report published by Hecht-Nielsen Neuro-Computer Corporation, San Diego, California.

Hecht-Nielsen, R. 1988. Applications of Counterpropagation Networks. *Neural Networks* 1:131-139.

Hines, Evor. 2004. Intelligent Systems Engineering (ES3770) Lecture Notes, University of Warwick.

Hinton, G., T. Sejnowski, and D. Ackley. 1984. Boltzmann Machines: Constraint Satisfaction Networks that Learn. Technical Report CMU-CS-84-119, CMU, Pittsburgh, PA.

Hinton, G.E., and J.L. McClelland. 1988. Learning Representations by Recirculation. *Proc. of the IEEE Conference on Neural Information Processing Systems*, November 1988.

Hopfield, John J. 1982. Neural Networks and Physical Systems with Emergent Collective Computational Abilities. *Proceedings of the National Academy of Sciences* 79.

Ivakhnenko, A.G. 1971. Polynomial Theory of Complex Systems. *IEEE Trans. on Systems, Man, and Cybernetics* 1(4):364-378.

Jain, A. S., and S. Meeran. Job-Shop Scheduling Using Neural Networks. *International Journal of Production Research* 36(5):1249-1272.

Kemsely, D., T. R. Martinez, and D. M. Campbell. 1992. A Survey of Neural Network Research and Fielded Applications. *International Journal of Neural Networks* 2(2/3/4):123-133.

Kohonen, T. 1988. *Self-Organization and Associative Memory*, Second Edition. Springer-Verlag, New York.

Kosko, Bart. 1987. Adaptive Bidirectional Associative Memories. *Applied Optics* 26.

Lippmann, Richard P. 1987. An Introduction to Computing with Neural Nets. *IEEE ASSP Magazine*.

Lisboa, Paulo J.G., Emmanuel C. Ifeachor, and Piotr S. Szczepaniak (Eds). 1999. *Artificial Neural Networks in Biomedicine, Perspectives in Neural Computing Series*. Springer-Verlag.

Lisboa, PJG. 2002. A Review of Evidence of Health Benefit from Artificial Neural Networks in Medical Intervention. *Neural Networks* 15 (1):11-39.

Madala, H.R. and A.G. Ivakhnenko. 1994. *Inductive Learning Algorithms for Complex Systems Modeling.* CRC Press.

Martinez, Tony. 1989. Neural Network Applicability: Classifying the Problem Space. *Proceedings of the IASTED International Symposium on Expert Systems and Neural Networks.*

Michalski, R.S. 1983. A Theory and Methodology of Inductive Learning. *Artificial Intelligence* 20:111-116.

Müller, J.-A. and F.Lemke. 2000. Self-Organizing Data Mining. BoD Hamburg.

Parker, D.B. 1987. Optimal Algorithms for Adaptive Networks: Second Order Back Propagation, Second Order Direct Propagation and Second Order Hebbian Learning. *Proc. of the 1st ICNN*, Volume II.

Paul, Jody. 2004. Adaptive Resonance Theory Course Notes [online]. Denver, CO: Metropolitan State College of Denver, 2003 [cited May 10, 2004]. Available from the World Wide Web: (http://www.jodypaul.com/cs/ai/ART.pdf).

PlanetMath.org. 2004. Zermelo's Well-Ordering Theorem [online]. [cited April 20, 2004]. Available from the World Wide Web:
(http://planetmath.org/encyclopedia/WellOrderingPrinciple2.html).

Poulton M.M. 2002. Neural Networks as an Intelligence Amplification Tool: A Review of Applications. *Geophysics* 67(3):979-993.

Quinlan, J. R. 1986. Induction of Decision Trees. *Machine Learning* 1:81-106.

Rumelhart, D. and McClelland J. 1986. *Parallel Distributed Processing: Explorations in the Microstructure of Cognition.* MIT Press, Cambridge, MA.

Seiffert, U. and B. Michaelis. 2001. Directed Random Search for Multiple Layer Perceptron Training. In: D.J. Miller et al. (Eds): *Neural Networks for Signal Processing XI.* IEEE, Piscataway, USA.

Sima, J. and P. Orponen. 2003. General Purpose Computation with Neural Networks: a Survey of Complexity Theoretic Results. *Neural Computation* 15:2727-2778.

Smith A.E., C.D. Nugent, and S.I. McClean. 2003. Evaluation of Inherent Performance of Intelligent Medical Decision Support Systems: Utilizing Neural Networks as an Example. *Artificial Intelligence in Medicine* 27(1):1-27.

Zhang, H.C. and S. H. Huang. 1995. Applications of Neural Networks in Manufacturing: a State-of-the-Art Survey. *International Journal of Production Research* 33(3):705-728.

Chapter 5

STABILITY PROPERTIES OF NEURAL NETWORKS

Edgar J. Fuller[1], Sampath K. Yerramalla[2], Bojan Cukic[2]
[1]Department of Mathematics, West Virginia University,
[2]Lane Department of Computer Science and Electrical Engineering, West Virginia University

1. INTRODUCTION

Neural networks are key elements in the implementation of adaptive software. Fixed structure neural networks such as multi-layer perceptrons and higher-order neural networks have a well-established history as controllers for a variety of systems in industry. More complicated neural networks such as dynamic self-organizing maps and systems of neural networks are being used as more flexible architectures are needed for deployment in more complex environments. In this section, the stability and convergence properties of a few classes of neural networks are explored and an overview of the techniques used to analyze their behavior is given.

A common approach to analyzing neural network behavior is to view the learning mechanism of the network as a dynamical system in the sense that each neuron and weight in the network represents a state of the system and each training adjustment represents a discrete differential equation for the system.

1.1 Lyapunov Stability

It is a general observation that the process of adaptation in online learning neural networks resembles in many ways the behavior of dynamical systems [Yerramalla 2003a]. Based on the interpretation of neural networks as a dynamical system, the stability and convergence of online adaptation can be considered as heuristic measures of correctness for the sake of system safety. The idea is to first characterize the process of online adaptation in neural networks in the context of dynamical systems and then apply existing dynamical system stability analysis techniques for neural network analysis. One of the foremost dynamical stability analysis techniques is based on Lyapunov stability theory. The interesting feature about Lyapunov stability analysis is that it can be systematically applied to validate the existence (or nonexistence) of stable states in dynamical systems [McConley 1998].

The objective of this chapter is to develop a framework for a non-conventional V&V procedure suitable for evaluation and testing of non-deterministic neural networks. Since the concept of applying Lyapunov theory for stability analysis of neural networks is a relatively novel validation approach, this section provides the reader with a basic understanding of the fundamental concepts of stability according to Lyapunov's theory. For additional details on the use of Lyapunov's theory for stability analysis of dynamical systems the reader is referred to [Passino 1994].

1.2   Stability of Dynamical Systems

A dynamical system is an evolution rule on a set of states, the phase space, defined as a function of time as a parameter. The evolution rule can be deterministic or stochastic, depending on the nature of the system. A system is deterministic if for each state in the phase space there is a unique consequent, i.e., the evolution rule is a function taking a given state to a unique, subsequent state. Stochastic systems are non-deterministic: a standard example is the idealized coin toss. The process of adaptation in neural networks evolves over time in an unpredictable manner, and therefore is mostly stochastic and can be characterized in context of stochastic dynamical systems.

The mathematical theory of stability analysis deals with validating the existence (or nonexistence) of stable states within a dynamical system using rigorous mathematical proofs and analysis techniques. Stability of a dynamical system is usually defined in terms of the system's equilibrium point and not the system. Therefore, it is necessary to understand the definition of an equilibrium point of a dynamical system.

Definition 5.1 Equilibrium Point: Consider a nonlinear time-invariant system, $\dot{\mathbf{x}} = f(\mathbf{x})$, where $\mathbf{x} = [x_1, x_2, ..., x_m]^T$ are the states of the system, $f : \Omega \rightarrow \mathfrak{R}^n$ is a continuously differentiable function, and $\Omega \subseteq \mathfrak{R}^n$ is a subset of Euclidean space. A point, $\mathbf{x}_e \in \Omega$, is an equilibrium point of the system if $f(\mathbf{x}_e) = 0$.

It should be noted that x_e is an equilibrium point $\Rightarrow \mathbf{x}(t) = \mathbf{x}_e$ is a trajectory of the system. Considering the origin as the equilibrium point of

$\dot{\mathbf{x}} = f(\mathbf{x})$, i.e., $\mathbf{x}_e = 0$, the following definitions introduce the notion of stability of dynamical systems. For further details on the concept of stability of dynamical systems, the reader is referred to [Friedland 1996; Passino 1994].

Definition 5.2 Local Stability: If for every $\varepsilon > 0$, and $t_0 \in \mathfrak{R}$, there exists $\delta(\varepsilon, t_0) > 0$ such that if $|\mathbf{x}(t_0)| < \delta$ then $|\mathbf{x}(t)| < \varepsilon$ for all $t \geq t_0$, then the equilibrium point $\mathbf{x}_e = 0$ of the system $\dot{\mathbf{x}} = f(\mathbf{x})$ is said to be locally stable at time t_0.

The concept of stability given in Definition 5.2 is illustrated in Fig. 5-1, where a system's trajectory starting close to the equilibrium is shown to remain arbitrarily close. Note that in the case of Fig. 5-1, the equilibrium point is the origin, $\mathbf{x}_e = (0,0)$. An equilibrium state is unstable if the above condition is not satisfied. In linear systems, instability means approaching different trajectories arbitrarily close in any given time. However, this is not the case with nonlinear systems, which makes nonlinear stability analysis a challenge.

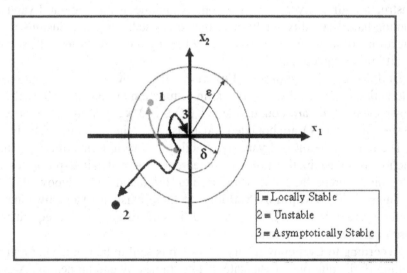

Figure 5-1. Graphical Illustration of the Concept of Local Stability for a Dynamical System (The system's equilibrium point is assumed as the origin)

Definition 5.3 Local Asymptotic Stability: If the equilibrium point $\mathbf{x}_e = 0$ is locally stable and if for every $t_0 \in \mathfrak{R}$, there exists $\delta(t_0) > 0$ such that if $|\mathbf{x}(t_0)| < \delta$ then $|\mathbf{x}(t)| \to 0$ as $t \to \infty$, then the equilibrium point $\mathbf{x}_e = 0$ is said to be locally asymptotically stable.

In other words, Definition 5.3 implies that a system trajectory starting sufficiently close to the equilibrium point will eventually approach the equilibrium point, i.e., the origin.

Definition 5.4 Global Asymptotic Stability: If the equilibrium point $\mathbf{x}_e = 0$ is locally stable and if for every initial condition $\mathbf{x}(t_0)$, $|\mathbf{x}(t)| \to 0$ as $t \to \infty$, then the equilibrium point $\mathbf{x}_e = 0$ is said to be globally asymptotically stable.

Definition 5.4 implies that if the asymptotic stability condition holds for any initial condition, then it can be said the equilibrium point of the dynamical system is global asymptotically stable.

1.3   Lyapunov Function Based Stability Analysis

Most of the previously discussed notions of stability are based on the solution (equilibrium point) for the difference equation governing the system dynamics. In general, it is inherently difficult to solve higher order difference equations, and there is no guarantee for the existence of a solution for certain higher order nonlinear difference equations. This difficulty in finding a solution for the difference equations can be overcome by the construction of a Lyapunov function. A unique feature about Lyapunov function-based stability analysis is that one establishes conclusions about trajectories of a system without actually finding the trajectories, i.e., solving the difference equations.

Definition 5.5 Lyapunov Function: If $V : \Re^n \to \Re$ is continually differentiable and locally positive definite function around $\mathbf{x}_e = 0$ such that all sublevels of V are bounded and $\dot{V}(\mathbf{x}) \le 0$ $\forall \mathbf{x}$, then all trajectories of the system $\dot{\mathbf{x}} = f(\mathbf{x})$ are bounded and V is called the Lyapunov function.

The relevant result of Lyapunov stability theory in terms of a Lyapunov function is given in the following theorem. For a detailed proof for the following theorem, the reader is referred to [Friedland 1996, Zubov 1957].

Theorem 5.1 Lyapunov Stability: If there exists a Lyapunov function for the system $\dot{\mathbf{x}} = f(\mathbf{x})$, then $\mathbf{x}_e = 0$ is said to be a stable equilibrium point in the sense of Lyapunov.

According to Lyapunov theory, a system is said to be stable near a given solution if all solutions of the state that begin nearby end up nearby. A good measure representing the notion of "nearby" is the size of the domain of the Lyapunov function by a Lyapunov function, V over the states of the system.

By constructing the function V, all trajectories of the system can be guaranteed to converge to a stable state, i.e., if they lie in the domain of the definition of V. The function V should be constructed keeping in mind that it needs be scalar $V : \Re \times D \to \Re$ and should be non-increasing over the trajectories of the state space (at least negative semi-definite). This is required in order to ensure that all limit points of any trajectory are stationary. A strict Lyapunov function should force every trajectory to asymptotically approach equilibrium state. Even for a non-strict Lyapunov function, it is possible to guarantee convergence by LaSalle's invariance principle. For detailed proofs for the following theorems, the reader is referred to [Zubov 1957, Friedland 1996, Bhatia 1970].

Theorem 5.2 Asymptotic Stability: If $\mathbf{x}_e = 0$ in addition to being Lyapunov stable, $\dot{V}(\mathbf{x})$ is locally negative definite, then $\mathbf{x}_e = 0$ is a asymptotically stable equilibrium point.

Asymptotic stability adds the property that in a region surrounding a solution of the dynamical system trajectories are approaching this given solution asymptotically.

Theorem 5.3 Global Asymptotic Stability: If $\mathbf{x}_e = 0$ in addition to being Lyapunov stable, $\dot{V}(\mathbf{x})$ is negative definite in the entire state space and $\lim_{t \to \infty} \dot{V}(\mathbf{x}) = 0$, then $\mathbf{x}_e = 0$ is a global asymptotically stable equilibrium point.

A notable difference between asymptotic and global asymptotic stability is the fact that the latter implies that any trajectory beginning at any initial point will converge asymptotically to the given solution unlike the former where only those trajectories beginning in the neighborhood of the solution approach the solution asymptotically. The types of stability defined above have increasing property strength, i.e., Global Asymptotic Stability $\Rightarrow$ Asymptotic Stability $\Rightarrow$ Lyapunov Stability. The reverse implication however, does not necessarily hold.

Though the concept of Lyapunov stability was originally intended for use in mathematical theory, it can be simplified for use in many practical applications including neural networks [Yerramalla 2003a; Yu 2001]. In mechanical systems, a Lyapunov function is considered as an energy-minimizing term and in economy and finance evaluations it is considered as a cost-minimizing term, and for neural networks, the construction of a Lyapunov function can be based on the error-minimizing states of the neural network learning.

The central goal of an adaptive system is to calculate the present state of the system and determine a strategy to drive the system to a desired operating state. It must be realized that by accommodating for changing dynamics of the system, online adaptive components play a critical role in the functionality of the adaptive system. Therefore, it is necessary to ensure correct behavior of the online adaptive components before their deployment into the actual safety-critical system [Hull 2002, Schumann 2002, Taylor 2003].

A provably stabilizing online adaptation ensures that the learning in an embedded adaptive component converges to a stable state within a reasonable amount of time without bifurcating towards instability. In the context of the V&V of online adaptation, the goal of theoretical stability analysis is to delineate stability boundaries of online adaptation for certain specific domains of adaptive system data using mathematical theories of stability analysis.

2.   APPLICATIONS TO FIXED TOPOLOGY NEURAL NETWORKS

Several authors have applied Lyapunov theory to the study of neural network behavior. Calise, et al. [Calise 2001] have shown that certain neural networks with fixed connectivity such as Sigma-Pi neural networks evolve stably over time.   In their work, a traditional Sigma-Pi architecture is adopted and an error measure for network performance is defined. Fig. 5-2 is a representation of a typical Sigma-Pi neural network.

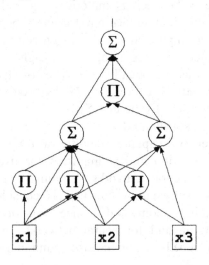

Figure 5-2. A Sigma-Pi Neural Network with Inputs x1, x2, x3

In the figure, the nodes of the network (circles) take sums and products of the inputs that are weighted by values associated to the connections (arrows).   These weights are modified during training using a back-propagation algorithm which attempts to minimize the error of the network. In this way a function, usually a polynomial of some specified degree, is constructed that approximates the values of the data signal being analyzed by the neural network. In [Kim 2003] the error between the signal and the approximation is combined with the update rule to define a Lyapunov function for the online neural network. The reader is referred to their work for more details.

3.   APPLICATION TO SELF-ORGANIZING MAPS

Self-organizing maps (SOM) pose a different kind of problem for this type of analysis. Many authors have attempted to understand the behavior of self-organizing maps using Lyapunov theory. Cottrell and others [Cottrell 1998] have shown that fixed topology self-organizing maps admit Lyapunov functions only in dimension one. It is conjectured that no Lyapunov function exists for higher dimensional fixed topology SOMs.

SOMs in their most general form are vector quantizers in the sense that they partition a set of data into clusters that are then represented by vectors called *neurons* that are then connected to each other. In the case of fixed topology SOMs, there are a fixed number of neurons and each is connected to the same set of neurons in the network for the entire training cycle. Adaptation occurs when neurons are moved in order to find the minimum Euclidean distance between that neuron and the data points it represents. This *best-matching neuron* or best matching unit (BMU) for a subset of the data is stimulated by the data in this way during training. In the case of dynamic SOMs, the number of neurons may change as well as the connectivity of the network. This allows for greater flexibility in training, particularly when the data being analyzed is multi-dimensional.

An example of a dynamically changing SOM is the Dynamic Cell Structures (DCS) neural network [Bruske 1995]. To illustrate how Lyapunov theory can be applied here, the following questions should be answered:

- How can a systematic approach to delineate stability boundaries of online adaptation in a dynamic self-organizing neural network such as the DCS be derived?
- To what specific domains of the adaptive system data are the delineated stability boundaries confined?

It is observed as a part of the ongoing research that the learning process in neural networks evolves over time in a manner similar to the behavior of dynamical systems [Yerramalla 2003b, Yerramalla 2004]. The idea then is to characterize neural network learning in the context of dynamical systems and analyze its stability properties using dynamical system analysis techniques. One of the foremost dynamical system stability analysis techniques is Lyapunov's theory. The interesting feature about Lyapunov's stability theory is that it can be systematically applied to validate the existence (or nonexistence) of stable states in a dynamical system. The research therefore, proposes the extension of the Lyapunov's stability theory for analysis of the stability properties of online learning DCS neural network.

Due to the stochastic nature of learning in self-organizing neural networks, the stability analysis in this chapter is restricted to neural network adaptation from stationary or fixed data manifolds. Learning from a stationary data manifold implies that once a certain data manifold is presented to the online adaptive component (neural network), the configuration of the data remains unchanged throughout the learning process.

3.1   Dynamics of DCS Neural Network

This section aims to characterize the learning process in neural networks in the context of a dynamical system. The first step in this stability analysis is the identification of stable-states involved in the DCS neural network. The learning process involved in the DCS was discussed elsewhere in this work. A state-space representation is a commonly preferred method for representation of the states within a dynamical system. It is important to represent the states of the dynamical system (online learning neural network) using a state-space representation technique as it can prove to be effective during the construction of a Lyapunov function.

Consider D-dimensional input and output manifolds, $\mathbf{I} \subset \mathfrak{R}^D$ and $\mathbf{O} \subset \mathfrak{R}^D$, respectively. The DCS is a self-organizing neural network consisting of neurons that are positioned in the output space $\mathbf{O} \subset \mathfrak{R}^D$ using weight vectors. Consider N as the number of neurons in the DCS network at any time. The weight vectors of the DCS neural network can be then be represented as, $\mathbf{w}_i \in \mathbf{O} \subset \mathfrak{R}^D \quad \forall i \in \{1,2,...,N\}$. The lateral connections between neurons in the DCS are expressed in terms of real constants known as connection strengths, $c_{ij} \equiv c_{ji} \in [0,1] \quad \forall i \neq j \quad i,j \in \{1,2,...,N\}$. Unlike feed-forward neural networks, the lateral connections between neurons in a self-organizing neural network are not static but evolve over time [Ahrns 1995, Bruske 1995]. A D-dimensional DCS neural network consisting of N neurons can therefore be represented in the output space $\mathbf{O} \subset \mathfrak{R}^D$ using a $D \times N$ position matrix, $\mathbf{W}_{D \times N} \ni \mathbf{w}_i$ and a $N \times N$ connection strength matrix, $\mathbf{C}_{N \times N} \ni c_{ij}$. For a given input space $\mathbf{I} \subset \mathfrak{R}^D$, the DCS is essentially an undirected graph of $\mathbf{W}_{D \times N}$ and $\mathbf{C}_{N \times N}$ that can be defined in the following manner.

Definition 5.5 DCS Neural Network Mapping: For a given input space, $\mathbf{I} \subset \mathfrak{R}^D$, the DCS neural network mapping is an undirected graph of $\mathbf{W}_{D \times N}$ and $\mathbf{C}_{N \times N}$, $G(\mathbf{W}_{D \times N}, \mathbf{C}_{N \times N}) : \mathbf{I} \subset \mathfrak{R}^D \to \mathbf{O} \subset \mathfrak{R}^D$ that can be considered as an Nth order neural network representation of the input manifold,

$\mathbf{M} \subset \mathbf{I} \subset \mathfrak{R}^D$ in the output space, $\mathbf{O} \subset \mathfrak{R}^D$ generated by assigning N neural units using the DCS training algorithm.

3.2 State-Space Representation of the DCS Neural Network

Based on the Hebb and a Kohonen-like adaptation rules, a state-space representation of the DCS neural network is provided. Let the states of the DCS neural network due to the adaptation of weight vectors using a Kohonen-like rule and the Hebb update be represented by $\mathbf{x}_W$ and $\mathbf{x}_C$ respectively. The dynamics of the state changes in the DCS due to the adaptation of weight vectors using a Kohonen-like rule and the Hebb rule can be represented in the following manner.

$$\frac{\Delta \mathbf{x}_W}{\Delta t} = f_W(\mathbf{x}_w, \mathbf{x}_C) \tag{5.1}$$

$$\frac{\Delta \mathbf{x}_C}{\Delta t} = f_C(\mathbf{x}_C, \mathbf{x}_W) \tag{5.2}$$

The nonlinear functions $f_W, f_C : \mathbf{I} \subset \mathfrak{R}^D \to \mathbf{O} \subset \mathfrak{R}^D$ are continuous and provide the required adjustments to the states $\mathbf{x}_W$ and $\mathbf{x}_C$ respectively of the DCS neural network. Considering the DCS as a discrete-time dynamical system, the states of the DCS training algorithm can be represented in the following manner in a state-space representation form using Eq. (5.1) and Eq. (5.2).

$$\frac{\Delta \mathbf{X}}{\Delta t} = \begin{bmatrix} \dfrac{\Delta \mathbf{x}_W}{\Delta t} \\ \dfrac{\Delta \mathbf{x}_C}{\Delta t} \end{bmatrix} = \begin{bmatrix} f_W(\mathbf{x}_W, \mathbf{x}_C) \\ f_C(\mathbf{x}_C, \mathbf{x}_W) \end{bmatrix} \tag{5.3}$$

3.3 Construction of a Lyapunov Function for the DCS Neural Network

Lyapunov's direct method (also known as Lyapunov's second method) in particular can be easily and systematically applied to validate the existence of stable states of nonlinear dynamical systems. In order to extend its use for the online learning DCS neural network, one first needs to construct a

Lyapunov function based on the states of the neural network training algorithm (Eq. 5.3).

The goal of the DCS is to overlay neurons (using weight vectors) over the presented data manifold in a topology-preserving manner such that nearby data patterns are mapped using neighboring neurons of the DCS network [Ahrns 1995, Bruske 1995]. In order to generate a topology-preserving feature map of the presented data manifold, $\mathbf{M} \subset \mathbf{I} \subset \Re^D$, the DCS network is initialized with two neurons that are connected to each other with connection strength of value 1. If it is determined that the error in the DCS network falls below a predefined threshold, additional neurons are introduced into the network. This process is repeated until the map generated by the DCS reaches a pre-specified degree of accuracy in its representation of the presented data [Yerramalla 2003b].

The addition of new neurons into the DCS network is based on resource values, a local error associated with every DCS neuron. In most cases, the Euclidean distance between the data patterns of the training data manifold, $\mathbf{m} \in \mathbf{M} \subset \mathbf{I} \subset \Re^D$ and the positions of the best matching units, $\mathbf{w}_{bmu} \in \mathbf{W}_{D \times N} \subset \mathbf{O} \subset \Re^D$ serves as a measure for resource. Since resource is a measure of the local error associated with each neuron, an average resource value can serve the purpose of a Lyapunov function for the DCS neural network. While considering the DCS adaptation as a discrete-time dynamical system, the end of a learning cycle followed by the addition of a new neuron can be treated as a time step. A Lyapunov function for the DCS can then be formulated in the following manner.

$$V = \frac{\sum_{\forall \mathbf{m} \in \mathbf{M}} \left\| \mathbf{m} - \mathbf{w}_{bmu(\mathbf{m})} \right\|}{N} \tag{5.4}$$

The Lyapunov function of Eq. (5.4) is the average resource value of the neural network that in essence is a measure the amount of topology of the input data manifold that is being preserved by the map generated by the neural network. The constructed Lyapunov function of Eq. (5.4) is known in the neural network community as the quantization error.

Using this framework, the following can be stated:

Theorem 5.4: Let $V(G,t) : \mathbf{O} \subset \Re^D \to \Re$ be a scalar function constructed for the map $G(\mathbf{M}, \mathbf{W}_{D \times N}, \mathbf{C}_{N \times N}) : \mathbf{I} \subset \Re^D \to \mathbf{O} \subset \Re^D$ generated by the online learning neural network from an input manifold $\mathbf{M} \subseteq \mathbf{I} \subset \Re^D$. If $\mathbf{M}$ remains fixed, then for any $\varepsilon > 0$, an integer $\delta > 0$ can be found such that for all $t > \delta$, $V(G,t) < \varepsilon$.

This result holds as long as the input data being trained by the neural network is fixed. In the case of online training where data may be dynamically changing as well, another approach must be taken. This is the subject of another chapter in this work.

4. SUMMARY

Lyapunov theory is a powerful tool for understanding the stability of neural networks. Once a measure of error is defined for the system, suitable Lyapunov functions can be described which then provide a rigorous characterization of network behavior across all of the possible set of states for the network for which the Lyapunov function is defined. In combination with probabilistic methods such as those of Schumann and Gupta [Schumann 2003], a high degree of reliability may be obtained for systems that integrate neural networks into their structure.

REFERENCES

Ahrns, I., J. Bruske, and G. Sommer. 1995. "Online Learning with Dynamic Cell Structures". *In Proceedings of the International Conference on Artificial Neural Networks (ICANN'95)*, Vol. 2, pp. 141-146, Paris.

Bhatia, N. P., and G. P. Szego. 1970. *Stability Theory of Dynamical Systems*. Springer-Verlag, Berlin.

Bruske, J., and G. Sommer. 1995. Dynamic Cell Structures Learns a Perfectly Topology Preserving Map. *In Proceedings of the Advances in Neural Information Processing Systems (NIPS'95)*, Vol. 7, No. 4, pp. 845-865.

Calise, Anthony, Naira Hovakimyan, and Moshe Idan. 2001. Adaptive Output Feedback Control of Nonlinear Systems using Neural Networks. *In Automatica Special Issue Neural Networks for Feedback Control*, Vol. 37, No. 8.

Cottrell, M., J.C. Fort, and G. Pages. 1998. Theoretical Aspects of the SOM Algorithm. *Neurocomputing Journal*, Vol. 21, No. 1-3, pp.119-138, November.

Friedland, Bernard. 1996. *Advanced Control System*. Prentice Hall Inc.

Hull J., D. Ward, and R. R. Zakrzewski. 2002. Verification and Validation of Neural Networks for Safety-Critical Applications. *In proceedings of the American Control Conference*, Vol.6, No.8-10, pp. 4789-4794, May.

Kim, Nakwan. 2003. Improved Methods in Neural Network-Based Adaptive Output Feedback Control, with Applications to Flight Control. PhD thesis, Georgia Institute of Technology, School of Aerospace Engineering, Atlanta, GA, November.

McConley, M. W., B. D. Appleby, M. A. Dahleh, and E. Feron. 1998. Computational Complexity of Lyapunov Stability Analysis Problems for a Class of Nonlinear Systems. *Industrial and Applied Mathematics Journal of Control and Optimization*, Vol. 36, No. 6, pp. 2176-2193.

Passino, K. M., N. Michel, and P. J. Antsaklis. 2002. Lyapunov Stability of a Class of Discrete Event Systems. *IEEE Transactions on Automatic Control*, Vol. 39, No. 2, February 1994.

Schumann, J., and S. Nelson. Towards V&V of Neural Network Based Controllers. Workshop on Self-Healing Systems.

Schumann, J., P. Gupta, and S. Nelson. 2003. On Verification & Validation of Neural Network Based Controllers. *In Proceedings of the Engineering Applications of Neural Networks (EANN'03)*.

Taylor, B. J., and M. A. Darrah. 2003. Verification and Validation of Neural Networks: a Sampling of Research in Progress. *In Proceedings of the AeroSense*, Orlando, FL, 21-25 April.

Yerramalla, S., E. Fuller, and B. Cukic, M. Mladenovski. 2003a. Lyapunov Analysis of Neural Network Stability in an Adaptive Flight Control System. *In Proceedings of the Sixth Symposium of Self-Stabilization Systems (SSS'03)*, June.

Yerramalla, S., E. Fuller, and B. Cukic. 2003b. Lyapunov Stability Analysis of DCS Quantization Error. *In Proceedings of the IEEE International Joint Conference on Neural Networks (IJCNN'03)*, July.

Yerramalla, Sampath, Edgar Fuller, Bojan Cukic, Yan Liu and Srikanth Gururajan, 2004. An Approach to V&V of Embedded Adaptive Systems. Formal Approaches to Agent-Based Systems (FAABS) III, Lecture Notes in Computer Science, Springer-Verlag.

Yu, Wen and X. Li., 2001. Some Stability Properties of Dynamic Neural Networks. *IEEE Transactions on Circuits and Systems*: Part 1, Vol. 48, No. 2, pp. 256-259.

Zubov, V. I. 1957. Methods of A. M. Lyapunov and Their Applications. U.S. Atomic Energy Commission.

Chapter 6

NEURAL NETWORK VERIFICATION

James T. Smith
Institute for Scientific Research, Inc.

1.   INTRODUCTION

Neural network-based systems have truly become mainstream with their employment in safety- and mission-critical applications. Because a neural network is an *empirical* model, the model design and data requirements replace the functions served by knowledge representation and acquisition in symbolic reasoning. Issues and considerations that are deemed substantial regarding the assessment of neural network systems include:

- Assessing the quality of training and testing data,
- Relating training and testing data to defined safety margins, and
- Tracing neural network design features to overall specification requirements at the system level.

Critical issues of particular relevance to the V&V of neural networks include:

- Focusing in areas where significant data are available for training,
- Addressing difficulties with scaling systems from prototypes to full deployment, and
- Evaluating the system using real data.

The neural network system development lifecycle is very similar to that for decision systems involving statistical modules. Neural network system lifecycle stages also have parallels with the corresponding stages in the design of knowledge-based systems and to any inference system with substantial nonlinear components, whether using symbolic or distributed knowledge representations. However, the technical aspects of verification of neural network systems at the systems, integration, and unit levels have not been generally established.

This chapter examines the considerations and issues listed above in an attempt to provide the V&V practitioner a comprehensive view of how the generic verification process can be particularized to the verification of neural network-based systems.

1.1   Setting the Stage: Framing the Issues

The following quote from "Industrial Use of Safety-Related Artificial Neural Networks" [Lisboa 2001] identifies the need for the integration of additional neural network-specific methods with the more traditional linear design and verification methods that already are well understood.

It is clear from the applications reviewed that the key to successful transfer of neural networks to the marketplace is successful integration with routine practice, rather than optimization for the idealized environments where much of the current development effort takes place. This requires the ability to evaluate their empirically derived response using structured domain knowledge, as well as performance testing. In controller design, the scalability of solutions to production models, and the need to maintain safe and efficient operation under plant wear, have led to the integration of linear design methods with neural network architectures. [Lisboa 2001]

In particular, Dr. Lisboa then identifies the need for additional research in two directions. The first is to systematize current best practice in the design of a wide range of quite different neural computing systems, some for static pattern recognition, others for control, some in software and others embedded in hardware. The second is to formulate a unified perspective of each stage in the development lifecycle of high-complexity computation in safety-related applications, spanning the full range from empirical to structural process models. [Lisboa 2001]

He then offers a warning to the V&V practitioner regarding where most additional effort will be required. "In emerging computation, the complexity is often not in the software implementation, but in the interpretation and testing required to evaluate the operation of the model."

1.2   Expanding the Generic Software Lifecycle for Neural Networks

A generic lifecycle for computer systems incorporating neural network system components may be expressed in any of the standard ways. One such representation based on that used by the U.S. Food and Drug Administration in their software guidance for reviewers and industry [FDA 1998] is shown in Fig. 6-1.

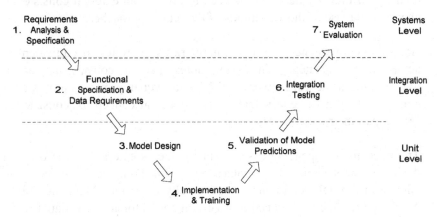

Figure 6-1. Generic Software Lifecycle Model

In tracing through the blocks in Fig. 6-1, Dr. Lisboa expressed the following observations and caveats of which both the designer and the V&V practitioner of neural network systems should be aware:

1. Expressing system requirements involves specifying against unwanted behavior in responses to unforeseen sequences of events. This point indicates the need not only to verify how the system performs under expected conditions, but also how the system reacts to unforeseen events. The handling of such events must be addressed not only for operational mode but also in regards to the training that the neural network receives.

2. Knowledge representation impacts generalization ability, i.e. correct operation for future situations. In particular, human expertise is not always consistent and complete and can be difficult to capture into an algorithmic representation. This point calls attention to the importance of the underlying knowledge representation in the ability of a system to generalize its applicability beyond a rigid constrained subset of a problem domain. The representational power of a neural network

depends not only upon the neural network architecture and topology, but also on other considerations such as choice of transfer function, learning rule, selection of training epochs, and mode of supervision.

3. There appears to be a convergence of knowledge-based, neural computing, and statistical modeling approaches. This point describes a convergence of system development methodologies that will necessarily require corresponding convergence of V&V practices. In particular, the methods of one approach can be used to provide an external consistency check for the use of those methods of the other approaches.

4. Assessing convergence in a neural network-based system is equivalent to achieving consistency. This point notes that the convergence of an online-learning neural network (OLNN) to ever improving outputs as it continues to learn is equivalent to the statistical concept of consistency for nonparametric estimators.

5. The need for independent assessment by agents external to the original design process should be emphasized. This point currently is being addressed through such concepts as novelty detection [Marsland 2003]. This is partly due to the need to ascertain and automatically signal if the inference is extrapolating outside, rather than interpolating within, the neural network's knowledge base. The V&V of the neural network is not complete without also addressing the appropriateness of these external agents.

6. Transparency of inferences is difficult for any complex system, and particularly so when knowledge is distributed. This point has become critical as neural network systems become increasingly large and complex. The traceability of their operation by direct inspection of the weights and hidden node activations in response to specific test patterns may not be sufficient to enable verification against established domain expertise. Methods such as rule extraction and decision tree extraction are examples of efforts to better infer and describe what the neural network "knows" [Darbari 2000, van der Zwaag 2002].

7. Any system may in principle be consistent and complete by design, yet contain knowledge that is incorrect. This point leads to the following observation: V&V requires adherence to formal methodologies at each level of the design lifecycle. However, where non-linear inferences from real-world data are involved, the emphasis appears to be shifting towards extensive trials with external data.

1.3 Verification Considerations for Neural Networks

The major considerations for the verification of a neural network system thus revolve around its realization: "Was it implemented as intended?" and its functionality: "Does it perform as expected?" More formally, these concepts may be defined thus:

- *Realization* is concerned with existence: what the neural network system is, what its components are, and how the network is put together.
- *Functionality* is concerned with purpose and action: what the neural network system does, how well it does what it does, and how its activity relates to the problem it is supposed to address.

The two areas, realization and functionality, approach the verification process from different perspectives.

Verification of the realization of the neural network based system is focused on assuring that the system has the appropriate resources, organization, data flow, etc. to perform the tasks or to satisfy the purpose for which it is developed. Realization verification is more static and precise: it performs an assessment of what the system, when properly implemented, could and should be capable of performing. Realization verification confirms that the system is "a completed operable body awaiting life to be breathed into it," that it is able and ready to begin functioning as intended.

Verification of the functionality of the system is focused on assuring that the system executes as planned and that the execution accomplishes what is expected of it within the bounds and constraints set for it. Functionality verification is more dynamic and qualitative: it performs an assessment of what level or degree of functionality is ultimately demonstrated regarding the system.

The various perspectives overlap, at least in the supporting tools and techniques they may employ. However, the questions that are raised, and the results and conclusions being sought are different. The functional or integration testing of the system involves evaluation of the total system package – including the neural network architecture, neural network parameters (e.g., number of nodes, transfer function), the learning algorithm, and the actual training epochs. Before the system components are brought together for such verification, each individual component should be verified independent of the others.

In addition to and dependent upon the above core dimensions of neural network verification are two other potentially critical aspects of neural network verification. They are:

- *Adaptation*, which is concerned with what modifications to a system's structure and behavior are permitted over time, and how well they are implemented, and
- *Fault management*, which is concerned with protecting a system from potential failures, whether due to its environment or to itself.

The requirements for which an adaptive system is designed necessarily include statements regarding what the nature of the adaptation is to be. Two examples of adaptation types are supervised vs. unsupervised or explicitly bounded and focused vs. open-ended where the adaptation is limited only by the capabilities and resources of the underlying computing platform. The adaptation can involve changes in the system's architecture and thus realization, as well as changes in its behavior, or functionality. That the developed system indeed satisfies the described adaptation strategy must be verified. Each of these adaptation choices will affect the approaches taken to verify the system.

Complex systems may be safety critical, where human safety is at risk, or mission critical, where system failure could impact the total mission the system is supporting. The purpose of fault management is to enable a complex system to continue to perform through faulty situations less than optimally, intended, or desired, and yet well enough to accomplish significant aspects of the original task (mission preserving) and without loss of life (risk aversion). Evaluation of how well a system achieves this goal must be part of the total verification process.

1.4   Organization of the Chapter

The rest of this chapter addresses Dr. Lisboa's seven points in section 1.2 with further discussion based upon the four verification considerations from section 1.3 (realization, functionality, adaptive systems, and fault-management). Section 2.1 Realization Verification, addresses points 2, 6, and 7. Section 2.2 Functionality Verification, discusses points 6 and 7 with further detail. Section 2.3 Adaptive Systems Verification discusses points 3 and 4. Section 2.4 Fault Management-Based Verification addresses points 1 and 5.

2.   NEURAL NETWORK VERIFICATION

Neural network-based systems have truly become mainstream with their employment in safety- and mission-critical applications. They are being used in cutting edge research conducted by NASA and the U.S. Department of Defense as well as finding uses within commercial technologies including medical and automotive devices. This section will discuss the verification techniques needed to provide software assurance for these highly critical adaptive systems.

2.1   Realization Verification

Realization verification is essentially a white-box testing activity. The system components must be produced to specification. They must fit together properly, which can involve many aspects. In the case of digital information processing, for example, communications interfaces and protocols must be properly implemented among the individual internal components, as well as externally with the environment of the system. The components must share the available resources that can consist of time allocation, memory, processing elements, and external interfaces.

In the case of a neural network system, the major components required for the realization are:

- *Structure*, which is its architecture, or topology, and parameterization, and
- *Knowledge*, which is captured (encapsulated) within that structure.

The neural network structure will typically be realized as some combination of neural network architecture and neural network parameterization. Some of the more common neural network architectures include the multi-layer perceptron (MLP), self-organizing map (SOM), and radial basis function (RBF). The parameterization can control the specifics of the architecture or the architecture functionality. Example parameterizations would be the number of layers, number of nodes, or choice of transfer functions.

The knowledge of a neural network is encapsulated implicitly within the neural network by the connections between nodes, the weights stored with the node, and the transfer functions applied to the various links between connected nodes. Knowledge must be ingested into the system and demonstrated empirically through the use of appropriate training and testing examples.

These two major components of a neural network based system, its architecture and its knowledge, need to be evaluated from the following perspectives:

- *Independently*, or component-wise, as to how well each accomplishes its intended purpose, and

- *Systemically*, or collectively, in terms of their fit, or appropriateness, to each other, so that the sum of the parts indeed equals the whole.

These two components, architecture and knowledge, need to be verified independently and systemically as if they represented interoperable components of a final product. In particular for neural network systems, there is a need to verify the appropriateness of the neural network structure (architecture and architecture parameters) against the type of knowledge to be encoded and training to be performed. Such verification involves an analysis of the potential of success for encoding and for utilizing the knowledge with the given neural network architecture.

In Chapter 4, the discussion of validation addresses the appropriateness of various neural network architectures, learning rules, etc. to adequately encapsulate or represent the necessary knowledge, and to respond with appropriate outputs to given sets of inputs. A set of guidelines and suggested mappings of various problem domain classes to generally appropriate neural network architectures is provided. The reader may wish to review that chapter at this point.

The purpose of verification at this same systems level is to confirm the accuracy of such determinations made regarding the specific system as part of its validation. Specific to neural network systems, each of the following major verification tasks are considered:

- Verify the neural network structure as an independent system component. The verification of the neural network structure includes correct use of hardware, implementation of software, and selection of system parameters.

- Verify the knowledge sources to be encoded. The knowledge sources should be analyzed for completeness, consistency, quality, and accuracy. External checks and balances that are supposed to assure the required levels are achieved should be verified. In the case of online learning systems, the consistency of the knowledge and the maintenance of these checks and balances over time also must be addressed.

- Verify the appropriateness of the pairing of the neural network structure with the knowledge to be encoded. How well the identified knowledge characteristics, its strengths and limitations, complement those of the neural network architecture must be addressed. The appropriateness can be ascertained to a great extent prior to and independent of the actual encoding (training) of the given neural network architecture with the targeted knowledge that constitutes the functional verification of the total system.

2.1.1 Independent Verification of the Neural Network System Structure

Verification of the neural network structure independent of the particular knowledge to be encoded can be decomposed further, based on encoded knowledge-base considerations:

1. Some aspects to be evaluated, such as the correctness of the software code and hardware that implements the neural network architecture, are independent of the knowledge being encoded.
2. Some aspects can be considered independent of the actual knowledge that is encoded, but do depend on characteristics of the knowledge.

General verification tools and techniques can be utilized for those aspects of the neural network structure verification that are independent of the knowledge that will be encoded within the neural network system. A plethora of formal static analysis tools may be employed to verify the correctness of the program that implements the neural network system, e.g., from logic, data-flow, and resource management perspectives, such as memory, bandwidth, and timing constraints. Such tools are able to verify the data structures that implement the neural network layers, nodes, and links, as well as the functional expressions that implement the transfer functions. However, such tools are not able to determine algorithmetically whether the knowledge encoded due to a given training epoch will produce the desired outputs.

Neural networks, at least in theory, represent a parallel computing model, and various efforts have been proposed to capitalize on this parallel nature of neural networks. Methods can include the use of both generic non-neural network-specific and neural network-specific parallel-based hardware [Saratchandran 1998], as well as custom parallel hardware, including programmable hardware approaches.

One example is the potential to use readily available commodity priced graphics chips as vector processors to implement some of the vector oriented neural network architectures, such as support vector machines (SVM) and SOMs. Such hardware processors are optimized for vector processing and for data streaming [Dally 2003], both characteristics of SVMs and SOMs. Another example of such promising technology is the use of field–programmable gate arrays that enable the use of adaptive hardware as opposed to adaptive software to implement neural network systems [Nichols 2003].

Such newly emerging approaches to the development and implementation of neural network-based systems will require the application of new V&V methods, at least new to the field of neural networks to support those approaches. Fortunately, the field of hardware design already has in place well-developed V&V processes. These range from the use of sophisticated modeling and simulation design tools to the incorporation of built-in test [Richards 1989] and built-in self-test [Mohamed 2000] technologies for real-time error detection and recovery.

From a practical viewpoint, most neural network systems are implemented on von Neumann hardware designed around a serialized computational model [Backus 1978]. The processor found in most PCs and Macs are von Neumann hardware. Serialization of the neural network parallel computing model is based on multiple considerations that involve resource and performance trade-offs. One implementation may be more memory intensive while another may be more processor intensive. Various data structures may be employed in an effort to accelerate some functions.

Appraisal of these trade-offs and optimizations is part of the verification process. Some implementation choices may be explicitly mandated in the system requirements, while others are discretionary, allowing the design engineer to chose how to do things. General verification concerns include how appropriate they are to accomplish the intended purpose, and whether they are correctly implemented.

Numerical computations such as the calculation of values propagated through the network are constrained by the representational capabilities of the underlying hardware, as well as by software program effects such as the ordering and scaling of the computations. Standard numerical techniques such as data scaling and computation reordering can improve the accuracy and stability of the computed results.

The analysis of such numerical processing is the realm of numerical analysis. Methods of numerical analysis such as approximation theory may be applied to evaluate the accuracy and precision, as well as the operational efficiency like operations count or memory required. Evaluations can be taken from multiple perspectives including best case, worst case, and average. Which perspective is deemed more relevant depends on various factors. Real-time and safety critical systems may emphasize a worst-case scenario; whereas, a non-real time but heavily employed system may emphasize an average case scenario.

Other aspects of computational appropriateness to be considered include computational resource requirements such as processor speed, memory, computational operation counts and I/O bandwidth. Scalability and order of magnitude considerations also should be considered. Later, during the system's functional verification (see Section 2.2), the estimates of required resources can be confirmed for the actual implementation of the system.

Such aspects of software and systems verification are not specific to neural network systems and will therefore not be refined further in this assessment of neural network verification. Instead, the remainder of this discussion will focus on neural network-specific considerations.

Numerical analysis methods such as an algorithm analysis may be applied to evaluate the efficiency of the system implementation for a specifically targeted execution environment. For example, such an analysis can be particularly important in the case of embedded systems with limited resources, and in the case of real-time systems where the time required for neural network, processing can be critical.

This analysis ranges from considerations regarding the most appropriate neural network architecture, to the choice of transfer function, to the data structures, and to the characteristics of the hardware used to implement the system. What otherwise might be deemed a reasonable design for general-purpose systems and applications may prove sub-optimal or even impossible to achieve with the targeted execution environment.

Another consideration occurs when the development and target platforms are different and each requires special treatment. Toolsets such as MathWork's Neural Network Toolbox [MathWorks 2004] may provide a reasonable choice of platform for iterative prototyping and experimentation as a neural network architecture is crafted, transfer functions selected or defined, and preliminary knowledge is captured in the network through trial-and-error training.

However, the final deployed system may require porting to a targeted embedded platform with quite different capabilities, or specific limitations. The inherent accuracy and precision of the targeted platform may be quite different from that of the development platform. Complex mathematical functions may require software versions, in lieu of hardware acceleration. The conversion or porting process by autocode or cross compilation is subject to verification.

In addition to the theoretical, mathematical, and formal aspects of numerical analysis or algorithm analysis of a neural network implementation is the need to consider empirical results. Ultimately, the neural network system will be trained with empirically collected data. That empirical process itself needs to be verified, both in terms of the methodology by which it is accomplished and in terms of what quality of results can be expected. This can constitute a significant simulation effort in which artificial training epochs are employed that have been specifically designed to empirically test various characteristics of the neural network system. This stage in the verification process may make significant use of specialized test generation tools (see Chapter 9).

This empirical verification is driven from two perspectives:

1. Empirical verification of the neural network system's designed and predicted capabilities and performance, independent of what knowledge may eventually be encoded through neural network training with actual real-world data.
2. Empirical verification of the neural network's appropriateness to be encoded with knowledge having the expected characteristics of the training epochs.

This first perspective of empirical verification leads to an understanding of the capabilities of the neural network structure and implementation that is independent of a particular problem to be solved. The results of this stage of verification are of strategic value, since they may be reapplied in the appropriateness assessment of this system for any given problem, not just the particular one in hand.

Training epochs may be specifically designed to test the representational properties of the implementation like convergence, stability, or generalization. Each such training epoch constitutes a class of problems with specific characteristics. These epochs are distinct from those to be drawn later from live datasets for capturing the actual knowledge that ultimately is to reside in the deployed system. This type of training epoch is specifically designed to constrain and focus upon exactly what aspects or features of the neural network system architecture are being evaluated.

Special performance evaluation epochs, for example, may be employed to verify the neural network architecture's stability qualities. An example of a quality that could be considered is to construct a given test epoch purposely ill-conditioned from a numerical analysis perspective. This could allow determination of how much flexibility or brittleness the neural network system exhibits with respect to the data on which the neural network system will be trained and deployed.

The employment of carefully constructed training epochs thus empirically evaluates the performance of candidate neural network architectures, transfer functions, and other neural network parameters that may be compared against various criteria. Performance capabilities previously predicted are thus investigated systematically in a controlled laboratory setting. The results of this stage of the verification process are reusable since they do not presuppose a particular problem domain.

The second perspective takes the empirical verification process another step closer to the specific application problem, the one that the neural network system ultimately is expected to address. With the general capabilities of the neural network system established, this second step commences the meshing of the neural network system with the particular knowledge it is to encode and the problem it is intended to solve.

Again, the neural network system is trained using specifically designed training epochs, rather than actual real life training data. This time, however, the epochs are designed not to explore capabilities and limitations of the neural network architecture, but to explore those characteristics that are particular to the actual knowledge to be encoded and the ultimate problem to be solved [Cukic 2002].

This second phase of the empirical verification process could be viewed as a series of targeted trial runs. Before this phase can be accomplished, an analysis of the knowledge to be encoded that is independent of any particular neural network system is required. The discussion of this independent analysis process and the characterization of the knowledge to be encoded within the neural network system is presented in Section 2.1.2. The results of that analysis effort are employed in the generation of the previously described testing epochs, and in the analysis of their results.

With completion of this second phase, the neural network system verification independent of the actual knowledge with which it is to be trained is considered completed. What then remains is the functional evaluation and verification of the system using the actual training epochs that complete the actual neural network system's development.

2.1.2   Independent Verification of the Neural Network System Knowledge Source

Hand in hand with an independent analysis and verification of the total neural network structure, including the specification of all its parameters, is the need for a corresponding independent analysis and verification of the knowledge that is to be encoded within the neural network. Two major areas of analysis are identified:

1. Knowledge analysis, which considers the inherent nature of the knowledge to be employed in the system.
2. Application analysis, which considers how that knowledge is to be applied within the given system.

Knowledge analysis covers both the knowledge that is used to train the neural network system as well as that which describes the problem to which the neural network system is directed. In contrast, application analysis positions the knowledge particular to the neural network system with respect to the total knowledge and processing required by the total system of which the neural network system may be one component.

Simply stated, the first point addresses the question: "What knowledge is available?" The second point addresses the question: "How will this knowledge be employed in the particular problem domain?"

Analysis of the knowledge to be encoded in a neural network system includes considering the following:

1. Completeness of the available knowledge
2. Significance of missing knowledge or gaps, e.g., cases not adequately covered
3. Representative coverage of the total problem space by the available knowledge
4. Organization or partitioning of the knowledge, whether natural (obvious) or identified via data mining methods
5. Knowledge characteristics, e.g., static, dynamic, evolving, adaptive, and conditional

This information is critical to the application analysis which considers what types of inferences are expected based upon or at least supported by this knowledge.

With symbolic or logic-based systems (e.g., expert systems) the knowledge typically is expressible as symbolic rules, logic clauses, etc. In the case of traditional procedural or process-oriented systems, the knowledge is usually in the form of scientifically, formally derived algorithms, equations, and procedures that typically are expressible in some high-level procedural or object-oriented modeling language. In both cases, the knowledge readily is reviewed and critiqued by human experts.

Methods such as rule extraction, discussed in Chapter 8, represent efforts to deconstruct the knowledge that is encapsulated in a trained neural network. Those same methods can be applied in the analysis of proposed training data, independent of any particular neural network implementation [Darbari 2000, van der Zwaag 2002].

In the case of neural network systems, by contrast, the knowledge is not so clearly or explicitly described, nor so easily compartmentalized, as is the case with an identifiable rule or equation to represent some specific theory, knowledge, or fact. Rather, the knowledge is implicitly expressed within what otherwise could be considered a body of raw data, which either previously has been or is yet to be collected from the problem domain. This body of implicit and empirical knowledge could be considered the ultimate use-case, as it is a collection of selected examples drawn from the problem domain for which the neural network system is developed.

Before such a body of implicit knowledge is encoded in a neural network, the system evaluator needs to formulate a sufficient understanding of what that knowledge consists. Considerations to be addressed include:

1. What is known or can be determined, directly or by inference, about that knowledge embedded in the data,
2. How the manner, process, and circumstance by which the data is collected affects its potential use,
3. Whether this information can be expressed and collected by multiple, perhaps independent, means, and
4. Reasons for preferring one expression or approach over the others.

Independent verification of the epoch knowledge that is contained within the neural network should be traceable back to the epochs that constitute the neural network's training. Such verification involves a closer examination by means other than the neural network encoding of the data that constitutes that epoch, independent of the neural network structure.

The report by Dr. Lisboa [2001] discussing verification requirements for safety critical systems emphasized the importance of independent assessment by agents external to the original design process. This independent assessment should cover all aspects of the neural network solution, both its structure and the knowledge that it encodes.

Various analysis methods and tools are available to support such an analysis. The data can be tested for how well it fits hypothesized principles, particularly those under which the neural network system is designed. For example, such analysis can determine what type of decision curves or surfaces best fit, bind, and partition the empirical data into meaningful subclasses. On the other hand, the data may be described in terms of its statistical and clustering properties. Analysis of how the data varies with time can be very important.

The tools of numerical analysis [Pai 2000], multivariate statistical analysis [Anderson 2003], and data mining [Hand 2001] can be employed to perform such an analysis of the data constituting the knowledge source to confirm system design hypotheses as well as to identify unanticipated issues, like conflicts with those hypotheses. In particular, some data mining methods incorporate neural network techniques as part of their data analysis.

Machine learning [Mitchell 1997] may appear at first to constitute an attempt at circuitous reasoning, using one neural network to analyze data to be used in another neural network. The major difference between the two applications of neural network technology lies in how they are used. In this case the emphasis is on characterizing and understanding the available knowledge, whereas in the original case (the one being verified) the emphasis is on applying the knowledge to solve a particular problem.

This machine learning exercise could be considered an automated or computer-assisted brainstorming session to explore and to determine just what information or knowledge is contained in the proposed data that will be used to train the neural network system that is to be deployed. The results of this effort at knowledge analysis are apropos not only to the particular application of this knowledge that is the current focus, i.e., the current problem to be solved, but more generally whether the knowledge might be appropriate to any other problem that may even tangentially involve this knowledge.

In addition to providing a detailed characterization of the knowledge implicit in the training data, this analysis also facilitates a better determination of engineering concerns, such as how much data is needed to properly capture within the neural network system the knowledge or mechanisms that supposedly are exhibited in the data to the levels or degrees of accuracy, precision, coverage, or generalization specified in the system design requirements.

The results of this knowledge analysis can also benefit the actual operation of the neural network system by providing a foundation for evaluation of the operational epochs that are passed through the deployed neural network system. This knowledge can be employed proactively in the development of real-time monitors that evaluate when the inputs to the operational neural network system should be questioned.

Complementary to knowledge analysis is the consideration of the suitability of the knowledge implicitly expressed in the proposed training epochs in accomplishing the purpose of the total system. The task of application analysis utilizes the insight gleaned by the knowledge analysis task regarding the nature of the knowledge source (KS) to explicitly and purposefully relate that KS to the problem that it is supposed to address.

The goal of application analysis is to ascertain how well the proposed KS addresses the problem being solved. Identified deficiencies may indicate the need to expand or otherwise modify the knowledge collection, to incorporate other external knowledge, or to modify neural network system architecture and parameters.

Major issues and concerns to be addressed by the application analysis task include, for example, the following considerations:

1. Extent to which the KS covers all possibilities (scenarios),
2. Uniqueness and relevance of the KS to the particular problem,
3. Alternative or additional KS that are more relevant,
4. Generalization, levels and what types, required of the KS,

5. Ambiguity of multiple, equally plausible and acceptable generalizations,
6. Accuracy and precision expected from the KS,
7. Safety-critical requirements on the KS,
8. Mission-critical requirements on the KS,
9. Fault management requirements on the KS,
10. Confidence levels to which results are judged, and
11. External mechanisms or KSs available by which to judge and confirm generalizations.

The functional verification activities discussed in Section 2.2 will consider whether the final implemented neural network system does indeed generalize as expected. However, before that determination is addressed, the more immediate concern is to what extent the underlying knowledge itself, independent of any particular neural network architecture, can be expected to satisfy the application requirements. Otherwise, the determination of what knowledge to use or whether the problem should be solved with a neural network system remains in question.

In addition to the identification of the major issues to be addressed, another major aspect of this task is to identify the criteria by which to judge the findings of the analysis.

The use of neural network-based systems in medical diagnosis provides an example of such systems design and V&V considerations [Lisboa 2002]. Neural network-based medical diagnostic systems are safety-critical, and so their predictions must be externally confirmable by a medical exam or other independent medical procedures. The determination of which instances of the system's usage should be second opinioned can depend on many factors. A medical system must attain a series of certification levels on its way to full certification, moving from limited trial to broad based trial, and finally to full deployment.

The source of the knowledge should be carefully considered. The eventual target environment of the neural network system can be quite complex. Proper training of the neural network system can be greatly affected by the quality of the data that constitutes its training epochs. The collection of production data will certainly be required for the training as well as for the final functionality verification and acceptance testing of the neural network system. Production data will likely characterize the type of data typically available to the deployed neural network system. However, the neural network development and verification in some cases may necessitate the use of additional designed data.

Designed data [Coit 1998] is not simulated or fabricated data. Rather, designed data is indeed actual observable, collectible data. However, it is collected under carefully controlled and specified conditions. When a data collection experiment is designed and performed, the data collected is much more tightly controlled. Exact levels of the input variables are stated. Experiments can be blocked to avoid confusion caused by questionable examples. Experiments may be replicated. The designer can control the sampling distribution.

Such planned experimental data often is collected with more care and attention than that normally given to production data. The setting is more controlled, so that the observations that are collected can be properly attributed to the correct circumstances and causes. For example, only a single operator, machine or ambient condition may participate. Additional special tests or measurements may be made that would be impractical during normal production.

Data analyzed during the course of the experiments may lead to the modification of the experimental design or the data collection procedures, as needed. Multiple iterations may be required to satisfy the data collector as to the usefulness and completeness of the data that is collected.

More information may be collected as part of the designed data collection than will be available for use by the neural network system when employed in normal production mode. Such additional sources of information are not to be used to train the neural network system, since they would not normally be available as inputs to the neural network system. However, such information may be available under special circumstances as in when the system is operated in a diagnostic mode observed by an external monitoring system. Thus, what otherwise might be considered extraneous data may yet have a valid purpose in one or more of the diagnostic operational modes of the system. It also may be useful in the determination or verification of overall system performance.

Other reasons for the collection of designed data include the need to capture atypical situations like failure modes that do not occur with sufficient frequency when the system environment is employed in typical production mode. If the neural network system is expected to detect the presence of faulty products in some production process or some anomalous situation, a sufficient number of such events may not occur frequently enough under normal operations to provide an adequate training set.

Dr. Alice Smith discusses the issues related to the need for and the use of both designed data and production data in the development of appropriate complete training and testing epochs [Coit 1995]. Such issues include the proper balancing of examples from both sources. Normal production data is more readily available than specifically collected designed data.

The need for a readily available external source of confirmation can be a vital concern in real-time safety-critical systems such as neural network-based aircraft flight controllers. For example, medical standards related to the deployment of new systems require the ready availability of independent means to confirm the results of the new system. Such external sources must be independent and not simply the result of partitioning available training epochs to support a cross-validation strategy.

For the case of systems that require such ready access, one alternative may be for novelty detection to be permanently built into the total system. In a sense, the novelty detector may be viewed as part of a real-time self-imposed V&V of the neural network system's performance (see Section 2.2).

The willingness of various industries to adopt and to trust neural network-based systems is following a predictable story-line similar to that of the development and deployment of fly-by-wire technology.

> Fly-by-wire is a means of aircraft control that uses electronic circuits to send inputs from the pilot to the motors that move the various flight controls on the aircraft. There are no direct hydraulic or mechanical linkages between the pilot and the flight controls. Digital fly-by-wire uses an electronic flight control system coupled with a digital computer to replace conventional mechanical flight controls.[2]

For a number of years, new fly-by-wire control systems were deployed with then traditional hydraulic systems as backup. Over time, the fly-by-wire system technology was in fact proven by accumulated experience to be more adaptive as well as more reliable (less prone to failure and less expensive to maintain) than the hydraulics that was replaced. Historically, the National Aeronautics and Space Administration (NASA) used an F-8C for its Digital Fly-by-Wire Program. This was the first digital fly-by-wire aircraft to operate without a mechanical backup system.

2.1.3 Appropriateness Verification of Neural Network Structure and Knowledge

Sections 2.1.1 and 2.1.2 discussed the roles of independent examinations of the neural network structure and of the knowledge that has been or will be encoded. The information gleaned during these independent examinations serves a crucial role in the evaluation of how well the two system components can be expected to mesh to form a total neural network-based system.

This section considers issues that should be addressed before the actual neural network training is performed and functionally evaluated. Emphasis is on how well the strengths and limitations of the chosen neural network

---

[2] Fly-by-wire, http://www.1903to2003.gov/essay/Dictionary/fly-by-wire/D183.htm

architecture complement the knowledge available for training the neural network and external constraints on the problem to be solved.

The appropriateness of matching the chosen neural network structure with the available knowledge should be considered at several levels. These aspects range from the high-level validation question of whether the choice of neural network architecture is appropriate to the problem being addressed, to how the neural network parameters should be set to best encode the training dataset, to planning how to verify the encoding of the domain KS that represents the problem domain knowledge.

Whether selected from a standard configuration, as from a development package such as MATLAB Neural Network Toolbox, or custom designed, the particular neural network architecture and its configuration parameters are determined based on a set of assumptions about the knowledge to be encoded and the data available for training and evaluating the final system.

To focus discussion of the appropriateness of the neural network structure, of the knowledge it is to encode, and of the problem to be solved or application to be performed, this section considers the two general statistical estimators of performance, bias and variance. In particular, this section analyzes the interplay of these two as typified in what has been termed the *bias-variance dilemma*. Geman, Bienenstock, and Doursat [1992] in "Neural Networks and the Bias/Variance Dilemma" provide a comprehensive discussion of this neural network design problem. The two statistical factors, in neural network terminology, may be defined thus:

1. *Statistical bias* is the complexity restriction that the neural network architecture imposes on the degree to which the target function is accurately fit.
2. *Statistical variance* is the deviation of the neural network learning efficacy from one data sample to another sample that could be described by the same target function model.

Statistical bias accounts only for the degree of fitting of the given training data, but not for the level of generalization. On the other hand, statistical variance accounts for the generalization of whether or not the neural network fits the examples without regard to the specificities of the provided data. While the two statistical measurements are interrelated, improvement of one of these measurements does not necessarily guarantee improvement in the other.

The performance of the trained network can depend on many factors, including the learning algorithm, number of layers, number of neurons, connections, overall network topology, and the transfer functions computed by each neuron. To avoid over- and under-fitting of the data, the bias–

variance trade-off should be balanced by matching the complexity of the network to the complexity of the data [Twomey 1998].

Fig. 6-2 depicts an idealization of the prediction risk, represented as the expected training error and expected test error, versus model size for models trained on a fixed finite training sample [Moody 1994]. The figure separates into two regions: under-fitting which is due to high model bias and over-fitting which is due to high model variance. The selection of the best model corresponds to an optimal tradeoff between the global low training error and the global low test error.

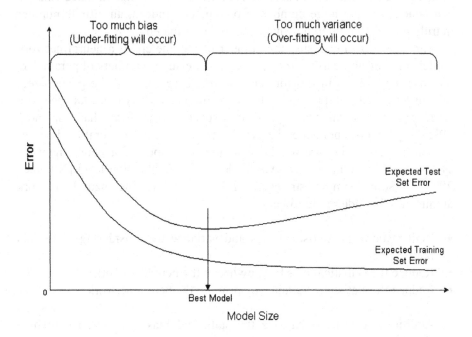

Figure 6-2. Idealized Depiction of Expected Training Test Error (Prediction Risk) vs. Model Size

The under-fitting situation of Fig. 6-2 occurs due to a lack of adequate training. On the other hand, too much training of a neural network system can result in over-fitting. This corresponds to the situation where the learned function fits very closely the training data however it does not generalize very well. Consequently, the neural network cannot model sufficiently well unseen data from the same task. General criteria for avoidance of over-fitting the training data and increasing the generalization are given by the statistical and generalization theories.

A neural network that fits closely to the provided training examples should have a low bias but could have a high variance. Incorrect neural network models can result in too high a bias. This is the situation where the neural network tightly matches the training set, but the training set does not in fact represent the true problem. On the other hand, truly model-free inference where the model is selected without any understanding of the training set suffers from high variance. Model-free approaches to complex inference tasks are slow to converge, in the sense that training epochs required to achieve acceptable performance can be quite large—to the point of being impracticable to collect. This is the effect of high variance and is a consequence of the large number of parameters; indeed, an infinite number in truly model-free inference that need to be estimated.

Simply stated, increasing the number of parameters of a neural network model can contribute to a large variance, while small numbers of parameters increase their bias. In the former case, more cases might be generalized, though less well, while in the latter case the network is more tailored to a given problem domain and should be expected to perform that task more efficiently but does not generalize well outside that carefully crafted domain.

Various strategies are available to the developer of a neural network system for fine-tuning to achieve the desired generalization level [Nikolaev 2003]. Some simple strategies that manipulate the neural network architecture include the following:

- Reduce both the statistical bias and variance by considering more data points.
- Reduce the statistical bias by growing of the neural network.
- Reduce the statistical variance by pruning the neural network.

Additional efforts to balance the statistical bias and variance involve tuning the network learning algorithm, providing training examples, or shaping the transfer function. Other efforts to balance the statistical bias and variance in an effort to avoid over-fitting can be made with the following neural network tuning strategies:

- Regularization
- Early stopping
- Growing neural networks
- Pruning neural networks
- Committees of neural networks

The neural network verification process should include an analysis of the following bias-variance aspects of the neural network system design and implementation:

- Bias-variance target that is mappable to the available data and the problem being solved.
- Approaches taken to achieve that target with combination of the above or other methods employed.
- Justification given bias-variance target and the choice of approaches used, including technical issues, cost and management issues, safety- or mission-critical concerns.

An obvious concern of the V&V practitioner is the determination of how well the neural network system addresses the bias-variance dilemma. Prior to the actual neural network training, the V&V analysis should leverage the resources previously discussed in Sections 2.1.1 and 2.1.2 to access how well the proposed combination of neural network system and training epochs will evaluate with respect to the general performance estimators of bias and variance.

During and following the training of the neural network, these general estimators again should be computed and compared with expected results as a component of the functional verification discussed in Section 2.2. Discretion to modify the training epochs or the neural network system via its available parameters in an effort to achieve better performance results certainly are options for the system developer and may be an option to the V&V practitioner, whether directly or via referral to the developer.

Neural networks have been proven capable of functioning as universal approximators. They can approximate an arbitrary continuous function on a compact domain with arbitrary precision given a sufficient number of neurons when they include nonlinear activation functions [White 1990]. The trained weights of a neural network are a vector-valued statistic, and training is the process of computing that statistic. The relationship between neural network models and statistical models has been the subject of several recent papers by well-known statisticians [Cherkassky 1994] with the general conclusion that there are many important parallels between the development of neural network models and the computation of statistical models.

Networks with neurons that produce Gaussian outputs also are examples of universal approximators. Two popular feed-forward neural networks models, the MLP and the RBF network, are based on specific architectures and transfer functions. MLPs use sigmoidal transfer functions, while RBFs use radial functions, usually Gaussians. Given such choices of transfer functions, both types of neural networks have been employed as universal approximators.

The employment of universal approximators as transfer functions does not always provide an optimal choice. Approximations of complex decision borders or approximations of multidimensional mappings by neural networks require flexibility that may be provided only by networks with a sufficiently large number of parameters. This leads to another method by which to address the previously discussed bias-variance dilemma.

More recently, a number of new transfer function types, as well as hybrids of previous types, are being applied in a variety of applications. The comprehensive 50-page paper, "Survey of Neural Transfer Functions" written by Duch and Jankowski [1999] provides an examination of general criteria by which to judge the appropriateness of these and other transfer function types for various classes of neural network applications. Their survey reinforces the argument by several neural network experts that the choice of transfer functions should be considered as important as the network architecture and the learning algorithm when developing a neural network solution.

Fig. 6-3 that follows is taken from another Duch and Jankowski [2001] paper. The transfer function types are hierarchically ordered according to their flexibility. Each similarly grayed row contains functions that exhibit similar flexibility. The top rows contain the most flexible function classes, and the bottom rows are the simplest. Along with the names of function types are numbers in parentheses to identify the equations in the Duch paper that describe each type, and mathematical symbols indicate the activation and output functions employed to form each transfer function type.

For simple problems, the selection of transfer function may not appear to be a significant system constraint. However, in the case of more sophisticated applications, the selection of transfer functions may make a significant difference in eventual performance or ease of training.

At one extreme, when the datasets are small and the dimensionality of the feature space is relatively large, the actual shape of decision borders determined by the choice of transfer function may seem irrelevant. Logical rules or decision trees, dividing the feature space into hyper-boxes, may be sufficient.

However, as more data samples are provided, the inadequacy of the generic transfer function models will appear and the need for flexible contours approximating real distribution of data may become apparent [Jankowski 2001]. As noted in Section 2.1.3, complexity of the neural network model may be controlled by Bayesian regularization methods using ontogenic networks that grow and/or shrink, and judicious choice of the transfer functions.

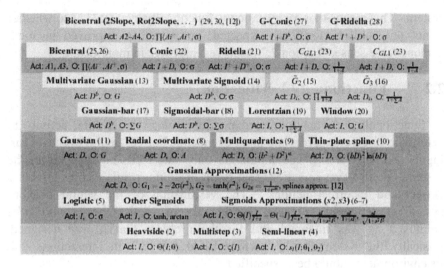

Figure 6-3. Hierarchy of Neural Network Transfer Function Classes [Duch and Jankowski 2001]

Much of the prior discussion has focused on correctness and performance, but there are other considerations such as efficiency. Efficiency involves not only the resources required by the neural network system when it is functioning in its intended application, but also the steps that lead to that neural network system's development as well as its V&V.

The optimal system may consume too many resources, computationally, to be deployed in the targeted environment. The choice of transfer function may not only improve the correct performance of the system, but also result in a system that is less complex and requires less training effort to achieve the desired performance level.

A variety of strategies have been explored for the incremental refinement of neural network systems so they are both more correct and more efficient [Ragg 1997a]. Some approaches attempt to modify the neural network topology [Ragg 1997b]. Other approaches include the employment of hybrid algorithms integrating genetic algorithm, simulated annealing, and other heuristic procedures that can be applied for the optimal design of a neural network architecture and correct parameters for the learning algorithm that yield a smaller, faster and better generalization performance [Abraham 2000]. More recently, researchers are considering transfer function adaptation as a means to improve neural network system performance and training efficiency [Chandra 2004; Abraham 2001].

Such efforts to iteratively, incrementally, and genetically evolve a neural network system to achieve better performance and efficiency require comparing the actual performance of successive versions of a neural network system. This means that each version is functionally evaluated as to whether it not only still performs as expected, but also has improved in some demonstrable sense. Section 2.2 discusses this topic in more detail.

2.2   Functionality Verification

Functionality verification is essentially a black-box testing activity to determine if, given appropriate input events, the correct output events occur. Inputs and outputs may encompass not only data feeds into and out of the system, but also system actions that result or do not result such as a robot's correct and incorrect actions.   The verification of the neural network system's functionality involves determination of whether the system can be employed as was intended and for the problem that it was designed. Basically, the system should "perform as advertised." Its interactions with its environment should be as specified.

The functional verification of a neural network system may be particularly challenging.   The same methods that are applied to the functional verification of a completed neural network system are also employed during the neural network learning/training process.

As Dr. Lisboa [2003] has previously noted regarding the V&V of safety-critical systems, the V&V process requires adherence to formal methodologies at each level of the design lifecycle. However, where non-linear inferences from real world data are involved, the emphasis appears to be shifting towards the employment of extensive trials with external data. This leads to a verification process that is performance-based.

Training is an iterative process; the knowledge encoded in the neural network system is changed with each additional training cycle of a training epoch.

Functionality verification is concerned not only with what the system is able to do but with also how well it performs those functions. Additional considerations include the stability and consistency of its performance over an expected diversity of operational settings.   The predictability and repeatability of the observed performance is considered.   Such considerations are important when judging adaptive systems.

Previous sections have discussed verification of the components that comprise the neural network system, namely, the total neural network structure, consisting of neural network architecture and system parameter choices, and the training epochs employed, where the knowledge to be captured implicitly resides.   Various approaches and techniques for the independent evaluation of each of these components have been discussed. The results of those independent verifications now are brought to bear on the functional verification of the total neural network system.

2.2.1 Simulated vs. Empirical Verification

In particular, Section 2.1.3 considered via an analysis of the ability of the neural network structure to encode especially crafted artificial knowledge via training epochs that supposedly exhibits the characteristics of the actual knowledge with which the neural network system is ultimately to be trained. This set of dry-runs permitted the carefully controlled analysis of how well the neural network system might be expected to behave under a variety of assumptions. Objectives and considerations served by such a preliminary training exercise include the following:

- The amount and quality of data available with which to test the neural network system's characteristics, performance, etc. is not limited by potential difficulties and costs in collecting real data.
- This flexibility in training epochs facilities a comprehensive analysis of the neural network system's ability to encode the desired knowledge.
- The training process itself can be thoroughly verified.

Some data sets, such as those that would be collected during a test flight of an aircraft, could be quite expensive. To perform repeat data capture sessions for multiple scenarios can quickly become cost prohibitive. Additional considerations that can arise and so must be addressed include recalibration between test collection runs and proper documentation of all pertinent constraints.

The simulated data sets may include not only training epochs designed to represent expected or typical scenarios, but also to mimic abnormal training epochs. Such epochs may be difficult, quite unsafe, and perhaps impossible to collect under normal conditions. These conditions could occur under plausibly realizable circumstances and should therefore be considered in the final analysis. The nature and quantity of designed data discussed in Section 2.1.2 can be identified, estimated, and confirmed.

A comprehensive analysis of the neural network system should include a sensitivity analysis to determine whether and under what circumstances the combination of this neural network system and the expected actual training data might result in an ill-conditioned system, and so require further engineering consideration and refinement.

Simulated data, generated from actually collected data, can be systematically deformed. Deformation would render the simulated data defective in some sense. This data can be employed to test the stability of the neural network system from two perspectives:

1. Training with less than optimal (desirable) epoch data

2. Executing with less than optimal (expected) run-time data input.

The first case is part of the stability analysis of the neural network system's training. The latter case constitutes part of the assessment of the system's expected run-time performance for scenarios where circumstances outside the system's control affect data on which the neural network system depends.

Additional considerations to be addressed include verification of the neural network training and verification of the process itself, including how to assure quality control of the actual training epochs, estimation of how much data should be collected, or what error metrics are more appropriate to use.

The training methods that are to be employed with the actual training epochs are presumed to have been employed previously with such artificial epochs. The process of capturing and training with actual training epochs should greatly benefit from such prior effort.

Of the two concerns of what vs. how that functional verification addresses, the easier one is that of how well the system performs. The more difficult analysis concerns appraisal of the correctness of the system. Given a neural network system and a set of training epochs, the training can be performed using a variety of approaches that are adaptable and flexible.

The following section examines the process for verification of the training of the system. The focus is on the generation of quantifiable appraisal of the neural network system's performance. The training process and its evaluation are interrelated. A given training process may perform poorly or well.

This process is not the counterpart of compiling the source code of a procedural program to generate executable object code, which either does or does not compile. A traditional program may have and eliminate compiler errors, only to reveal run-time errors.

2.2.2   Quantifiable Training Verification

The verification of the training needs to be measurable. Neural network systems may be viewed as implementing a function approximation task. Generally accepted standard error measurements include:

- mean absolute error (MAE),
- mean squared error (MSE),
- root mean square error (RMS), and
- percent good classification (PG). [Twomey 1997]

There is no consensus as to which measure is preferred.

A neural network system performing pattern classification typically will use an error metric that measures misclassifications along with, or instead of, an error metric that measures distance from the correct classification.

Misclassification error is further broken down into two components:

1. Type I errors, also called α errors or missed occurrences, are misclassifications where the input pattern, which belongs to one class, is identified as something other than that class.
2. Type II errors, also called β errors or false alarms, are misclassifications where the input pattern belongs to another pattern class, but is identified by the neural network as belonging that particular class.

The objective of a neural network system is to generalize successfully, that is, to predict successfully on data not used to train the neural network. A neural network system's success generally is measured in terms of the following three statistical error measurements [Efron 1982]:

1. True Error is statistically defined on "an asymptotically large number of new data points that converge in the limit to the actual population distribution." [Weiss 1991]
2. Apparent Error is the error of the neural network when validating on the same training set used to construct the model.
3. Testing Error is the error of the neural network when validating on a test set other than the training set.

Since any real application can never determine True Error, it must be estimated from Apparent Error and / or the Testing Error. This situation is expressed as

$$\text{True Error} = \text{Apparent Error} + \text{Bias} \qquad (6.1)$$

Most current neural network practitioners use Testing Error as the estimate for True Error, the so-called train-and-test validation method; however, some use Apparent Error, and a few use combinations of both. Typically the true error of a neural network system is estimated by testing the trained neural network on new data not used in model construction.

In many cases data may be severely limited; consequently, the true error is estimated using the same data employed to construct the model. Several sampling methods that reuse the training set data have been developed. These have two important aspects:

- They use all data for both model construction and model validation.
- Nonparametric techniques do not depend on functional form or probabilistic assumptions.

Some of the more prominent methods are briefly discussed below. There are trade-offs associated with using these methods for both neural network and statistical prediction models [Twomey 1993]. These methods are nonparametric or data driven. Benefits of nonparametric methods include the following:

- They demand minimal amounts of modeling
- They require few assumptions or analysis
- They are mechanistic or easy to apply for universal application
- They substitute computing power for theoretical analysis

The greatest benefit associated with such resampling methods is that they utilize all available samples in neural network system training. The first two methods below require the training only on neural network system. These methods are relatively inexpensive in computational resources, and may be appropriate for simpler, non-mission critical applications. The latter three methods generate multiple neural network systems but provide better error estimates, so they are appropriate for systems associated with higher value and risk.

Resubstitution substitutes the training data used to construct the model for estimating model error or training set error. This method is also called the apparent error method since it estimates True Error as equaling the Apparent Error, and Bias is treated as being zero. This estimate is thus biased downward to less than the true error, sometimes severely. This method does use all of the data both for model construction and for model validation and is computationally inexpensive because only one model is constructed.

The test-and-train methodology divides the available data into two sets. One set is used to train the neural network model, and the other set is used to validate the model. This is the most common method of neural network validation. True Error is estimated directly as the testing set error and Bias could be calculated by subtracting the Apparent Error from the testing set error.

The proportion set aside for training of the available data has ranged, in practice, from 25% to 90%. The training set error, and therefore the estimate of True Error, is highly dependent on the exact sample chosen for training and the exact sample chosen for testing. These two components are completely dependent on each other since they are mutually exclusive. This creates a highly variable estimate of True Error, especially for small sample sizes.

A modified version of this method divides the available data into three sets:

1. Training set,
2. Stop testing set used during training, and
3. Performance testing set used for validating the trained network.

The stop testing set is used during training to decide when training should stop. This stop-learning test set is intended to detect and prevent over-fitting. The second testing set then is used to estimate the True Error of the trained network. This method may result in a better generalizing final network, because of its avoidance of over-fitting, but the available data sample is divided three ways instead of two ways, decreasing the number of data points used for model construction.

Fig. 6-4 [Twomey 1993] provides an example of over-fitting due to neural network over-training. In this example, the best results were achieved with a training epoch of 180 items. Continuing to train with additional training items results in degraded statistical results.

Fig 6-4 is separated into two columns. The column on the left shows training with a training data set. The column on the right shows testing via cross-validation data. In row a), the training results in a poor fit as it is thus far insufficient. In row b), there is a slightly improved fit due to continued training. Row c) results in a near-perfect fit and would be an opportune time to stop training. Finally, row d) demonstrates over-fitting due to continued training where there is a low error in training and a higher error in testing

In terms of computational costs, for both versions of train-and-test, only one model is constructed, but both training and testing are performed on a subset of the available data.

Cross-validation and group cross-validation [Stone 1974] each divide the available data into k subgroups. A total of k distinct neural network systems are constructed, each using k-1 data groups for model construction, and the reserved group for k^{th} model validation.

In general, this method removes a sub-sample of data size k from the entire data set size n. The network is trained on the remaining n-k data points and tested on the k data points left out. The sub-sample of data then is returned into the training set. This extract-train-test-return procedure is repeated until all n points have been removed and n/k networks have been trained and tested. In the special case of k=1, this method is known simply as cross-validation.

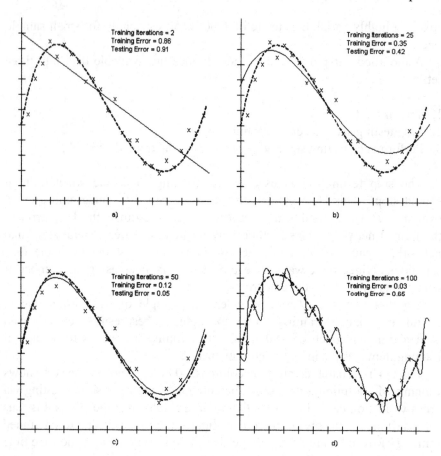

Figure 6-4. Training: An Example of Over-fitting

The final deployed neural network system then is trained using all the data. Some practitioners simply select the final network from the n/k networks that were constructed. Its True Error is estimated by using the mean of the Testing Errors of the k grouped cross validation neural network models.

This method uses all available data for both model training and model validation, but requires the construction of k+1 models, i.e. training k+1 neural networks. Its Bias is estimated by subtracting the Apparent Error of the application network from the estimate of True Error.

The jackknife methodology [Miller 1974] is identical to the grouped cross-validation except that the Apparent Error is determined by averaging the Apparent Error, rather than the Testing Error, of each jackknifed model. Each jackknifed model is the same as each grouped cross-validated model, described in the preceding section. The Bias is estimated by subtracting this new Apparent Error from the estimated True Error.

Simply stated, the validation using grouped cross validation and grouped jackknife will be identically determined and computed, except for the calculation of Apparent Error. Consequently, the computational costs are the same as that of group cross-validation.

With the bootstrap methodology, [Efron 1982] an initial data set of size n, called the bootstrap, is drawn with replacement from the original data set of n observations. The bias of each bootstrapped network is estimated by subtracting the Apparent Error of that network from the error of the network evaluated on the original total data set.

This process is repeated k times, each with a different randomly drawn data set. The overall estimate of Bias is obtained by averaging over the k estimates of bias. The final application model is constructed using all of the data. Therefore k+1 models are constructed. True Error is estimated by adding the estimate of Bias to the Apparent Error of the application model.

The bootstrap method is generally noted to be less variable than either the grouped cross validation or the grouped jackknife, but it can be downwardly biased. According to Efron, originator of the bootstrap, this method is the maximum likelihood estimate of the True Error. The bootstrap method constructs the final model using all n data points and estimates the bias via resampling.

Although the bootstrap methodology has been shown to provide very good estimates of error for statistical prediction models, there are few instances in the literature where the bootstrap method of error estimation has been applied to neural network prediction models. This is most likely due to the increase in computational effort of building additional models.

2.3   Adaptive Systems Verification

If the neural network system is an OLNN, it is adaptive while used in operation. This means the verification process becomes significantly more complicated. The requirements for which the adaptive system was designed necessarily included statements regarding what the nature of the adaptation is to be. Example requirements could specify that the network is supervised or unsupervised or that it is explicitly bounded and focused or open-ended where the neural network is limited only by the capabilities and resources of the underlying computing platform.

That the developed system indeed satisfies the described adaptation strategy must be verified. Each of these adaptation choices will affect the approaches taken to verify the system. Verification now includes not only the system's encoded knowledge at a given point in time, the case with a pre-trained neural network (PTNN), but also the discipline by which the OLNN is constrained to perform within the bounds set for it. The system cannot be allowed to "learn its way into a hole."

A significant difference exists between a PTNN and an OLNN in regard to the roll and objective of verification. With the PTNN, focus is on what the PTNN knows at the time of deployment; whereas, with the OLNN, the bounds of what the OLNN might yet learn in the future also is a major concern.

In particular, with adaptive systems, the verification process does not reach a definitive point in time. For example, the verification might not be considered complete at system rollout when system verification can be treated as a completed static event, since the knowledge encoded within the neural network is subject to change in response to events in its operational environment. On the other hand, to address the requirement of post-deployment verification by repeatedly reapplying the methods of static system verification is not practical, either.

To adequately address this situation, a middle-ground strategy is needed. This section examines how such a strategy may be implemented and verified. The following areas are examined:

- Sources or mechanisms for neural network adaptability
- Functionality required to oversee and assure the neural network adaptability
- Evaluation procedures and processes

The neural network system adaptability may be achieved in multiple ways:

- Neural network system weights, topology, etc. may be modified.
- Learning rules and constraints may be modified.
- New training may be integrated with prior neural network training in a variety of ways.
- New training may be integrated with external knowledge in a variety of ways.

Each of these modalities raises particular verification concerns to be addressed. In particular, these modalities of adaptation may be applied in multiple ways that may or may not be coordinated with one another.

2.3.1   Adaptive Neural Network Architectures: A Primer

The simplest form of neural network adaptation is the adjustment of neural network weights during the training process, whether this adaptation is performed as pre-training or online learning. Examples of such neural network architectures that employ this approach include the widely employed feed-forward, back-propagation architecture developed in the early 1970's by several independent sources, including Parker [1987], and Rumelhart [1986]. Such architectures are generally employed in prediction-class problems and require supervised learning.

With some neural network systems, not only are the various weights subject to modification, but so is the neural network structure. The SOM developed by Teuvo Kohonen in the early 1980's [Kohonen 1998] is such a neural network architecture. The input data to an SOM is projected to a two-dimensional layer that preserves order, compacts sparse data, and spreads out dense data.

Another significant difference between this neural network type and many others is that training of the SOM involves unsupervised learning. Hybrid applications involving SOMs also are possible. When the SOM topology is combined with other neural layers for prediction or categorization, the network first learns, in PTNN mode, in an unsupervised manner. It then switches, in OLNN mode, to a supervised mode for the trained network to which it is attached.

The counter-propagation network was developed by Hecht-Nielsen [1988] as a means to combine an unsupervised Kohonen layer with a teachable output layer. This is yet another neural network topology to synthesize complex classification problems while attempting to minimize the number of processing elements and training time. The operation of the counter-propagation network is similar to that of the learning vector quantization network in that the middle Kohonen layer acts as an adaptive look-up table, providing the closest fit to an input stimulus and outputting its equivalent mapping [Ellingsen 1994].

More recently, efforts to apply adaptive technologies such as genetic algorithms and simulated annealing techniques to the adaptation of a neural network architecture have been explored [Alander 2001]. Other researchers have attempted comprehensive strategies, such as the Adaptive Learning by Evolutionary Computation system [Abraham 2001], an automatic computational framework for optimizing neural networks wherein the neural network structure and the learning algorithms are adapted according to the problem.

From a verification perspective, the means and the mechanisms of neural network architecture adaptation for the system in hand, whether restricted to weight changes, or including topological modifications, should have been verified as described previously in Section 2.1.1 before any pre-training or online-learning is implemented. Similarly, the appropriateness of the chosen means of modification should have been at least simulated with artificial adaptation scenarios. Those aspects of neural network architecture verification are not repeated in this section; rather, the emphasis in Section 2.3 is on the special problems and conditions that real-time online adaptation introduces, and how the verification process may address them.

2.3.2   Adaptation Through Learning: Supervised and Unsupervised

The verification process must take into account whether the OLNN training is supervised, unsupervised, or some combination of the two. In one sense, all neural network systems are supervised; that is, mechanisms and procedures at some level of system control must be provided to constrain and oversee when and what the neural network system is permitted to learn, and thus how it will adapt. Validation through determining the applicableness and verification through determining the correctness of those supervision mechanisms must be considered a core fundamental component of the neural network system verification process, whether such supervision is considered to be a component of the total neural network system or external to it. Some of the more prevalent learning mechanisms are considered here.

In the traditional neural network sense, supervised learning refers to the neural network being explicitly presented with a set of examples, the supervised training epoch that includes not only the inputs that the neural network is to observe, but also the outputs that the neural network is to recall. This learning experience is explicitly controlled by an external source or mechanism. This mechanism shall be termed the supervisor, and such learning is termed supervised learning. The neural network initiates new learning when toggled into learn-mode and presented an epoch on which to train. Otherwise, the neural network functions in application-mode, producing outputs to the inputs it is presented, based on its current state of training.

In the case of unsupervised learning, the neural network is not presented with matching sets of neural network inputs and outputs, such as may have been prepared by an external supervisor. Instead, the learning rule, which is part of the total neural network system, determines how appropriate outputs are generated. Unsupervised learning is generally associated with pattern classification-like problems in which a collection of data inputs are sorted into several potential classes. The neural network may be indirectly supervised by the external modification of learning rule parameters.

The learning rule parameters include such considerations as the number of distinct classes to which an input may be classed, the similarity metric for evaluating the similarity of an input to one class vs. another, and the transfer functions that determine the shape of the functional hyper-planes that delineate the separate classes. For example, when in learning mode, an SOM-based neural network system will adjust its weights and vectors to reflect modification of how the solution space of all potential classes is partitioned among the various classes.

The application of the unsupervised learning rule behaves the same whether the system is training in PTNN mode on a training epoch, or is being presented individual epoch data in OLNN mode. The learning rule computations of weights and topological changes involve the same types of computation for both PTNN and OLNN training.

The issues previously discussed in Section 2.1 regarding the verification of training and learning of a PTNN are again apropos to an adaptive OLNN. For example, the contents of the new epoch that forms the OLNN training session still need to be quality controlled. While the learning rule algorithm or heuristic automates the processing of inputs to generate new modifications to neural network weights and topology, it does not perform prescreening or pre-selection on the input data.

2.3.3 Novelty Detection: Implicit Supervision of Learning and Operation

Additional preprocessing to filter out the potential of learning based on inappropriate or incorrect data comes under the discipline of novelty detection [Marsland 2003]. Statistical outlier detection [Williams 2002] from the field of statistical theory is a similar concept. Novelty detection applies both to learning and non-learning modes when inappropriate inputs would lead to inappropriate outputs, which would be viewed as an example of the "garbage in, garbage out" mantra. In this case, novelty detection processing could be considered functionally to be one particular form of supervision.

Novelty detection represents one approach to achieving quality control. In the case of the PTNN, such qualification of the training epoch often may occur prior to the training exercise, so that the novelty detection processing effectively may be decoupled from the training process.

In the case of OLNN training, such a priori novelty detection is not possible; however, other general approaches to providing such supervision of the learning process exist:

1. The novelty detection function may be integrated into the OLNN training process, so that all necessary supervision is available in real-time.
2. Partial novelty detection may be performed as part of the real-time OLNN training, so that the new learning may be conditionally verified, while ultimate verification is performed post facto.

Previously, Section 2.2.2 discussed Type I and Type II error situations. Dependent on the purpose and functionality of the total system, of which the neural network system is one component, the conditional verification may refer to either of the above two situations. The Type I error situation would be treated as a missed opportunity of not learning when one could have. The Type II error situation would be treated as a false alarm of learning that occurred when it should not have and that needs to be reversed.

To support a two-stage conditional-final verification strategy, the ability and the resources to perform a post mortem analysis are needed. Given that the OLNN training is to be subject to a post-mortem review as part of its verification, the implication for system design and operation is that the results of such OLNN training should be not only re-viewable but also reversible, so that the undesirable results of incorrect, inappropriate, or simply poor training may be reversed.

The additional functionality in support of this verification strategy may be achieved in a variety of ways. For example, the state of the OLNN preserved before the questionable training could be re-loadable. In such a situation, the training epoch including the supervised response may need to be archived, as well as the state of the network before and after the training. This approach would imply a universal systems verification requirement for the ability to archive and to recall the state of the OLNN for some point in time. The implementation of those mechanisms that address such requirements in turn must be verified.

For a complete, post facto verification, the analysis must consider both the epochs on which the neural network was permitted to train and those epochs that were rejected by the novelty detection process. Thus, both Type I and Type II error situations are fully considered.

Such complete post facto verification serves more than just the original purpose of verifying that the neural network is learning as it is currently configured. This analysis also can support consideration of how the system might be enhanced and improved to handle other scenarios currently beyond its capability but reachable with appropriate modification to the original neural network design and implementation.

2.3.4   Long-Term Verification: Maintaining Consistency

Statistically speaking, the asymptotic convergence of an estimator to the object of estimation is called consistency. In the case of an adaptive OLNN that learns and evolves over its lifetime of deployment, learning consistency is a very important factor. Neural networks can be viewed mathematically as being statistical estimators.

Most nonparametric algorithms are consistent for essentially any regression function. Depending on the particular algorithm and the particular regression, however, the convergence of such methods can be extremely slow. Neural networks modeled after these algorithms, like those based on the universal approximators discussed in Section 2.1.3, may require significantly large training epochs.

There exist many consistent nonparametric estimators. Consequently, given enough training examples, optimal decision rules can be arbitrarily well approximated. Those studied extensively in the statistical literature include: Parzen windows and nearest neighbor rules [Duda and Hart 1973], regularization methods [Wahba 1982], and alternating conditional expectations [Friedman 1991], as well as feed-forward neural networks [Rumelhard 1986], and Boltzmann machines [Ackley 1985].

Section 2.1.3 discussed how the bias-variance dilemma can affect neural network learning performance. In the case of the PTNN, considerable care is required in the formation of appropriate training epochs. In the case of adaptive continually learning OLNNs, this dilemma re-manifests itself through the concept of consistency. The desired level of bias and variance achieved during pre-training of the OLNN may later become degraded, rather than improved, unless care is given to the online learning process to preserve consistency.

White [1990] has described a procedure by which a feed-forward neural network can be extended in a consistent manner. Major elements of the method are:

1. Strategic goal, which is to decrease both bias and variance. The typical manifestation of the bias-variance dilemma is to accept the expense of increasing one while decreasing the other.
2. Implementation strategy, which is to gradually decrease both bias and variance in a coordinated manner by increasing network size as new epochs are applied.

Bias can be diminished by increasing network size through the number of nodes and links in coordination with additional training from new epochs at such a rate that the variance also is managed. If nodes are added too quickly, bias can increase beyond acceptable tolerance. If they are added too slowly, variance can increase beyond acceptable tolerance.

This procedure for achieving consistency of feed-forward networks also can be applied as a general mechanism to manage learning consistency for other OLNN architectures. The procedure is not trivial to implement since the bias and variance both must tend to zero in coordination with each other. The reduction must proceed slowly, in small incremental steps. Otherwise, bias or variance will dominate the training, and the conditions of over-fitting and under-fitting may occur as the OLNN continues to learn.

From a practical standpoint, no neural network can be expected to grow in size indefinitely. Consequently, the above described consistency procedure must be adapted to the particular problem constraints and engineering limitations. On the other hand, the general principle of selecting sufficiently small steps by which to train and grow is still valid.

2.3.5   Incremental Verification: By Degrees

The previous discussion of consistency naturally leads to the concept of incremental verification. The NASA sponsored RIACS Workshop [Pecheur 2000] on the V&V of adaptive systems raised the issue of incremental verification: "How to dynamically verify at 'run-time' a continuously adapting system (on-board V&V, incremental V&V, how to recover from errors?)"

As the previous section discussed, neural network learning should proceed in relatively small, incremental steps to achieve consistency, i.e., to maintain control of bias and variance. Assuring that the bias-variance trade-off is maintained within the levels planned for the OLNN as the OLNN continues to learn is a significant aspect of the ongoing, quasi real-time, V&V process.

The term incremental has multiple dimensions in the context of V&V:

- Temporal, which is new knowledge acquired incrementally, also may be verified incrementally as it is learned.
- Component, which is verification of new training, may not cumulatively re-verify all previous training.
- Layered, which means the verification may be tiered in levels of confidence, with higher confidence levels achieved as additional testing is performed and case history accumulated.

Dependent on the problem domain being addressed, the verification process may emphasize one or more of these dimensions of incrementality.

As new training is presented to the OLNN over time, learning based on prior training may need re-verification. To what extent prior learning should be revisited depends on the underlying nature of the knowledge and the problem to which it is applied. The temporal nature of OLNN learning falls into two general scenarios [Lange 1993]:

1. Monotonic learning: New training represents knowledge complementary to prior training.

2. Non-monotonic learning: New training represents knowledge partially contradictory to prior training.

At least in theory, the monotonic learning case should be easier to maintain a verified status. However, the practical problem is that while the underlying knowledge may be monotonic, the learning process is not. The previous discussions of the bias-variance dilemma and learning consistency explained the impact of over-fitting and under-fitting. As a consequence of the new training, the neural network performance on the prior test epoch typically is degraded; although, total performance based on both prior and new training may have improved.

The new training may be incrementally applied to the previously trained OLNN in temporal order. In this case, the cumulative training epoch is not composed of a randomized sampling of all underlying knowledge, since a chronological ordering is imposed. This behavior may be acceptable and is indeed desirable when a problem domain is time varying and the OLNN is expected to track the underlying knowledge.

Other approaches for incorporating the new training that reduce and even eliminate the time dependency in the training epoch are also available. For example, to remove the chronological underpinning, a new cumulative training set may be constructed as a randomized epoch that is a sampling drawn from all current and prior training, and presented to an initialized OLNN from which prior training has been removed. One draw back of this approach is the need to accumulate an ever-growing dataset from which to sample the new cumulative training epoch. Based on the bias-variance dilemma discussion, this epoch, hopefully, will grow slowly.

Incremental verification of an adaptive OLNN-based controller in an aircraft may emphasize temporal aspects since a given flight situation may exist only momentarily, and thus the knowledge to be used is momentary. A physical control element of an aircraft may become stuck or otherwise perform sub-optimally, and the OLNN is to adapt to this situation, until the situation is corrected. In such a scenario, the re-verification of prior training may be counter-productive, since the current state of the dynamic environment is what matters. In this case, some version of a sliding-window verification strategy may be more appropriate.

The underlying knowledge and its application may be decomposed along functional dimensions rather than based on chronological considerations. In such cases, the training of each functional component may be independently verified. However, interactions among the training of two or more independent components may occur. This is the situation with a classification problem where membership between two classes may be ambiguous.

An example of incremental verification that emphasizes componentization is an interactive voice response unit, such as found in one of today's cell phones. Each epoch, the voiceprint of the name of a person to be called, represents a separate, conceptually independent, unit of knowledge on which the OLNN is trained. Pragmatically, the potential exists with each additional epoch for the contamination of prior training epochs, dependent upon how similar the voiceprint may be to an earlier entry.

The typical operational strategy is for a new voiceprint to be verified when it is first entered. As the implementation of a simple version of cross-validation, the user must enter the training phrase twice. The first time is employed by the neural network to train and a second time verifies that training. With successful completion of this point, the ability to recognize the new voiceprint when it is spoken is considered verified. However, any prior entries have not been re-verified, and some may no longer be correctly processed due to contamination of their prior training by the recent training. This is another example of the Type I vs. Type II error consideration introduced in Section 2.2.2.

In the case of the voice-activated dialing of the cell phone, the Type I error situation is addressed during the actual training, but the Type II situation is deferred in a lazy incremental verification mode. In other words, "Don't fix it until it is determined to be broken." The potential of having introduced a Type II error situation is not deemed serious enough to have the cell phone user retest each of the previously trained voiceprints each time a new one is introduced.

The above example is but one of the many ways that the total verification of the system can be decomposed based on a multitude of considerations including: distinctness or independence of functional components or knowledge, Type I vs. Type II error remediation, and urgency to verify sooner vs. relaxation to verify later.

In contrast to the lazy incremental verification approach is the employment of neural network systems in safety-critical problem domains. The verification of neural network systems in such scenarios can include their extensive exercise in a real-world setting, but with the additional requirement of independent confirmation by other independent means, until a sufficiently broad and complete case history of successful use has been accumulated [Lisboa 2001]. With continued successes, such an OLNN system may be promoted through a series of confidence levels. A typical set of confidence levels could be:

- Apprentice, in which every response must be independently confirmed,
- Novice, in which an ever enlarging well-defined subset of frequent situations no longer requires independent confirmation, and ultimately
- Expert, in which the system itself has become an independent confirmation source.

In the case of an advisory medical diagnostic system, a medical expert may review the results produced by the system prior to any action based on its recommendations. Providing for independent expert verification of the learning and performance of an OLNN in real-time may not be so easily realized.

In lieu of a full expert review by an independent source, other more readily mechanized approaches may be employed that:

- Provide a level of confidence, e.g., Type I error management, and
- Reduce the likelihood of catastrophic results, e.g., Type II error management.

Real-time techniques such as previously discussed novelty detection are apropos to such an approach [Marsland 2003].

2.4 Fault Management-Based Verification

Defining characteristics of complex systems, such as are found in flight control and robotics applications, include the following attributes:

- Adaptive, or the capacity or suitability for, or the tendency toward change, modification, etc.
- Autonomous, or being free from external control and constraint in action and judgment, independent in mind or judgment, self-directed.
- Non-deterministic, or the property that a computation or execution may yield multiple plausible results.

Complex systems also may be safety critical, where human safety is at risk, or mission critical, where system failure could impact the total mission the system is supporting.

Such complex real-world problems must be solved as best they can be, in spite of inherent uncertainties. Consequently, complex systems often may perform less than optimally, less than intended or desired, and yet well enough to accomplish significant aspects of the original task, and without loss of life.

This situation complicates not only the systems design and development process, but also the V&V process. When the design of complex systems incorporates these concepts and means, the V&V of such systems also must address the implications of these concepts from a V&V perspective. Recent research has focused on the V&V of such complex systems [Pecheur 2001].

2.4.1   Fault Management Framework

Systems design methodologies developed within the field of fault management that address the uncertainty inherent in complex systems include the following:

- Fault avoidance: Systems can be designed to be fault-free
- Fault removal: Faults can be removed from systems following their design and implementation.
- Fault tolerance: Measures can be taken to ensure residual faults do not cause failure.
- Graceful degradation: Perform sub-optimally, rather than cessation of function [Fed Std 1037C 2003].

These principles and methods not only constitute a framework to guide the design, development, and deployment of complex systems, but also provide the basis for a V&V framework for complex systems from a fault management perspective.

The cumulative online learning experience of an OLNN changes with each new learning epoch. The new epoch may:

- Strengthen prior learning,
- Represent new situations not previously addressed by prior pre-training or online learning epochs,
- Contradict prior learning, a non-monotonic situation, or
- Lie outside the domain that the OLNN is intended to learn.

Each of the last three situations is prototypical of the situations addressed by fault management.

2.4.2   Judging the Total Learning Experience

Determination of whether an OLNN should continue to be deemed V&V certified at any given point in time involves an analysis of the cumulative learning experience of the OLNN. That judgment encompasses three areas:

1. Nature of the data applied as an OLNN learning epoch
2. Learning mechanism capabilities
3. Context surrounding that data

The first area refers to the quality of the inputs to the OLNN including correctness, accuracy, and precision. If design assumptions made regarding data quality are not satisfied, then the usefulness of results produced by the OLNN is questionable. Concern also exists as to whether such data should be the basis for further learning. This topic was addressed in Section 2.1.2.

Various aspects of the neural network system determine the learning mechanism capabilities. This topic was explored in Section 2.1.1.

The context of the epoch encompasses additional information not directly ingested by the OLNN that, nevertheless, could be pertinent to whether the epoch ought to be learned or ignored, or requires special treatment.

Based on faulty management principles, the contextual space of the OLNN may be partitioned into normal operations for which the system is designed or abnormalities for which the system is not explicitly designed

Abnormalities are further decomposed into abnormalities the OLNN is expected to accommodate, and those that cannot or purposely should not be accommodated.

2.4.3 Context Safety Monitoring

The approach to V&V of accommodating anomalies complements the fault management concepts of fault avoidance and fault tolerance. It assesses to what extent and by what means the OLNN can tolerate various types of abnormalities or faults.

Dr. Bojan Cukic has considered the concepts of data sniffing and novelty detection as potential approaches to address this problem [Liu 2002a]. Data sniffing involves real-time monitoring of inputs and outputs of the OLNN to identify the two situations: one to be learned by the OLNN, the other to be ignored [Liu 2002b]. Novelty detection is defined as the process of finding or detecting novel events or data.

Novelty detection serves two roles:

1. OLNN learning: Identify abnormal inputs that should not be part of a learning regime.
2. Non-learning mode: Avoid inputs outside the scope that the OLNN is to handle.

In both cases, the OLNN's corresponding outputs are judged novel, as they would be based on novel or questionable inputs.

Researchers have proposed and investigated various implementations of this technique. The approaches fall within two general categories:

1. Statistical, including certain data mining strategies, and
2. Machine learning, which employs neural networks or other connection models to predict novelty.

Marsland [2003] has completed a comprehensive survey of novelty detection and its relationship to learning systems. Novelty defined by statistical models is based on the unconditional probability density function of data. In machine learning approaches, novelty is based on pre-defined classification of data and on the learning performance of such models.

2.4.4   System Adaptation: Specialization

This first step, recognition of a novelty, is the easier aspect of fault management. The more complicated aspect is determination of what should be done regarding detected novelties. Actions directed at the neural network can include adjustment of the OLNN's learning epochs, algorithms, and neural network architecture. Other actions may be directed toward the neural network environment.

Perhaps the simplest action is data blocking:

- Blocking inputs to the OLNN reduces potential of incorrect or inappropriate learning.
- Blocking outputs from the OLNN prevents delivery of questionable results to downstream system components.

In terms of fault management, such an approach necessarily presumes that fall-back, or fail-over, methods are available to the total system external to OLNN processing so the total system is able to function in such cases without benefit of the OLNN.

Such simplistic actions may be apropos for the case where only normal well-defined situations constitute the total operational domain of the OLNN. Outlier situations [Hodge 2004] are categorically rejected.

This scenario is typical of a skills-based problem domain where the purpose of online learning is to improve upon prior learning, but otherwise to avoid new or novel situations. OLNN learning in this scenario falls into the category termed specialization. Since emphasis is on achieving system improvement, the emphasis of fault management is on its first two dimensions: fault avoidance and fault removal.

In what are otherwise normal contexts where no novelty is detected, the OLNN through learning becomes increasingly matched to the addressed problem. The specialization scenario constitutes continual refinement and improvement of what already is known. This is a monotonic learning situation, one in which the system does not learn knowledge that contradicts what already is known [Mili 2002].

2.4.5   System Adaptation: Generalization

More complex than specialization is the problem space category termed generalization, to successfully perform an increasingly varied set of tasks. In the case of generalization, what is considered and treated as abnormal is continually changing. To detect a novel situation and simply ignore it like it was in the previously discussed data-blocking scenario, is not an acceptable solution.

The novelty judgment process includes both the detection of a novelty, and an assessment of what should be done. The OLNN system is to learn that total judgment.   For this type of system, the emphasis of fault management is on system robustness through its last two dimensions: fault tolerance and graceful degradation.

The generalization scenario expands the domain of operations and hence breadth of knowledge of the OLNN.   The system must continually redistribute its finite set of resources; it can learn, recall, and execute only so much, so quickly. Consequently, the generalization of the OLNN may result in it performing a prior task less well than before, yet still within accepted tolerance. This is an example of a non-monotonic learning situation [Bain 1991].

As the OLNN system adapts to current anomalies, they become subsumed into the normal operational domain of the system. For this class of system, the previously introduced normal vs. abnormal dichotomy is further expanded:

1. Normal today, or part of normal operations
2. Conditionally abnormal, or today abnormal, but can accommodate via neural network training
3. Absolutely abnormal, or always to be avoided

Absolutely abnormal events are handled in the same manner for both the generalist and the specialization scenarios.   Absolutely abnormal circumstances are to be detected and avoided – absolutely! Furthermore, they need to be absolutely determinable, likely by algorithmic methods.

For example, a fighter plane absolutely is not to accelerate beyond a pre-determined critical velocity. This value is an external system design constraint that can be algorithmically determined and enforced.

The boundary between the conditionally abnormal and the absolutely abnormal may be continuous, which is a situation where graceful degradation becomes an issue. In the case where this boundary is discontinuous, an arbitrary margin of safety may be suggested.

2.4.6   Conditionally Abnormal Novelties

Novelty management involves two components:

1. Detection, which is recognition of the situation, be it by data sniffing or novelty detection.
2. Judgment, which is assessment of how to respond, both now and in the future.

Novelty judgment can involve many possibilities ranging from categorically ignoring a detected novelty, to the potentially complex process of capturing relevant information for the construction of an appropriate learning epoch that responds to anticipated future occurrences of that novelty.

A simple form of novelty detection is for the system component providing input to the OLNN to also indicate a confidence in the validity and accuracy of the input. This judgment could range from a simple "go/no go" flag, to a detailed analysis of that input. The simplest novelty detection provides the OLNN with no guidance as to why particular inputs have been flagged.

Introduction of boundary artifacts, such as margin of safety rules, leads to other considerations. A particularly interesting case involves determination of "when to break the rules," a problem found of human-in-the-loop systems. This problem has been studied extensively by human factors analysis (HFA) [Naval Safety Center 1996], a special subset of fault management that focuses on human-in-the-loop systems. Based on HFA, a priori decisions are made regarding how human-in-the-loop systems can be better designed and operated [Reason 1990]. This insight is generally apropos to complex systems, with or without a human-in-the-loop, and to OLNNs in particular [Smith 2003].

2.4.7 Managing System Inertia and Momentum

More detailed examples of novelty detection analysis and novelty judgment could consider not only absolute changes of input values, but also the rate of change of inputs within an otherwise normal absolute range.

Rather than the use of arbitrary margin of safety rules, the concept of system inertia and momentum leverages rate-of-change information collected via data sniffing together with knowledge of the system's absolute boundaries to provide a foundation for predicting the system's likelihood of having sufficient time, flexibility, and resources to adapt to impending or evolving situations.

The novelty management process may be incorporated into the OLNN learning process so that an OLNN's novelty detection and response can improve through online learning. The novelty management subsystem may itself be implemented as another OLNN or embedded within the original OLNN.

2.4.8 Fault Avoidance vs. Fault Tolerance

The discussion of fault management verification up to now has focused on fault avoidance in the sense of preventing any occurrence of improper learning or inappropriate processing by the OLNN. This perspective presumes that all novelties are detectable and that appropriate actions can always be taken in a timely manner. The existence of perfect estimators and predictors enable fault avoidance.

In the absence of such perfection, fault removal, fault tolerance, and graceful degradation move to center stage. A fault can occur in a variety of ways and for a variety of reasons. It could be an isolated event, or it could be the result of a chain of events, as typified in human factors analysis [Bird 1974].

The novelty may be improperly recognized or diagnosed, resulting in a false positive, a situation is treated as a novelty when in fact it isn't, or in a false negative, where a given novelty deserving treatment is not detected. Such situations are further complicated when the true nature is not or cannot be resolved conclusively until after the fact.

From a fault tolerance perspective, data sniffing and novelty detection are applicable not only to guide correct and proper learning, but also to detect and remediate incorrectly or inappropriately learned information. Such fault tolerance principles are embodied, for example, in the two-phase commit employed by distributed database systems.

Finally, an OLNN may be employed in complex systems where the handling of what would be novelties for most systems is in fact the norm for that OLNN. The verification of such complex systems must be able to support such fault management concepts as fault removal, fault tolerance, and graceful degradation. The V&V of such systems should address not only their implementation of fault avoidance, but also their support of fault removal, fault tolerance, and graceful degradation.

3.   SUMMARY

The reader is presumed to have a general knowledge of V&V methodologies. This chapter has attempted to provide a solid grounding and understanding regarding major verification issues that are peculiar to neural network based systems.

Four general areas have been addressed:

1. White-box verification: Verification of the major system and structural components, which include not only the neural network architecture and topology, but also the learning process and the knowledge to be encapsulated within the neural network.
2. Black-box verification: Verification of the neural network functioning and processing, which includes both its learning and its generalization modes of operation.
3. Adaptive verification: Verification issues focused on adaptive neural network systems.
4. Fault management verification: Verification of the neural network system to avoid or recover from error or fault situations.

The references are selected to provide the reader with a comprehensive set of survey references that are readily assessable to those with limited knowledge of neural network technology.

REFERENCES

Abraham, A, and B. Nath. 2000. Hybrid Heuristics for Optimal Design Of Artificial Neural Networks. *Third International Conference on Recent Advances in Soft Computing (RASC2000)*. England, June.

Abraham, A. and B. Nath. 2001. ALEC-An Adaptive Learning Framework for Optimizing Artificial Neural Networks. *Computational Science*. Edited by Vassil N. Alexandrov et. al. Germany: Springer-Verlag.

Ackley, D.H., Hinton, G.E., and Sejnowski, T.J. 1985. A Learning Algorithm for Boltzmann Machines. *Cognitive Science* 9.

Alander, Jarmo T. 2001. An Indexed Bibliography of Genetic Algorithms and Neural Networks, University of Finland, Report Series No. 94-1-NN, Draft, March 11.

Anderson, T.W. 2003. *An Introduction to Multivariate Statistical Analysis.* 3rd Edition. John Wiley & Sons.

Backus, John. 1978. Can Programming Be Liberated From the Von Neumann Style? A Functional Style and Its Algebra of Programs. *Communications of the ACM* 2(8).

Bain, M. Bain and S. Muggleton. 1991. Non-Monotonic Learning. In *Machine Intelligence* 12. Edited by J.E. Hayes-Michie and E. Tyugu. Oxford University Press.

Bird, Jr. Frank E. 1974. *Management Guide to Loss Control.* Atlanta: Institute Press.

Chandra, P., Y. Singh. 2004. A Case for the Self-Adaptation of Activation Functions in FF Neural Networks. *Neurocomputing* 56:447-454.

Cherkassky, V., J.H. Friedman, and H. Wechler (Eds.) 1994. *From Statistics to Neural Networks: Theory and Pattern Recognition Applications.* (NATO ASI Series) New York, NY: Springer-Verlag.

David W. Coit and Alice E. Smith. 1995. Using Designed Experiments to Produce Robust Neural Network Models of Manufacturing Processes. *Proceedings of the Fourth Industrial Engineering Research Conference,* Nashville, TN, May 1995, 229-238.

Coit, D. W., Jackson, B. T. and Smith, A. E. 1998. Static Neural Network Process Models: Considerations and Case Studies. *International Journal of Production Research* 6:2953-2967.

Cukic, Bojan, Brian J. Taylor, and Harhsinder Singh. 2002. Automated Generation of Test Trajectories for Embedded Flight Control Systems. *International Journal of Software Engineering and Knowledge Engineering* 12(2):175-200.

Dally, William J., Patrick Hanrahan, Mattan Erez, Timothy J. Knight, François Labonté, Jung-Ho Ahn, Nuwan Jayasena, Ujval J. Kapasi, Abhishek Das Jayanth Gummaraju Ian Buck. 2003. Merrimac: Supercomputing with Streams. *SC'03,* November 15-21.

Darbari,Ashish. 2000. Rule Extraction from Trained Neural Network: A Survey. Technical Report, Institute of Artificial Intelligence, Dept. of Computer Science, TU Dresden, Germany.

Duch, Wlodzisaw, and Norbert Jankowski. 1999. Survey of Neural Transfer Functions. *Neural Computing Surveys* 2:163-212.

Duch, W., and N. Jankowski. 2001. Transfer Functions: Hidden Possibilities for Better Neural Networks. In *9th European Symposium on Artificial Neural Networks* 81-94, Bruges, Belgium.

Duda, R. and P. Hart. 1973. *Pattern Classification and Scene Analysis.* NY:Wiley.

Efron, B. 1982. The Jackknife, the Bootstrap, and Other Resampling Plans. *SIAM NSFCBMS, Monograph* 38.

Ellingsen, B.K. 1994. A Comparative Analysis of Backpropagation and Counterpropagation Neural Networks. *Neural Network World* 4(6):719-734.

FDA. 1998. Guidance for FDA Reviewers and Industry. Office of Device Evaluation, US Department of Health and Human Services, May 29.

Fed Std 1037C. 1996. Telecommunications: Glossary of Telecommunication Terms. Federal Standard 1037C, General Services Administration, August 7.

Friedman, J.H. 1991. Multivariate Adaptive Regression Splines. *Ann. Statist.* 19:1-141.

Geman, S., E. Bienenstock and R. Doursat. 1992. Neural Networks and the Bias/Variance Dilemma. *Neural Computation* 4(1):1-58.

Hand, David J., Heikki Mannila, Padhraic Smyth. 2001. *Principles of Data Mining (Adaptive Computation and Machine Learning.* MIT Press.

Hecht-Nielsen, R. 1988. Applications of Counterpropagation Networks. *Neural Networks* 1:131-139.

Hodge, V. J. and J. Austin. 2004. A Survey of Outlier Detection Methodologies. *Artificial Intelligence Review*.

Jankowski, N. and W. Duch. 2001. Optimal Transfer Function Neural Networks. *9th European Symposium on Artificial Neural Networks*. 101-106.

Kohonen, T. 1988. *Self-Organization and Associative Memory*, Second Edition, New York: Springer-Verlag.

Lange, Steffen and Thomas Zeugmann. 1993. Monotonic Versus Non-monotonic Language Learning. In *Proc. 2nd International Workshop on Nonmonotonic and Inductive Logic. Lecture Notes in Artificial Intelligence* 659:254 – 269. Edited by G. Brewka, K.P. Jantke and P.H. Schmitt. Springer-Verlag.

Lisboa, P.J.G. 2001. Industrial Use of Safety-Related Artificial Neural Networks. HSE/Liverpool John Moores University HSE Books.

Lisboa, P.J.G. 2002. A Review of Evidence of Health Benefit from Artificial Neural Networks in Medical Intervention. *Neural Networks*, Invited Paper, 15(1):3-9.

Liu, Yan. 2002a. Verification and Validation of Online Adaptive Systems. Doctoral Proposal, Lane Department of Computer Science and Electrical Engineering, West Virginia University.

Liu, Yan, Tim Menzies, and Bojan Cukic. 2002b. Data Sniffing – Monitoring of Machine Learning for Online Adaptive Systems. *14th IEEE International Conference on Tools with Artificial Intelligence (ICTAI'02)*.

Marsland ,Stephen. 2003. Novelty Detection in Learning Systems. *Neural Computing Surveys* 3:157-195.

MathWorks. 2004. Neural Network Toolbox. http://www.mathworks.com/products/neuralnet/.

Mili, A. Mili, B, Cukic, Y. Liu and R.B. Ayed. 2002. Towards the Verification and Validation of Online Adaptive Systems. *Accepted for Special Volume of CI in SE*.

Miller, R.G. 1974. The Jackknife a Review. *Biometrika* 61:1-15.

Mitchell, Tom M. 1997. *Machine Learning*. McGraw-Hill.

Mohamed, Abdil Rashid. 2000. Built-In Self-Test (BIST), Embedded Systems Laboratory (ESLAB) Embedded Systems Laboratory (ESLAB), Linköping Linköping University, University, Sweden. http://www.ida.liu.se/~zebpe/teaching/test/lec12.pdf.

Moody, J. 1994. Prediction Risk and Architecture Selection for Neural Networks. In *From Statistics to Neural Networks: Theory and Pattern Recognition Applications*. Edited by V.Cherkassky, J.H.Friedman and H.Wechsler. NATO ASI Series F. New York: SpringerVerlag. 147-165.

Naval Safety Center. 1996. Quality Management Board Charter - Reducing Human Error in Naval Air Operations.

Nichols, K. 2003. A Reconfigurable Computing Architecture for Implementing Artificial Neural Networks on FPGA. Masters Thesis. University of Guelph.

Nikolay Nikolaev. 2003. Neural Network Tuning and Overfitting Avoidance, CIS 311: Neural Networks. Department of Computing, Goldsmiths College, University of London. http://homepages.gold.ac.uk/nikolaev/311over.htm.

Pai, D. V. and H. N. Mhaskar. 2000. *Fundamentals of Approximation Theory*. C R C Press.

Pecheur, Charles, Reid Simmons, and Willem Visser. 2000. Issues in Verification and Validation of Autonomous and Adaptive Systems. *RIACS Workshop On the Verification and Validation of Autonomous and Adaptive Systems*. Asilomar, CA, 5-7.

Pecheur, Charles, Willem Visser, and Reid Simmons. 2001. RIACS Workshop on the Verification and Validation of Autonomous and Adaptive Systems. Technical Report 01-20, RIACS, USRA.

Ragg, Thomas, Heinrich Braun, and Heiko Landsberg. 1997a. A Comparative Study of Neural Network Optimization Techniques. In *Proceedings of the ICNNGA 97*, Norwich, UK.

Ragg, Thomas, Steffen Gutjahr, and Hai Ming Sa. 1997b. Automatic Determination of Optimal Network Topologies based on Information Theory and Evolution. *Euromicro '97. Track on Computational Intelligence.*

Reason, James. 1990. *Human Error.* New York: Cambridge University Press.

Richards, D.W. 1989. Smart BIT: a Plan for Intelligent Built-in Test. *Aerospace and Electronic Systems Magazine* 4(1):26-29.

Rumelhart, D. and J. McClelland. 1986. Parallel Distributed Processing: Explorations in the Microstructure of Cognition. Cambridge: MIT Press.

Sundararajan, N. and P. Saratchandran. 1998. *Parallel Architectures for Artificial Neural Networks : Paradigms and Implementations,* 1st edition. Wiley-IEEE Computer Society Press.

Smith, James. 2003. Certification of On-Line Learning Neural Networks. Artificial Intelligence and Soft Computing (ASC 2003). Banff, Canada, July 14-16.

Stone, M. 1974. Cross-Validatory Choice and Assessment of Statistical Predictions. *Journal of the Royal Statistical Society*, Series B 36:111-147.

Twomey, Janet M., and Alice E. Smith. 1993. Nonparametric Error Estimation Methods for Validating Artificial Neural Networks. *Intelligent Engineering Systems Through Artificial Neural Networks* 3:233-238. Edited by C. H. Dagli, L. I. Burke, B. R. Fernandez, and J. Ghosh. ASME Press.

Twomey, Janet M., and Alice E. Smith. 1997. Validation and Verification. In *Artificial Neural Networks for Civil Engineers: Fundamentals and Applications* 44-64. Edited by N. Kartam, I. Flood and J. Garrett. ASCE press.

Twomey, Janet M. and Alice E. Smith. 1998. Bias and Variance of Validation Methods for Function Approximation Neural Networks Under Conditions of Sparse Data. *IEEE Transactions on Systems, Man, and Cybernetics*, Part C 28(3):417-430.

van der Zwaag, B.J., C.H. Slump, and L. Spaanenburg. 2002. Process Identification Through Modular Neural Networks and Rule Extraction. In *Computational Intelligent Systems for Applied Research (Proceedings of the 5th International FLINS Conference* 268-277. Edited by D. Ruan, P. D'hondt, and E.E. Kerre. World Scientific.

Wahba. Constrained Regularization for Ill-Posed Linear Operator Equations, with Applications in Meteorology and Medicine. In *Statistical Decision Theory and Related Topics*. Edited by S.Gupta und J.Berger. 2:383-418. New York: Academic Press.

Weiss, S. M. and C. A. Kulikowski. 1991. *Computer Systems that Learn.* San Mateo, CA: Morgan Kaufmann Publishers, Inc.

White, H. 1990. Connectionist Nonparametric Regression: Multilayer Feed-forward Networks Can Learn Arbitrary Mappings. *Neural Networks* 3:535-549.

Williams, Graham, Rohan Baxter, Hongxing He, Simon Hawkins and Lifang Gu 2002. A Comparative Study of RNN for Outlier Detection in Data Mining. *Proceedings of the 2nd IEEE International Conference on Data Mining (ICDM02).*

Chapter 7

NEURAL NETWORK VISUALIZATION TECHNIQUES

Marjorie Darrah
Institute for Scientific Research, Inc.

1. INTRODUCTION

Visualization techniques are important for the verification and validation (V&V) of neural networks. Designers, end-users, and V&V practitioners need to understand the design and performance of the neural network system. Visualization can be useful in meeting these goals.

Understanding the design and operation of neural networks is no elementary task. Neural networks used for solving real-world problems may have several thousand connections. Understanding the connections formed by the network during the learning process requires making sense of a vast amount of real-valued parameters. Visualization can help bridge the cognitive gap by representing relationships in the neural network and by examining how those relationships evolve.

In this chapter various visualization techniques are presented. Several commonly used commercial neural network design packages will be introduced along with a discussion of their visualization capabilities. Also included is a discussion of how visualization techniques can be used for V&V at various stages across the software development lifecycle.

Understanding the design and operation of neural networks is no elementary task. Neural networks used for solving real-world problems may have several thousand connections. Understanding the connections formed by the network during the learning process requires making sense of a vast amount of real-valued parameters. Visualization can help bridge the cognitive gap by representing relationships in the neural and by examining how those relationships evolve.

There are two types of neural network visualization techniques that may provide benefit: *whitebox* and *blackbox*. Whitebox techniques provide a view of the internal workings and processes of the neural network. These techniques could be used together with flow analysis to assist understanding of the interactions of the neural network nodes, links, and weights. Blackbox techniques provide representations that correlate inputs to outputs. The interpretation of the visual representation in a blackbox technique is left up to speculation or intuition. An example of such a blackbox technique would be a 3D flight simulation that shows the reaction of the aircraft with a neural network controller in use.

Visualization may assist neural network users in discovering data features whose importance was not previously recognized. Humans have highly developed abilities for visual pattern recognition that can be capitalized when vast quantities of data are transformed into a qualitatively different form. Changes that occur during training may also be detected using these techniques because errors or patterns may appear as visual anomalies. Additionally, visualization software can provide an interactive mechanism that enables the user to adjust parameters and quickly see the effects of the changes.

Visualization can aid in both developing and understanding systems involving neural networks. Personnel involved in verifying and validating such systems may have little or no knowledge of the workings of a neural network. Through the use of visualization techniques, such as simple neuron models, the MATLAB Neural Network Toolbox, or even 3D visualizations, the understanding can be increased.

2.   VISUALIZATION TECHNIQUES FOR NEURAL NETWORKS IN ACADEMIC LITERATURE

The first step in understanding a neural network is to comprehend the design. For most neural networks there are representations that present network structure and the way connections are formed to create the flow of data from input to output. Chapter 4 gives an overview of various neural network structures and provides visual representations of these structures.

Many visualization techniques that assist in the understanding of neural networks have been discussed in the academic literature. Craven and Shavlik [1992] discussed several visualization techniques in an overview paper titled "Visualizing Learning and Computation in Artificial Neural Networks." Many of the techniques summarized in this section can be further studied in their survey paper. Other authors, such as Vesanto [1998], have even used virtual reality 3D models to try to gain understanding of the networks. These techniques provide insight into the decision-making and the learning processes of neural networks. This section introduces several techniques with a brief description of how they assist in the understanding of the neural network.

The Hinton diagram, developed in 1986, was one of the first visualization methods. It provides a compact visual display of the weights and biases related to a particular neural network [Hinton 1986]. Fig. 7-1 depicts a neural network and the Hinton diagram to visualize the network.

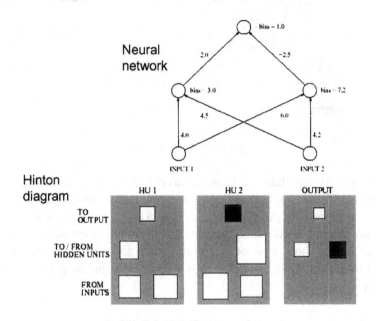

Figure 7-1. Simple Neural Network and Related Hinton Diagram

These diagrams show the two hidden units and the output unit of the network. The boxes in the lower part of each diagram depict weights from hidden units, and the boxes in the middle of each diagram depict a weight to the output unit. A unit's bias is drawn in the position in the unit's diagram where weights to and from the unit are shown in the other diagrams. The Hinton diagram is a rather weak method for visualization because the topology is not readily apparent from the diagram, and it does not clearly show how a unit partitions its input space.

Wejchert and Tesauro [1990] developed the bond diagram. This visualization method illustrates the sign and magnitude of each weight and bias in the network, but, unlike the Hinton diagram, it does show the topology of the neural network. In the bond diagram each unit is represented as a disk. The size of the disk indicates the magnitude of the unit's bias.

The bonds that link the disks represent the weights. The amount (width) of the bond indicates the magnitude of the weight, and the color represents the sign. Fig. 7-2 below shows a bond diagram for the simple neural network structure presented in Fig. 7-1 on the previous page.

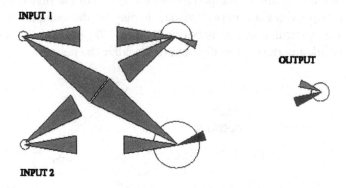

Figure 7-2. Bond Diagram

One way to visualize the learning process is to graphically display the movement of the hyperplane in the input space of the unit that the hyperplane represents [Munro 1991; Pratt 1991]. A hyperplane diagram can show how hidden units make decisions in an input space defined by input units, or it can show how output units make decisions in an input space defined by hidden units. Fig. 7-3 shows the hyperplane diagram of a neural network.

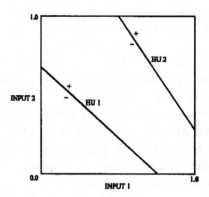

Figure 7-3. Hyperplane Diagram

The axes of the diagram denote the range of activations that may be propagated to the units through their incoming connections. Data points that a network is learning to classify may be plotted in the space. Each hidden unit of the network is represented by the hyperplane (in this case the line) that indicates how the unit is partitioning the input space. The learning process is automated by showing the movement of the hyperplane as the weights and biases of the network are changed.

One limitation of a hyperplane diagram is that only two- or three-dimensional input spaces can be depicted. Selecting a two- or three-dimensional projection of the actual input space may be used to depict an input space of higher dimensionality. There may be a problem choosing which projection to view. Statistical techniques, such as principal component analysis or canonical discriminant analysis, may be useful in determining which projections would provide the most information.

Hyperplane representation can also be animated. Pratt and Nicodemus [Pratt 1993] reported on case studies using a hyperplane animator that they developed, pictured in Fig. 7-4. The animator is able to display the relationship between a network and the training data, and is also able to show the changes in that relationship during learning.

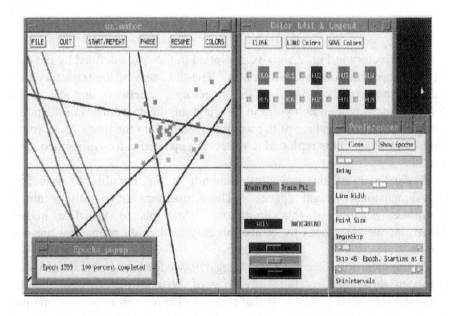

Figure 7-4. Sample Screen from Hyperplane Animator (© 1993 IEEE)

The trajectory diagram is another visualization method developed by Wejchert and Tesauro [1990]. The trajectory diagram is designed to provide insight into the weight space for a given problem. A trajectory diagram depicts the movement of a given unit through the weight space. Fig. 7-5 shows the trajectory over a hypothetical training session.

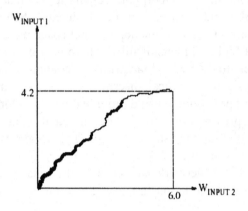

Figure 7-5. Trajectory Diagram

The trajectory in Fig. 7.5 above is plotted in the space defined by the two weights impinging on this hidden unit. The thickness of the trajectory line indicates the network error along the trajectory. A network unit at a given point in time is plotted as a point in the diagram; the coordinates of the point are specified by the values of the weights feeding into the unit. As learning progresses, the point is replotted to reflect the updated values of its incoming weights.

A weakness of the trajectory diagram is the inability to visualize high-dimensional weight spaces. These diagrams have only minimal usefulness because of this limitation. Attempts to visualize higher dimension weight spaces by projection may lead to diagrams that are not unique.

A graphical interface for visualizing knowledge-based neural networks has been developed by the University of Wisconsin. A weakness of conventional neural networks is that they provide no way to exploit existing knowledge about the problem to be solved. The knowledge-based neural network (KBANN) algorithm [Towell 1990] provides an approach to incorporating existing knowledge into a neural network. The KBANN algorithm uses a knowledge base of domain-specific inference rules in the form of PROLOG-like clauses to determine the topology and initial weights of a neural network. The domain theory does not need to be complete or correct; it needs only to support approximately correct domain reasoning.

KBANN translates a domain theory into a neural network in which units and links correspond to parts of the domain theory. Consider the domain theory for recognizing cups, which is depicted in Fig. 7-6.

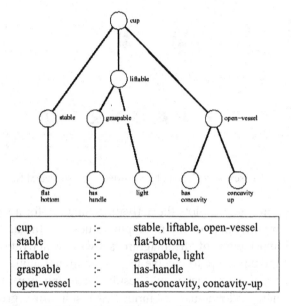

cup	:-	stable, liftable, open-vessel
stable	:-	flat-bottom
liftable	:-	graspable, light
graspable	:-	has-handle
open-vessel	:-	has-concavity, concavity-up

Figure 7-6. Hierarchical Structure of Cup Domain Theory

The hierarchical structure of the domain determines the topology of the knowledge-based neural network: the input units of the network represent the base-level facts of the domain theory, the hidden units represent intermediate conclusions, and the output unit represents the final conclusion. After the network topology and initial weights have been determined by KBANN, the network is trained using the back-propagation algorithm and a set of training examples. After training, refined rules can be extracted from the network [Towell 1991].

Lascaux is another tool developed by the same group at the University of Wisconsin. It assists in further visualizing the neural network both during and after learning. This tool enables visualization of the learning process by depicting forward propagation of activations, backward propagation of error, and changes to the weights and biases of the network. Each box represents a network unit. Lines that connect the units represent network weights. The thickness of each line indicates its magnitude, with positive weights drawn as solid lines and negative weights as dashed lines. Fig. 7-7 on the next page shows the interface provided by the Lascaux tool.

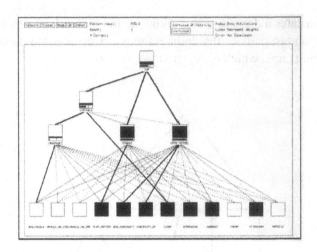

Figure 7-7. Lascaux Depiction of a Knowledge-based Neural Network

The diagram in Fig. 7-7 plots the activation function for a unit on a scale that is defined by the range of the net input values that the unit could have. Thus, the rightmost edge of the diagram shows the activation value that would result if the unit were to receive its maximum net input. The leftmost edge shows the activation that would result if the unit were to receive its minimum net input. The actual net input that results for a given pattern is displayed as a solid vertical line in the diagram. This displays the effective activation. It is valuable to describe the nature of the activation function relative to its weight space and to show the relative influence of the weights and biases. Lascaux also provides a mechanism to specify a "freeze" display that lets the user progress step-by-step through a set of input patterns.

Lascaux provides the same functionality whether it is used with conventional neural networks or with KBANNs. The tool aids in understanding the refinements that occur during learning by animating the weight changes. This can help explain why the network has made a particular decision.

Vesanto [1999] has developed several techniques for visualizing a Self-Organizing Map (SOM). An SOM is an unsupervised neural network that organizes a set of model vectors during training so as to represent the distribution and topology of the training data. One of the advantages of the SOM is that the structure is highly visual. When the model vectors are organized on a 2D grid, the SOM can be visualized using methods like component planes view and the unified distance matrix (u-matrix). Typically the visualization is done using color images.

Fig. 7-8 on the next page represents the overall shape of the data cloud by making projection of the prototype vectors to a lower dimension. Although the reproductions of these figures are in grayscale, the color in the original figures adds much to the information. The reader is encouraged to look at the original figures for further investigation. Two projections of the SOM trained on data have been made, one is 2D (a) and the other is 3D (b). In (a) each dot corresponds to one map unit, the color of which has been taken from the color-coding in (c). Each map unit has been connected to its neighbors with lines. From (a) several clusters can be seen as concentration of data. The 3D-projection in (b) provides a better view of the separation.

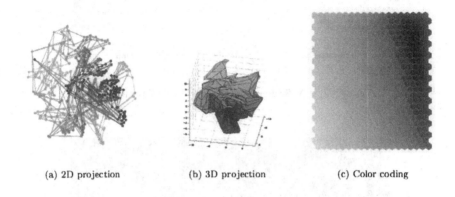

(a) 2D projection   (b) 3D projection   (c) Color coding

Figure 7-8. SOM Visualizations [Vesanto 1999]

Vesanto provides other visual techniques for understanding SOMs. In Fig. 7-9 (a) on the next page each dot corresponds to one map unit. The x- and y-coordinates of the dots have been taken from two variables of the vectors. Each dot is also given a color according to the color-coding of the map units shown in (b). In addition to color-coding, (b) also uses size to indicate clusters in the map. It can be seen that for most units, especially yellow color-coding, the two components are linearly correlated. Conversely, the units with orange color have another distinct pattern that tells information about the relationship of the two variables.

Along with the many other visual techniques for SOMs discussed by Vesanto in his paper, he also has a website [Vesanto 1998] that shows how he used Virtual Reality Modeling Language (VRML) to develop 3D visualization tools for the analysis of the SOM. VRML offers powerful and easily useable methods for visualizing 3D objects and scenes and enables the user to interact with the VRML model. Fig. 7-10 is a 3D model of a SOM that has been visualized using VRML. Several views are available and the model can be manipulated and moved in the virtual space.

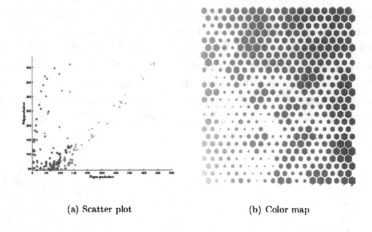

(a) Scatter plot   (b) Color map

Figure 7-9. SOM Scatter Plot and Color Map [Vesanto 1999]

Figure 7-10. 3D Model of a SOM using VRML [Vesanto 1998]

3.   COMMERCIAL SOFTWARE PACKAGES WITH VISUALIZATION CAPABILITIES

There are many commercial packages for developing neural networks. These packages offer various graphical user interfaces (GUI) and various visualization techniques. This section focuses on what several different software products offer with respect to the visualization of neural networks to facilitate understanding.

3.1   MATLAB® Neural Network Toolbox

The MATLAB® Neural Network Toolbox[3] is an additional software package for MATLAB that provides functions, utilities, and help for creating and training neural networks. Its usefulness in regards to the V&V of neural networks lies with simulation and visualization.

The tool allows for construction of most types of neural networks and even provides special utilities for back-propagation networks, radial basis functions, SOMs, and recurrent networks. Once in a model within MATLAB/Simulink®, the network can be trained, tested, simulated, and studied. Since MATLAB was designed as a mathematical analysis tool in general, data anywhere in a network is easily accessible for viewing and further manipulation. This means the data is available for analysis utilities like interpolation, statistical analysis, equation solvers, optimization routines, and any of the other powerful MATLAB functions. A system analyst can plot the training error function, watch the change in the weight matrix, and get real-time network outputs to verify their correctness. The toolbox can be used in both MATLAB and Simulink.

MATLAB Simulink and Neural Network Toolbox provide comprehensive support for many proven neural network paradigms, as well as a graphical interface that allows design and management of neural networks. The Neural Network Toolbox simplifies the creation of customized functions and neural networks. It has a GUI for creating, training, and simulating neural networks and has visualization functions for viewing performance.

One feature of MATLAB Simulink is the automatic generation of neural network simulation blocks. In Fig. 7-11, a three-layer neural network has been converted into Simulink blocks indicating its structure. This tool can be used in the design activity to achieve a detailed design for the software component.

Another visualization capability offered by this tool is the ability to model control system applications. Neural networks have been applied to the identification and control of nonlinear systems. The Neural Network Toolbox includes descriptions, demonstrations, and Simulink blocks for popular control applications: model predictive control, feedback linearization, and model reference adaptive control.

---

[3] http://www.mathworks.com/products/neuralnet/

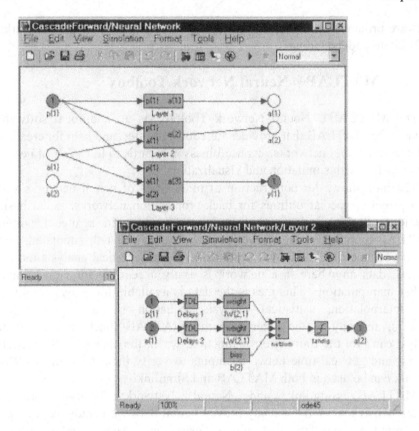

Figure 7-11. A Three-Layer Neural Network Converted into Simulink Blocks
(Reproduced courtesy of The Mathworks)

For testing activities, a Simulink model that includes the neural network control block and plant model could be used. The example below shows a model for predictive control of a continuous stirred tank reactor (CSTR). In Fig. 7-12, the upper left window shows the CSTR plant model that includes a neural network block. The other windows allow one to visualize validation data (top right), to manage the neural network control block (lower left), and the plant identification (lower right). These visualization features of Simulink could enhance the integration testing activities.

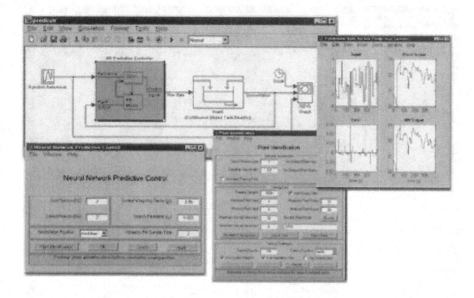

Figure 7-12. Simulink Model that Includes the Neural Network
(Reproduced courtesy of The Mathworks)

3.2   BrainMaker by California Scientific Software

BrainMaker Neural Network Software[4] has application to areas such as business and marketing forecasting, stock, bond, commodity, and futures prediction, pattern recognition, and medical diagnosis. No special programming or computer skills are necessary to use the software. All that is needed is a PC or Mac and sample data to build a neural network.

BrainMaker offers a GUI that allows some analysis of the neural network. After the network is trained, you can switch the display over to show numeric values, allowing you to edit the exact value of the inputs directly on the screen. The network instantly runs your new numbers and predicts an output.

BrainMaker has extremely flexible input and display formats. Below in Fig. 7-13 BrainMaker is learning optical character recognition. The input is a graphic picture of the number nine; the network is indicating with its output that the probability is very high that this is a picture of a nine, and very low that this is a picture of any other digit.

---

[4] http://www.calsci.com/

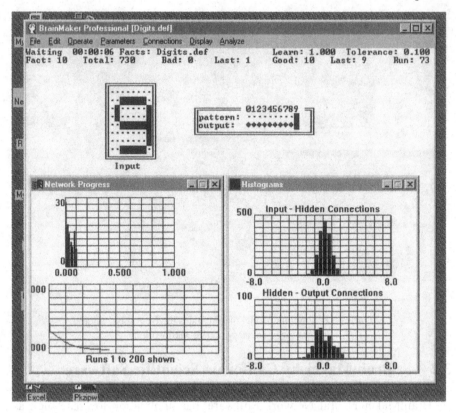

Figure 7-13. BrainMaker

Also, shown in Fig. 7-13 are two of BrainMaker Professional's graphs: the network progress display, which shows us graphically how the average error has declined over the course of training, and the connection histograms, which indicate to us how much of the network's capacity is being used. The histogram display shows us if the network has too many neurons (good memorization, poor generalization), too few neurons (not enough capacity to learn this problem) or just right (optimum generalizing).

BrainMaker also includes the following analysis tools:

1. Sensitivity Analysis to show which inputs determined results
2. Neuron Sensitivity to show the total effect of one input on results
3. Global Network Analysis reports how your network reacts to all facts overall
4. Contour Analysis shows color peaks and valleys of response to pairs of inputs
5. Data Correlator finds important data and optimum time delays
6. Error Statistics Report to check network error rate during training

7. Print or Edit Weight Matrices to examine and customize network internals
8. Genetic Training Option to train variations of the design and shows which was the best

3.3   NeuroShell® 2 by Ward Systems Group

NeuroShell® 2 combines neural network architectures, an icon driven user interface, utilities, and options to give users a neural network experimental environment. It is recommended for academic users, or those users who are concerned with classic neural network paradigms like back-propagation. Users interested in solving real problems should consider other Ward Systems Products[5] such as NeuroShell Predictor, NeuroShell Classifier, or the NeuroShell Trader.

NeuroShell 2 includes graphics utilities such as line charts, bar charts, scatter plots and high- low-close graphs. Options allow the user to add 3-D effects and change colors or types of graphs. These graphics facilities enable the user to look for patterns in the data

Before and after network processing, the Variable Graphs module may be used to create different types of graphs:

1. Graph Variable(s) Across All Patterns - graph different types of variables, such as advertising expenditures and cost of goods sold, across all patterns in a file. This graph is also used for graphing time series data.
2. Graph Variable Sets in a Pattern – this graph can be used to examine data if all of the variables in a pattern are of the same type, e.g., 100 points in a physiological signal such as an electrocardiogram.
3. Correlation Scatter Plot - this graph is a scatter plot of one variable against another through all patterns. The linear correlation coefficient is computed for each graph.
4. High-Low-Close Graph - this graph allows the user to select variables from the data file that are displayed as the high, low, and close values of a stock price. The graph reveals trends in the user's data.
5. Training Graphs - NeuroShell 2 allows the user to display graphs of training set/test set errors while training back-propagation networks. When training Kohonen networks, the user can display a graph of category distributions in either a bar or pie chart. The Probabilistic Neural Networks and General Regression Neural Networks Learning

---

[5] http://wardsystems.com

Modules allow the user to display a smoothing factor optimization graph. GMDH nets graph the criterion value for the created formula against the layer number.

The graph below in Fig. 7-14 shows an example of a graph generated by NeuroShell 2 that could be used to look for patterns in the data.

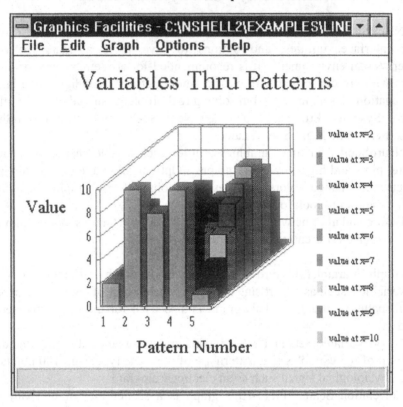

Figure 7-14. NeuroShell 2 Graph

3.4   NeuroShell® Predictor

This product is used for forecasting and estimating numeric amounts such as sales, prices, workload, level, cost, scores, speed, capacity, etc. NeuroShell® Predictor is a simple step-by-step process that uses recognized forecasting methods to look for future trends in the user's existing data. It contains the both neural network and statistical prediction algorithms.

Figures below show two different graphical representations that allow the user to gain insight into the neural network. Fig. 7-15 shows the network training status, giving information on network performance, hidden neurons and a graph of actual vs. predicted values. Fig. 7-16 shows the estimated relative importance of each variable in the model.

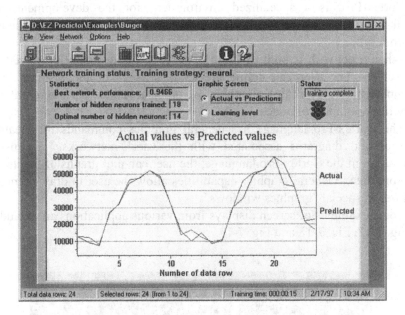

Figure 7-15. NeuroShell Predictor Training Status

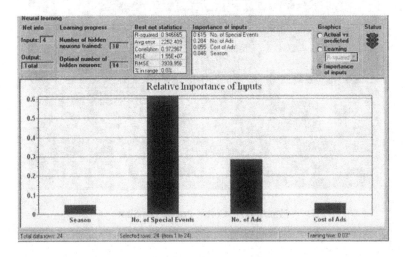

Figure 7-16. NeuroShell Predictor Relative Importance

3.5   Cortex Pro by Michael Reiss

Cortex-Pro[6] is a specialized environment for the development and simulation of neural networks. Cortex-Pro can handle a variety of neural network types.

When a network is built in Cortex-Pro, it is automatically displayed on the screen. The user can define the characteristics of the display. For example, size, gray scales, numbers, or other attributes can represent the activities or outputs of nodes.

The Cortex-Pro language has general graphics commands for creating pictures and diagrams associated with the user's networks. By using commands in the Cortex-Pro language, the user can plot graphs of the user's network data. General graphics capabilities allow the user to draw complex pictures in special "graphics windows".

Some examples of screen displays from various applications are included in Fig. 7-17, Fig. 7-18 and Fig. 7-19.

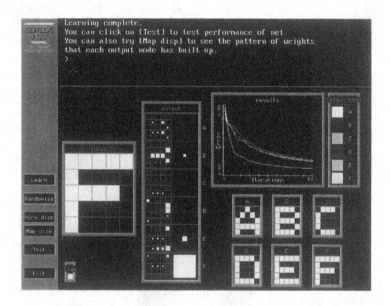

Figure 7-17. Cortex Pro Screen Shot

---

[6] www.reiss.demon.co.uk/webctx/intro.html

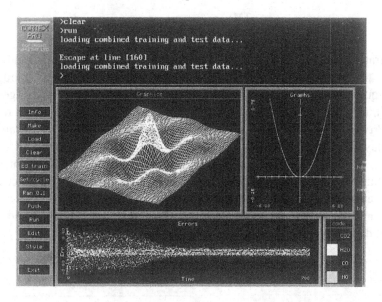

Figure 7-18. Cortex Pro Screen Shot

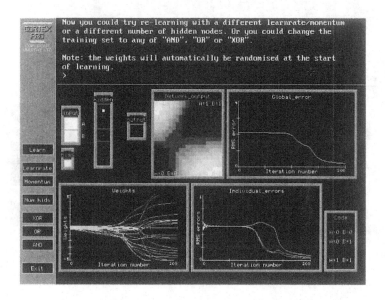

Figure 7-19. Cortex Pro Screen Shot

3.6 Partek Predict™ by Paratek Incorporated

Paratek[7] provides software and services for data analysis and modeling. These tools provide a combination of statistical analysis and modeling techniques and modern tools such as neural networks, fuzzy logic, genetic algorithms, and data visualization. Partek Predict™ is an advanced toolkit for *Predictive Modeling*. This software package includes a trainable Multilayer Perceptron neural network.

Fig. 7-20 on the next page is an example of the graphical interface depicting the numerically selected structural properties that are predictive of drug activity. A neural network was used to build a predictive model. Selecting a point with the mouse displays the corresponding compound. The screen display shows the visual tools available.

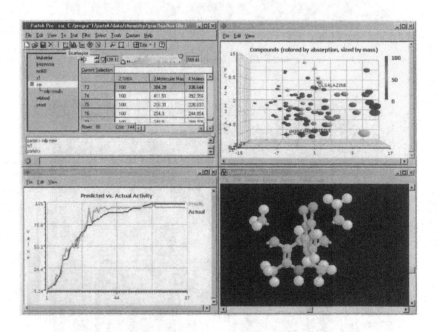

Figure 7-20. Partek Predict Screen Shot

[7] http://www.partek.com/

3.7 havBpNet++, havFmNet++, and havBpNet:J by hav.Software

havBpNet++ and havBpNet:J by hav.Software[8] are, respectively, C++ and Java class libraries that implement feed-forward, simple recurrent (sequential), and random-ordered recurrent nets trained by back-propagation and can be used for both stand-alone and embedded network training and consultation applications.

havFmNet++ and havFmNet:J are, respectively, C++ and Java class libraries which implement Self-Organizing Feature Map nets. Map-layers may be from one to any dimension. havFmNet may be used for both stand-alone and embedded network training and consultation applications.

havETT is a simple demo program written in Visual Basic which uses the DLL version of the havBpNet++ library to allow a user to define, train, save, restore and consult a simple 3 layer network with optional use of recurrent layers.

In havBpETT, the main screen in Fig. 7-21, which can be found on the following page, presents both a toolbar and an information display. The toolbar may be used to select overall actions (such as data or network control). Both buttons and menu items are provided for all main actions. The information display presents a summary of certain layer and network parameters. Also provided is an information display line in which messages will appear as the cursor is placed on various buttons and fields.

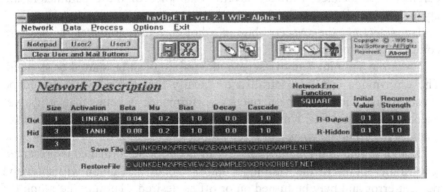

Figure 7-21. Network Description Screen

The Network Control screen in Fig. 7-22 is used to describe the overall network's configuration. Connections between layers are enabled/disabled

[8] http://www.hav.com/

by clicking on the connectors located under a layer. Inactive connections are dashed light-gray lines. Active connections are color coded according to their type: Forward, Weighted-Copy Recurrent and Random-Order Recurrent. Layer parameters are entered for each layer individually. A layer is selected by clicking on that layer.

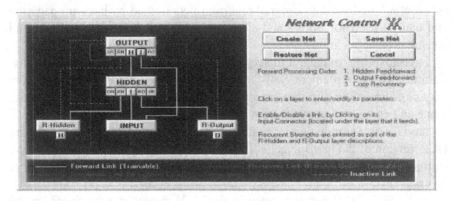

Figure 7-22. Network Control Screen

The Layer Description screen in Fig. 7-23 allows the user to set various layer parameter values.

When a layer button in the Network Control screen is clicked, a sub-screen is opened that allows the user to set/select the values of various parameters associated with the layer. Examples of these parameters are layer-size, learning-rate (Beta), momentum (Mu), etc.

By selecting the Accept button, the current parameter values are communicated to the system.

From the Training Control screen, the training can be started or stopped. The error-mode can be controlled to specify that the network should be saved to disk each time the network's performance is better than it has yet been. On the training window, selecting the appropriate items can make changes to certain network and layer parameters.

Both a digital and graphical display of network performance is presented toward the bottom of the Training Control window. A graph will show the percent-error and may be turned on or off as desired. Turning the graph off will noticeably increase training speed for smaller nets with relatively small training-data sets. When the graph is off, it is still updated for use at a later time if desired.

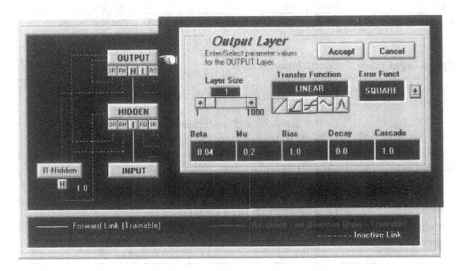

Figure 7-23. Layer Description Screen

4. USEFULNESS OF VISUALIZATION

Visualization techniques can be evaluated in a variety of ways. Many books and articles have dealt with visualization issues from web page design to scientific visualization. The criteria in Table 7-1 can provide a means to evaluate a specific visualization technique or software application to determine whether it provides useful visual information. Freitas [2002] in a paper titled "On Evaluating Information Visualization Techniques" outlines four classes of criteria for testing usability of visual representations. The four classes are completeness, spatial organization, codification of information, and state transition. Other authors use similar criteria and classification schemes.

4.1 Visualization Techniques Used Across the Development Process

Many visual techniques can assist V&V in the Development Process for neural network software. Development V&V activities, such as concept (selecting architecture), requirements (defining functional and performance requirements), design (designing for software component and training of the neural network), implementation (transforming design into executable

Table 7-1. Criteria for Evaluating Visual Techniques [Freitas 2002]

Criteria	Description	Affected By
Completeness	All the semantic content of the data is displayed	Geometric or visual constraints; Cognitive complexity
Spatial Organization	Overall layout of visual representation; Ease of locating information on the screen; Overall distribution of information elements in the representation	Presentation of context while displaying a specific element in detail
Codification of Information	Mapping of data elements to visual elements; Use of additional symbols or realistic characteristics used for building alternative representation	Perception of the user
Changes in Spatial Organization	Rebuilding the visual representation after a user action	Processing speed; Complexity of the visual display

representations), and testing (software testing and simulation), may be addressed through the use of visualization tools. Many of the examples provided below are related to the neural networks used by the Intelligent Flight Control System (IFCS) project (see Foreword for a description of this project).

4.1.1   Concept Activity

In the concept stage, a neural network developer will select an architecture for the neural network. Visualization can explain the design structure (see Fig. 7-24). Diagrams of the intended neural network architecture should be part of the documentation produced by the development process. Examples of such diagrams are given throughout Chapter 4.

4.1.2   Requirements Activity

Defining functional and performance requirement can be difficult for a neural network system. The DCS used by the IFCS project had to be reverse-engineered from two different sets of code, one in MATLAB and one written in C. This process became very confusing until diagrams of the DCS were introduced. A model of the DCS was built in MATLAB using the knowledge of the structure of the DCS, how the nodes evolved over time, and what connections meant. The DCS structure was then plotted across time and these plots were assembled into a movie (see Fig. 7-25 on

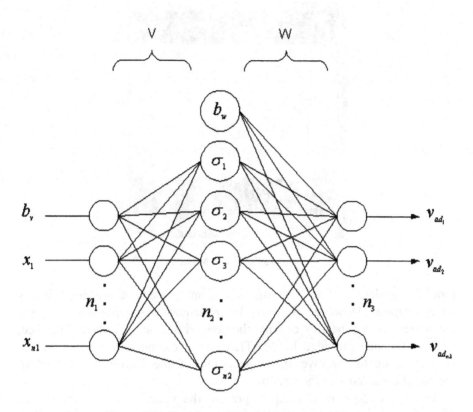

Figure 7-24. Feed-forward Neural Network Architecture

the next page). The movie was used at an early project-wide meeting to give the project team, who had limited knowledge of neural networks, a basic understanding of how the DCS works and adapts. This movie proved to be an excellent visual tool to promote understanding and help the project gain support. It was very useful in explaining to the participants of the team, especially managers, the workings of the DCS and how it would evolve over time. Now the project was at a point where the technical people had more understanding about the DCS (SOMs in general) and how it worked, and this in turn led the group to develop better requirements for the project.

4.1.3 Design Activity

Visualization can also play an important role in improving a system designer's supervision of neural network adaptation during training. Typically, training a neural network is an automated routine: collect training data, process training data, set up an automated function for training, check for errors, modify the neural network to some prior chosen method, and

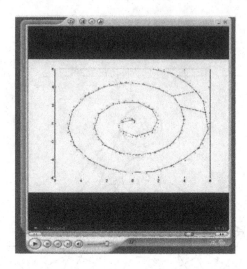

Figure 7-25. DCS Movie

repeat. The designer can leave the system unattended and return when it is done learning. However, this may be inadequate supervision because the developer may not be sure of what the network learned. A visual interface, such as the one provided by MATLAB or a custom one created by the developer, could improve the supervision of the learning and lead to increased confidence in the system.

Other visualization techniques present the neural network knowledge after it has been trained. These techniques are especially useful when examining neural networks, such as a SOM, that may change structure by growing new nodes as it learns. One example of a technique that applies to the DCS, a type of SOM, is representing the trained neural network using a Voronoi Diagram[9] (see Fig. 7-26).

The neural network may have actually learned a violation of the expected operation and this could be determined by examining a visual representation of what has been learned. For this purpose, visual techniques such as a Voronoi plot of a trained DCS, Fig. 7-27 on the following page, can be very useful. This type of diagram allows for the examination of how the regions are forming around the centroids to look for anomalies that may need explanation. This technique can be used when the input space is two- or three-dimensional, or it used by restricting a larger dimensional space to two or three dimensions at a time.

---

[9] Given a set of *n* points in the plane, a Voronoi partition is a collection of *n* convex polygons such that each polygon contains exactly one point as its centroid and every point in a given polygon is closer to its centoid than to any other of the *n-1* points.

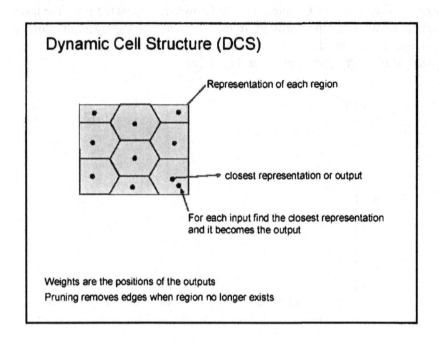

Figure 7-26. Voronoi Diagram representing the DCS [Mackall 2002]

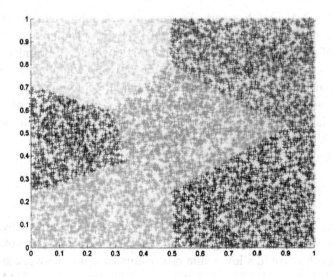

Figure 7-27. Diagram of a trained DCS

Other visual representations of knowledge can be used along with rule extraction results (see Chapter 8). The knowledge extracted from the trained neural network in the form of rules can then be displayed in plots and compared against domain requirements (Chapter 8, Section 2.2). An example of such a plot is below in Fig. 7-28.

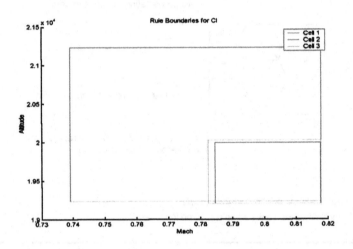

Figure 7-28. Visualization of Rule Antecedents for Trained DCS Network

4.1.4 Implementation Activity

MATLAB Neural Network Toolbox and Simulink can be used in the implementation activity. The Neural Network Toolbox simplifies the creation of customized functions and neural networks. Simulink can be used to achieve a detailed visual design for the software component and then the design can be transformed into executable representations using the autocode generation feature of the software. One feature of MATLAB Simulink is the automatic generation of neural network simulation blocks. In Fig. 7-29, a three-layer neural network has been converted into Simulink blocks indicating its structure.

4.1.5 Testing Activity

Testing is another process activity where visualization proves useful. Neural networks are often tested as a black box, but there are many visual techniques that would allow white box testing of neural network software by the developers or V&V practitioners. The capabilities of MATLAB's Neural Network Toolbox demonstrate some of these techniques that give

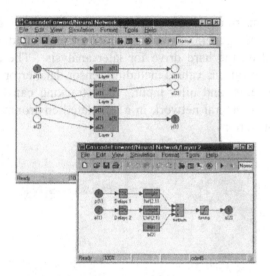

Figure 7-29. A Three-Layer Neural Network Converted into Simulink Blocks

visual examination to the internal workings of the neural networks learning process [Mathworks 1998]. For the IFCS project, several plotting scripts were developed in MATLAB to look at the various results from the DCS (both in simulation and from a C version) to determine if it was working correctly. These scripts are still being used by the IFCS project today.

Visualization capability offered by MATLAB Simulink can enhance the integration testing activities. Simulink has the ability to model control system applications. For testing activities, a Simulink model that includes the neural network control block system model could be used. The Neural Network Toolbox includes descriptions, demonstrations, and Simulink blocks for popular control applications.

Other low-fidelity visual tools can include off-the-shelf graphical packages or original software developed for a specific purpose. The neural network developer or V&V practitioner could use graphical packages or create specialized tools specific to the individual situation for visualization of various aspects of the neural network operation. Greg Limes[10], a NASA Ames Research Center (ARC) subcontractor working on the IFCS project, developed one such tool to watch the DCS adapt during training.

The WVU F-15 Simulator (Fig. 7-30) provides a 3D representation of an aircraft that can be used for testing a system that contains a neural network. This simulation developed for the IFCS project offers different viewing points, external and internal, to the vehicle [Perhinschi 2002]. It presents the

---

[10] Limes, Greg. Personal interaction with Brian Taylor on IFCS Project, 2001.

traditional pilot instrumentation overlaid on the flying aircraft. Real-time MATLAB plots are generated during the flight and are displayed on the screen or stored on the hard drive for later analysis. The plots are user-selected and show various values including sensor data, error tracking of the research components, and pilot input. This tracking can help assess the performance of the neural network in a simulated environment before it is deployed into operation.

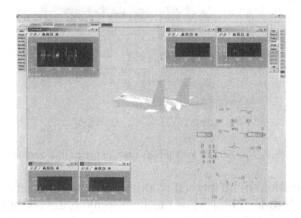

Figure 7-30. WVU F-15 Simulator

4.2   Visualization During the Operation Process

For an on-line learning neural network (OLNN), one that adapts during operation, visualization can provide a means by which to examine the neural networks inclination towards a certain direction of adaptation. If the direction of adaptation is incorrect, then the designer can remedy the situation before the OLNN is deployed or a monitoring device may be able to predict incorrect adaptation before it causes failure. An OLNN may, over time, begin to exhibit learning patterns that are considered unacceptable. Visual tools and techniques can be useful in examining these patterns so the neural network can be redesigned or reset to a previous state to prevent future occurrences of unacceptable behavior.

Two tools have been created for the IFCS project for the purpose of monitoring the OLNN performance. One is the Sensitivity Tool created by Soares [2002] for the NASA Dryden Flight Center and the other is the Confidence Tool created by Gupta and Schumann [2004] at NASA Ames Research Center.

The Sensitivity Tool [Soares 2002] applies Lyapunov's 2nd Method for the stability analysis of neural network-based flight control systems that guarantees the boundedness of the tracking error and network weights. The

Sensitivity Tool is used to determine whether the neural network-based flight control system model signals remain bounded and to exercise the gain sensitivity to determine changes to the weights and inversion errors while adding white noise to the adaptation algorithm.

The Tool is a GUI interface (Fig. 7-31 on the next page) to MATLAB/Simulink models that allows the user to vary gain and noise parameters and generate plots of desired variables. The plots include:

1. The trajectories of the neural network weights, as they remain bounded and converge to the desired value
2. The trajectories of the pitch, roll, and yaw rates, showing their stability and boundedness
3. The weights of the three channels versus time
4. Neural network estimation of the inversion errors
5. Error between the inversion error and the adaptive neural network

The Sensitivity Tool was modeled in Simulink. The GUI is modeled in MATLAB and can be used to plot the results. The tool includes time history plots of the weights and cross plotting of variables that show the boundedness of the weights and the tracking error for roll, pitch, and yaw channels, in addition to the neural network estimation for the inversion errors. Additional capability of the tool includes adding gains (perturbations) on selected gain parameters.

Fig. 7-32 shows the Noise Analysis interface (one of the features offered). The Noise Analysis introduces a Band-Limited White Noise to the error rates in each channel. By double clicking on the Noise option, the user can change the noise characteristics, and then plot the result in the presence of noise. This demonstrates how the cancellation of inversion errors changes with the addition of white noise. Individual random noise based on the system clock is input into each channel, two (2) per roll, pitch, and yaw axes respectively, with one representing the proportional and integral controller each.

Another tool that can be used to support the operation activity is the Confidence Tool created by Gupta and Schumann [2004] at NASA ARC. The tool was developed to measure the performance of the neural network during operation by calculating a confidence interval (error bar) around the neural network's output. The tool can be used during pre-deployment verification as well as during operation to monitor the network performance. The tool has been implemented in Simulink.

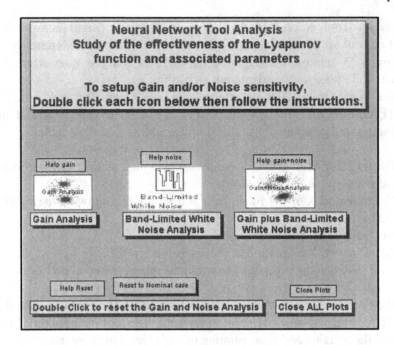

Figure 7-31. GUI for the Sensitivity Tool [Soares 2002]

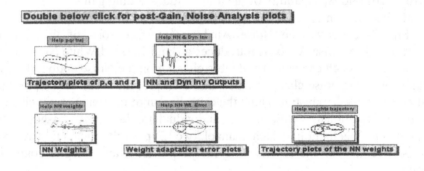

Figure 7-32. Additional Plots (Gain and/or Noise Analysis) [Soares 2002]

Fig. 7-33, Fig. 7-34, and Fig. 7-35 show a graphical representation of the tool's output for three simulation runs for three different operating conditions. In each graph, the output of the neural network over time is shown as a solid line and the dashed lines show the error bars (variance). A broad band corresponds to a low confidence value.

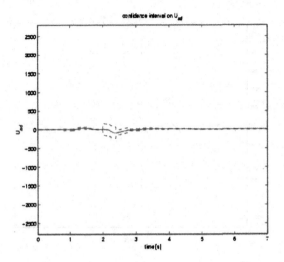

Figure 7-33. Confidence Tool (a) [Gupta 2004] (©2004 IEEE)

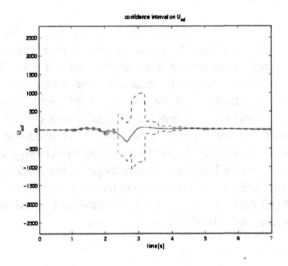

Figure 7-34. Confidence Tool (b) [Gupta 2004] (©2004 IEEE)

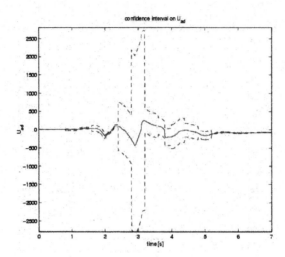

Figure 7-35. Confidence Tool (c) [Gupta 2004] (©2004 IEEE)

5.   SUMMARY

Visualization can help bridge the cognitive gap by representing relationships in the neural and by examining how those relationships evolve. Two-dimensional diagrams, three-dimensional plots, or even 3D simulations can be used to visually compare structures and adaptation of the neural networks.   These activities can be used as V&V activities to assess the constraints or limitations of the proposed neural network architecture.

Visualization can aid in both developing and understanding systems involving neural networks.   Personnel involved in verifying and validating such systems may have little or no knowledge of the workings of a neural network. Through the use of visualization techniques, such as simple neuron models, the MATLAB Neural Network Toolbox and Simulink, or even 3D visualizations, the understanding can be increased.

REFERENCES

Craven, Mark W. and Jude W. Shavlik. 1992. Visualizing Learning and Computation in Artificial Neural Networks. *International Journal on Artificial Intelligence Tools* 1 3:399-425.

Freitas, Carla M.D.S., Paulo R.G. Luzzardi, Ricardo A. Cava, Marco Winckler, Marcelo S. Pimenta, Luciana P. Nedel. 2002. On Evaluating Information Visualization Techniques. *In Proceeding of Advanced Visual Interfaces.* Trento, Italy, May.

Gupta, Pramod and Johann Schumann. 2004. A Tool for Verification and Validation of Neural Network Based Adaptive Controllers for High Assurance Systems. In *Proceeding of High Assurance Systems Engineering (HASE)*. Tampa, FL. April 2004. 277-278.

Hinton, G.E., McClelland, J.L., and Rumelhart, D.E. 1986. Distributed representations. In *Parallel Distributed Processing: Explorations in the Microstructure of Cognition*, eds. D.E. Rumelhart and J.L. McClelland. Cambridge: MIT Press. 77-109.

Mackall, Dale; Stacy Nelson; and Johann Schumman. 2002. Verification and Validation of Neural Networks for Aerospace Systems. NASA Dryden Flight Research Center and NASA Ames Research Center. June 12.

Mathworks, Inc. 1998. *Neural Network User's Guide (version 3)*.

Munro, P. 1991. Visualization of 2-D Hidden Unit Space. Technical Report LIS035/IS91003, School of Library and Information Science, University of Pittsburgh, Pittsburgh, PA.

Perhinschi, M. G., G. Campa, M. R. Napolitano, M . Lando, L. Massotti, and M.L. Fravolini. 2002. Modeling and simulation of a fault tolerant flight control system. Submitted to *International Journal of Modeling and Simulation* in April 2002.

Pratt, L.Y. and Mostwo, J. 1991. Direct Transfer of Learned Information Among Neural Networks. In *Proceedings of the Ninth National Conference on Artificial Intelligence*, Anaheim, CA. 584-589.

Pratt, L. Y., and Nicodemus, S. 1993. Case Studies in the Use of a Hyperplane Animator for Neural Network Research. In *Proceedings of the IEEE International Conference on Neural Networks, IEEE World Congress on Computational Intelligence*, 1:78-83.

Soares, Fola. 2002. Users Manual for the Generic Analysis Tool of Neural Network-Based Flight Control systems, Hypersonic Vehicles, Adaptive controllers, and Lyapunov Techniques.

Towell, G.G., Shavlik, J.W., and Noordewier, M.O. 1990. Refinement of Approximately Correct Domain Theories by Knowledge-Based Neural Networks. In *Proceedings of the Eighth National Conference on Artificial Intelligence*. Boston, MA: MIT Press. 861-866.

Towell, G.G., M.W. Craven, and J.W. Shavlik. 1991. Constructive Induction in Knowledge-Based Neural Networks. In *Machine Learning: Proceedings of the Seventh International Workshop*. Evanston, IL. Morgan Kaufmann. 213-217.

Vesanto J. 1998. http://www.cis.hut.fi/~juuso/vrmlsom/index.html.

Vesanto J. 1999. SOM-Based Visualization Methods. *Intelligent Data Analysis*. 3:111-126.

Wejchert, J., and Tesauro, G. 1990. Neural Network Visualization. In *Advances in Neural Information Processing Systems*, Vol. 2, 465-472. San Mateo, CA.: Morgan Kaufmann.

Chapter 8

RULE EXTRACTION AS A FORMAL METHOD

Marjorie Darrah, Brian J. Taylor
Institute for Scientific Research, Inc.

1. INTRODUCTION

The term *formal methods* refers to the use of techniques from formal logic and discrete math in the specification, design, and construction of computer systems and software. These techniques enable the formalization of software for development and testing so that it may be verified and validated in a more thorough way. When used for testing purposes, formal methods can reduce the reliance on human intuition and judgment by providing more objective and repeatable tests. Traditional formal methods techniques include model checking and theorem proving.

In the case of deterministic software, model checking can provide significant help for designing more efficient and reliable systems. Model checking starts from an initial state and repeatedly applies the transition relation to search all reachable states for a property violation, while remembering explored states to avoid looping [Pecheur 2000]. In theory, when this technique is applied to standard deterministic software, a thorough check of the state space may be accomplished, though in practice it may take a very long time.

Theorem proving is the use of logical induction over the execution steps of the program to prove system requirements. System requirements are translated into complex mathematical equations and solved by verification experts to prove the system is accurate [Pecheur 2002]. This technique can use the full power of mathematical logic to analyze and prove properties of any design but will require significant effort and expertise.

This chapter explores the idea of applying formal methods to adaptive neural network software in order to make the verification and validation

(V&V) process more objective. Both model checking and theorem proving were investigated to decide whether these techniques could be applied to adaptive neural networks.

Model checking seems less applicable when the state space is infinite or when the system is non-deterministic or adaptive. In "Verifying Properties of Neural Networks" [Rodrigues 2001], the idea of using model checking to verify properties of recurrent neural networks is discussed. The system presented in the paper, by the author's own conclusion, was clearly undecidable and therefore could not be automated. A finite version of the system was addressed using local model checking and was implemented, but Rodrigues fails to generalize these results to the infinite system. In current literature, no other research was found that applied model checking to neural networks. It is most likely that because of the infinite state space of the neural network, and the adaptive nature of some neural networks, model checking does not directly apply. Additionally, much more work in this research area will need to be done in order to make it a viable method for the V&V of neural networks.

Likewise, theorem proving in the traditional sense does not seem to be applied to adaptive neural networks. Rather than the traditional approach where the proof of requirements is done by logical induction over the structure of the program, the approaches for the adaptive neural networks deal with proving convergence and stability. Lyapunov or stochastic methods are commonly used and take the place of theorem proving for neural networks.

Although not specifically identified in the literature as a V&V formal method technique, rule extraction fits the basic definition by using techniques from formal logic to formalize neural network software so that it may be examined more completely.   There are many researchers investigating the use of rule extraction to acquire knowledge from the neural network and put it in a form that a human can understand and examine. In the past, rule extraction has been applied to various types of neural networks including multilayer perceptron (MLP), local cluster, and radial basis function [Andrews 1995; Andrews 2002; McGarry 1999]. This chapter examines whether rule extraction can be used as an effective tool for the V&V of neural networks and specifically can it be applied to the dynamic cell structure (DCS) neural network.

2. OVERVIEW OF NEURAL NETWORK RULE EXTRACTION TECHNIQUES

The internal knowledge of a neural network cannot be understood by examining the source code of the software. By design, neural networks change while training on a data set. After training, some networks are fixed while others are allowed to adapt during operation. It is a challenge to understand how the network will handle additional input. Testing can give some level of confidence but may not provide a satisfactory level in safety- or mission-critical cases. Other formal methods, such as model checking, do not apply in the case of neural networks.

The method of rule extraction can been used to model the knowledge that the neural network has gained while training or adapting. The rules will give insight into the workings of the neural network and may also be used to check against basic system requirements. The rules extracted are generally represented by a set of if-then statements that may be examined by a human. If the neural network is fixed after training, then the rules should, with some confidence, model the way the neural network will handle other data that is processed. If the neural network is a real-time adaptive neural network, then rule extraction can be done for one point in time to establish what the system looks like at that instance. Repeated application of rule extraction could yield an understanding of the progression of the network during adaptation.

In the current literature pertaining to rule extraction, two main survey papers give a good foundation for the study of this topic. The first is from the Neurocomputing Research Centre titled "A survey and critique of techniques for extracting rules from trained artificial neural networks" [Andrews 1995a]. The second survey paper was produced by the same group several years later titled "The truth is in there: directions and challenges in extracting rules from trained artificial neural networks" [Tickle 1998]. For a more detailed literature review of rule extraction please refer to "Toward Reliable Neural Network Software for The Development of Methodologies for the Independent Verification and Validation of Neural Networks" [ISR 2002].

Rule Formats
Rule extraction algorithms will generate rules of either conjunctive form or subset selection form, commonly referred to as M-of-N rules named for

the primary rule extraction that makes use of the form. All rules follow the English syntactical if-then propositional form. Conjunctive rules follow the format:

IF (condition 1) AND ... AND (contition N)

THEN RESULT
                                                                              (8.1)

Here the RESULT can be of a binary value (TRUE/FALSE or YES/NO), a classification value (RED/WHITE/BLUE), or a real number value (0.18).

The condition can be either discrete (flower is RED, ORANGE or YELLOW) or continuous (0.25 ≤ diameter ≥ 0.6). The rule extraction algorithm will search through the structure of the network, and/or the contents of a network's training data, and narrow down values across each input looking for the antecedents (conditions) that make up the rules.

Subset rules, or M-of-N rules, follow the format:

IF (M of the following N antecedents are TRUE)

THEN RESULT
                                                                              (8.2)

Cravin and Shavlik explain that the M-of-N rule format provide more concise rule sets in contrast to the potentially lengthy conjunctive rule format [Craven 1994]. This can be especially true when a network uses several input parameters.

Rule Extraction Techniques

Andrews [1995a] identifies three categories for rule extraction procedures: decompositional, pedagogical, and eclectic. Each approach may generate Boolean or fuzzy-logic rules. There are several dozen different rule extraction techniques; many are no more than a succeeding version of a previous technique. The techniques that appear prominently in the literature will be discussed below. Other techniques, such as fuzzy logic and Boolean rule extraction, discussed in Andrews' survey paper, do not seem to be widely used or are not well documented, as judged by the lack of information in the literature.

Decompositional

Decompositional rule extraction involves the extraction of rules from a network in a neuron-by-neuron series of steps. This process can be tedious and result in large and complex descriptions. The drawbacks to decompositional extractions are time and computational limitations. One advantage of decompositional techniques is that they do seem to offer the prospect of generating a complete set of rules for the neural network. These rules are also of a binary form; the outputs of the neurons are mapped into a yes/no condition that Andrews refers to as a rule consequent [Andrews 1995a].

KT and SUBSET are two well-known subset algorithms within decompositional rule extraction. Fu [1994] developed the KT algorithm that is able to handle neural networks with a smooth activation function, such as the back-propagation network with a sigmoid function, where the activation function is bounded in the region of [0, 1]. The SUBSET algorithm is an extension of the KT algorithm that was suggested by Towell and Shavlik [1993]. The SUBSET routine specifies a neural network where the output of each neuron in the network is either close to zero or close to one, as opposed to existing somewhere between the bounds of zero and one. This changes the importance of links between neurons in that the values that propagate on a link are close to the value of that link's weights or zero.

Pedagogical

Pedagogical rule extraction is the extraction of a network description by treating the entire network as a black box. In this approach, inputs and outputs are matched to each other. The decompositional approaches can produce intermediary rules that are defined for internal connections of a network, possibly between the input layer and the first hidden layer. Pedagogical approaches usually do not result in these intermediary terms. Pedagogical approaches can be faster than the decompositional, but they are somewhat less likely to accurately capture all of the valid rules describing a network's contents.

Thrun [1995] developed Validity Interval Analysis (VI-Analysis or VIA), the core technique within the pedagogical approach. The key idea in VIA is to attach intervals to the activation range of each input parameter looking for the network's activations that lie within these intervals. VIA checks whether or not a set of intervals is consistent, i.e. whether there exists a set of network activations inside the validity intervals. It does this by iteratively refining the validity intervals, excluding activations that are provably inconsistent with other intervals. The end result is a set of validity intervals for each input, a hypercube across all of the input dimensions.

Eclectic

The eclectic approach is merely the use of those techniques that incorporate some of a decompositional approach with some of a pedagogical approach or those techniques designed in such a way that they can be either decompositional or pedagogical. The Rule-Extraction-As-Learning (REAL) method, for example, is designed such that it can use either technique.

In a paper describing the REAL technique, Cravin and Shavlik discuss a way of extracting rules through supervised learning and network querying as opposed to the common search-based techniques from the previous sections [Craven 1994]. (They refer to the search methods as Rule-extraction-as-search approaches.) Many of the search algorithms try to find rules that explain the activations of hidden layer and output layer neurons in the networks. The REAL technique instead will learn from the training examples and query a network to determine if the specific instances from the training set are covered by the target output result.

2.1 Developing Rule Extraction Techniques for V&V of a Safety-Critical System

This section details the approach taken to determine whether rule extraction will be a viable tool for the V&V of the DCS neural network used in intelligent flight control (IFC). The Intelligent Flight Control System (IFCS) project is working towards developing a real-time adaptable flight control system utilizing neural networks. This project is a collaborative effort among the NASA Dryden Flight Research Center, the NASA Ames Research Center (ARC), Boeing Phantom Works, the Institute for Scientific Research, Inc. (ISR), and West Virginia University (WVU). The first generation (GEN1) flight control concept was designed to identify aircraft stability and control characteristics using neural networks and to use this information to optimize aircraft performance in both normal and simulated failure conditions.

Developers of the DCS neural network have been cautious about expanding their use into safety- and mission-critical domains due to the complexities and uncertainties associated with these complex, adaptive software systems. Since the DCS neural network and other adaptive neural networks are beginning to be used within high-assurance systems, NASA has encouraged research in the area of the V&V of neural networks to answer the question: How can we be sure that any system that includes neural network technology is going to behave in a known, consistent, and correct manner?

2.1.1 Overview of IFCS Use of the DCS Neural Network

The IFCS provides an example of neural networks used in a safety-critical application. Two types of neural networks are designed into the IFCS GEN1 scheme. A pre-trained, non-adaptive neural network component provides a baseline approximation of stability and control derivatives for the aircraft. The second neural network is an online adaptive network that learns and adapts during flight to account for aerodynamic changes, such as ones due to actuator failures.

In the fall of 2003, the IFCS GEN1 system completed successful testing in flight on the NASA F-15 Advanced Control Technology for Integrated Vehicles aircraft. This aircraft has been highly modified from a standard F-15 configuration to include canard control surfaces, thrust vectoring nozzles, and a digital fly-by-wire flight control system to enable the simulation of different actuator failures during flight.

The online adaptive neural network, the DCS, used in the IFCS GEN1 system is of special concern with respect to V&V. The DCS is a member of a group of neural networks known as self-organizing maps. The DCS algorithm, implemented in the GEN1 system by NASA ARC [Jorgensen 1997], was originally developed by Bruske [1994] and is a derivative of work by Fritzke [1994] combined with competitive Hebbian learning by Martinez [1993]. These neural networks are designed as topology representing networks whose roles are to learn the topology of an input space with perfect preservation.

The DCS neural network learns the function that describes a map of the input space, represented as Voronoi regions. The neurons within the neural network represent the reference vector (centroid) for each of the Voronoi regions. The connections between the neurons, c_{ij}, are then part of the Delaunay triangulation connecting neighboring Voronoi regions through their reference vectors.

This reference vector is known as the best matching unit (BMU). Given an input, v, the BMU is the neuron whose weights, w, are closest to v. Along with the BMU, the second BMU (SEC) is found using the Delaunay triangulation and nearby neurons are adjusted within the BMU neighborhood (with nearby neuron defined as the neurons connected to the BMU through the triangulation).

The DCS algorithm consists of two learning rules, Hebbian and Kohonen. Hebbian learning updates c_{ij} (Eq. 8.3) between neurons i and j to reflect the topology (triangulation) of the input space where the connection is a perfect fit of 1, if i and j are the BMU and SEC.

$$\dot{c}_{ij} = \begin{cases} 1 & i \in [BMU, SEC], j \in [BMU, SEC] \\ \alpha \cdot c_{ij} & \alpha \cdot c_{ij} > \theta \\ 0 & \alpha \cdot c_{ij} < \theta \\ 0 & i = j \end{cases} \qquad (8.3)$$

The forgetting constant, α, is included to produce a weakening between i and j if they are not currently the closest to the stimulus, and θ is the edge threshold, a minimum acceptable connection strength in order for the connection to be considered valid. Kohonen learning is used to adjust the weight vectors, w, of the neurons. The change in the weight vectors is represented by Eq. 8.4 and Eq. 8.5.

$$\Delta w_{BMU} = \varepsilon_{BMU} (v - w_{BMU}) \tag{8.4}$$

$$\Delta w_j = \varepsilon_N (v - w_j) \tag{8.5}$$

where ε_{BMU} is the BMU weight adjustment parameter and ε_N is the weight adjustment applied to the neighborhood of the BMU.

These two learning rules allow the DCS neural network to change its structure. The ability to add new neurons into the network as it grows gives the DCS neural network the potential to evolve into many different configurations. This adaptive nature can open up the possibility of sub-optimal or even erroneous solutions.

2.1.2   DCS Rule Extraction Algorithm

In order to determine whether rule extraction was a viable approach for the V&V of the DCS neural network used in the IFCS, an algorithm that applied to the DCS had to be found or developed. Several rule extraction techniques had been developed for neural networks similar to the DCS. RULEX is a tool offered by Robert Andrews and Shlomo Geva [1995b, 2002] that will extract rules from constrained error back-propagation (CEBP), MLP, and local cluster neural networks. Andrews and Geva provide MATLAB files that implement RULEX.

Another algorithm that seemed applicable to the DCS was the LREX rule extraction algorithm developed by McGarry, Wermter, and Macintyre [2001], School of Computing, Engineering, and Technology, University of Sunderland, England. These algorithms are used to extract rules from radial basis function (RBF) neural networks.

After examining both the RULEX and LREX techniques closely it was determined that neither technique could be used directly to extract rules from the DCS neural network in the IFCS. The literature reveals many techniques and tools available for rule extraction, although most of these techniques and tools are neural network specific. There is not one general rule extraction technique that can be applied to every neural network; rather there must be a collection of techniques to handle the different types. Therefore a new algorithm for extracting rules from the DCS was developed by ISR.

The algorithm developed for extracting rules from the DCS is a modification of the LREX algorithm by McGarry [1999] that was used to extract rules from a RBF neural network. After the DCS has been trained, the weights are used as inputs to the algorithm. During the training, the BMU corresponding to each data point is recorded and also used as input to the algorithm. The training data is divided into regions based on the BMU. Then for each region, x_{lower} is the smallest value of the independent variable that has a particular BMU and x_{upper} is the largest value of that independent variable that has that same particular BMU. These two numbers form bounds for the intervals in the antecedent of the rule. (Example: variable >= x_{lower} AND <= x_{upper}) An interval is determined for each of the independent variables and the statements are connected by AND to form the full antecedent. When the DCS was used as a classifier with the Iris data, the conclusion of the if-then statement was categorical. In this case the category associated with the BMU was reported in the rule as the conclusion. When the DCS was used to learn a function and the dependent variable was continuous, then the conclusion was stated the same way the antecedent was stated, intervals connected with ANDs. The algorithm used for the rule extraction is in Fig. 8-1. The rules will be explained in Sections 2.1.4 and 2.1.5.

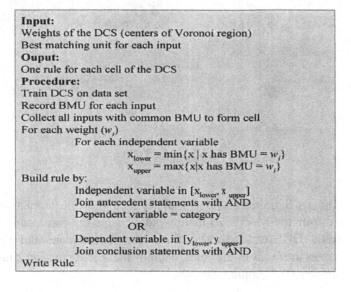

Input:
Weights of the DCS (centers of Voronoi region)
Best matching unit for each input
Ouput:
One rule for each cell of the DCS
Procedure:
Train DCS on data set
Record BMU for each input
Collect all inputs with common BMU to form cell
For each weight (w_j)
        For each independent variable
                $x_{lower} = \min\{x \mid x \text{ has BMU} = w_j\}$
                $x_{upper} = \max\{x|x \text{ has BMU} = w_j\}$
Build rule by:
        Independent variable in $[x_{lower}, x_{upper}]$
        Join antecedent statements with AND
        Dependent variable = category
                OR
        Dependent variable in $[y_{lower}, y_{upper}]$
        Join conclusion statements with AND
Write Rule

Figure 8-1. DCS Rule Extraction Algorithm

2.1.3   Implementation of the DCS Rule Extraction Algorithm

In order to test the DCS rule extraction algorithm, first a generic implementation of the DCS neural network was developed in MATLAB. This implementation has a GUI that allows different sets to be loaded for the purpose of training the neural network.   As reflected in Fig. 8-2, the command launchDCS brings up the window that, through a menu system, allows the user to load a data file, classify the variables in the file as independent or dependent, scale the data if necessary, configure the DCS, and then train the DCS.

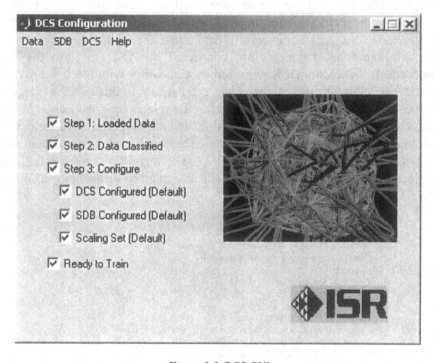

Figure 8-2. DCS GUI

After the DCS training was complete, then the rule extraction scripts were called from the MATLAB main window using the command results = extract_rules_DCS(dcs, data).   Since the independent and dependent variable names are used in the rules, each of the rule extraction source code files is specific to the training data set.

2.1.4 Testing Rule Extraction Algorithm on Benchmarking Data

To test the rule extraction algorithms, the DCS was trained on a benchmark data set available to developers for testing purposes. The data set chosen for this benchmarking exercise was the Iris data, available through the University of California at Irvine, because it is a common data set used by authors of other rule extraction techniques. The Iris plant database is from original work of Fisher [1936] and contains three classes of Iris plants (Iris_Setosa, Iris_Virginica, and Iris_Versicolor). There are four independent variables used to predict classification type (sepal_length, sepal_width, petal_length, and pedal_width). One of the Iris classes is linearly separable from the other two, but the other two are not linearly separable from each other.

A five-fold cross validation approach was used for the testing of the Iris data. This meant that the Iris data was divided into five equal parts, $\{S_1, S_2, S_3, S_4, S_5\}$, of which four parts were used for training and a fifth part is used for testing. The Iris data contains 150 data points; therefore, the data was partitioned into five groups of 30 random points.

After training on the Iris data, the DCS should have clustered the input data into different classifications representing the different Iris types: Setosa, Virginica, or Versicolor. To capture what the DCS learned, the rule extraction algorithm described in Section 2.1.2 was applied to the trained DCS. The output was a set of rules in the form of if-then statements. These rules in Fig. 8-3 represent one such set of rules that attempts to capture the Voronoi regions that the DCS formed to cluster the Iris data.

Since the extracted rules are a representation of the DCS, they should classify data in the same way that the DCS classifies data. To test the rules agreement with the DCS, the rules were implemented in MATLAB and applied to the S_5 subset partition of Iris data (the test set). The results from the extracted rules were then compared to the results from the same data classified by the DCS.

Five iterations of this procedure were completed to ensure that each subset was used as test data. This meant that iteration one used subsets $\{S_1, S_2, S_3, S_4\}$ to train and S_5 to test, iteration two used partitions $\{S_1, S_2, S_3, S_5\}$ to train and S_4 to test, and so on. When compared to the DCS, the extracted rules had an overall agreement of 82% in classifying the Iris data. Results are based on setting the minimum error for the network at 1.5. The minimum error controls the growth of the network. The network will continue to grow nodes until the minimum error is satisfied or the network size reaches a preset limit for number of nodes.

> **RULES FOR CELL1**
> IF (SL >=5.6 AND <=7.9) AND
> (SW >=2.2 AND <=3.8) AND
> (PL >=4.8 AND <=6.9) AND
> (PW >=1.4 AND <=2.5)
> THEN...Virginica
>
> **RULES FOR CELL2**
> IF (SL >=4.3 AND <=5.8) AND
> (SW >=2.3 AND <=4.4) AND
> (PL >=1.1 AND <=1.9) AND
> (PW >=0.1 AND <=0.6)
> THEN...Setosa
>
> **RULES FOR CELL3**
> IF (SL >=4.9 AND <=7) AND
> (SW >=2 AND <=3.3) AND
> (PL >=3 AND <=5) AND
> (PW >=1 AND <=1.8)
> THEN...Versicolor

Figure 8-3. Rules Extracted from Iris Data

2.1.5   Application of Rule Extraction Algorithm to DCS Trained on Flight Data

After a benchmark example had been executed and evaluated, the next step was to apply the rule extraction algorithm to the DCS trained on IFCS flight data. With the flight data, the DCS is used for function approximation (DCS was used for classification with the Iris data). The flight data used was obtained from an F-15 Flight Simulator developed at WVU for use in testing the IFCS GEN1 scheme. This data set contains seven independent variables and 26 dependent variables. These variables were introduced to one of five different DCS networks, one network for each of the aerodynamic derivative coefficients: Cz, Cm, Cl, Cn, and Cy. Each network learns the derivatives associated with a different coefficient. For example, Cz learns the stability and control derivatives associated with pitching moments due to normal force and uses the inputs of mach, altitude, alpha, and beta as the independent variables and cza, czdc, and czds as the dependent variables. After training the DCS on these variables the rules extracted take on the form seen in Fig. 8-4. The data in this case is all continuous data, so the rules give both antecedent and conclusion in the form of intervals.

RULES FOR CELL1
IF (mach >=0.78799 AND <=0.78945) AND
(altitude >=19860.484 AND <=19889.6526)AND
(alpha >=1.7003 AND <=1.8842) AND
(beta >=-0.029893 AND <=0.015156) AND
THEN (cza >=0.015062 AND <=0.019333) AND
(czdc >=0.22274 AND <=0.2287) AND
(czds >=0 AND <=0)

RULES FOR CELL2
IF (mach >=0.78455 AND <=0.8178) AND
(altitude >=19205.5546 AND <=19999.3379)AND
(alpha >=1.2545 AND <=1.7887) AND
(beta >=-0.20803 AND <=0.64913) AND
THEN (cza >=-0.076577 AND <=-0.002783) AND
(czdc >=0.22355 AND <=0.22448) AND
(czds >=0 AND <=0)

RULES FOR CELL3
IF (mach >=0.73926 AND <=0.78946) AND
(altitude >=19860.1718 AND <=21233.6014)AND
(alpha >=1.8854 AND <=2.4619) AND
(beta >=-0.079409 AND <=0.020729) AND
THEN (cza >=0.001184 AND <=0.015041) AND
(czdc >=0.20335 AND <=0.22271) AND
(czds >=0 AND <=0)

Figure 8-4. Rules from the Cz Network

As discussed above, in practice there are actually five different DCS implementations in the IFCS GEN1 system: Cz network, Cm network, Cy network, Cl network, and Cn network. Each of the networks has an individual variable list shown in Table 8-1. Each set of flight data contains all variables needed to train the five different networks. The flight data dcs_in1 was used to train the different networks and rules were extracted.

When trained on the Iris data, the DCS was used as a classifier, and thus, computing the agreement of the rules with the DCS for the Iris data was quite simple. With the flight data, the DCS is being used to approximate a function; as a result, determining the accuracy of the rules in this case is not as straight forward. The rules are evaluated by examining the domain coverage and the actual difference between the rule boundaries and the Voronoi region boundaries.

Table 8-1. DCS Networks Used for IFCS

Name of Network	Independent Variables	Dependent Variables
Cz	mach, altitude, alpha, beta	cza, czdc,czds
Cm	mach, altitude, alpha, beta	cma, cmdc, cmds, cmq
Cy	mach, altitude, alpha, beta, dstbd, drudd, daild	cyb, cydt, cyddc, cydr, cya
Cl	mach, altitude, alpha, beta, dstbd, drudd, daild	clb, cldt, clddc, cldr, clda, clp, clr
Cn	mach, altitude, alpha, beta, dstbd, drudd, daild	cnb, cndt, cnddc, cndr, cnda, cnp, cnr

Methods for refining the rule extraction algorithm and developing a deterministic rule set for the DCS flight data application were developed through funding provided through a NASA Ames STTR project titled *A Formal Method for Verification and Validation of Neural Network High Assurance Systems*. The original algorithm discussed in Section 2.1.2 is an uncomplicated way to capture the Voronoi regions that are created by the DCS. The refinement of the algorithm, discussed in the next section, generates expressions that completely capture the n-dimensional convex hulls that make up these Voronoi regions. These expressions are used as the antecedent for the new rules and a deterministic consequent was developed. The problem in refining the rules in this way is that the explicit description of Voronoi regions becomes overly complicated and can be less understandable than the information given by the initial rule type.

There is a definite tradeoff for rule sets between accuracy and understandability. A more simplistic, less accurate rule set may be useful to lend human understandability to the knowledge of the neural network. A more deterministic and accurate rule set may provide other methods of V&V, such as checking the rule set for inconsistencies in a model checker or theorem prover. Whatever format is used, it is important to ensure that any rules extracted are accurate, useful, and understandable.

2.1.6   Refining the Rule Extraction Algorithm

A new algorithm was developed to generate deterministic rules that utilize the structure of the DCS knowledge by considering the Voronoi regions that partition the input space.

As explained previously, the DCS partitions the input space into Voronoi regions. These regions are convex polygons in two dimensions and convex n-dimensional polyhedra in *n* dimensions. The original rule extraction algorithm did not capture the entire polygon or polyhedron region with the rules. The original algorithm used a "box" to represent that region and the rules represent the box. (See Fig. 8-5)

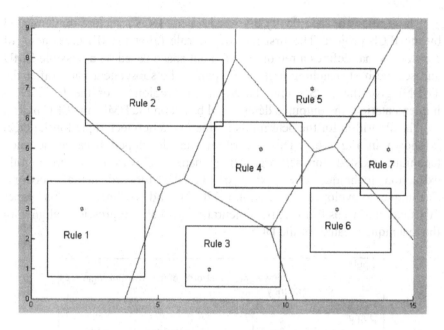

Figure 8-5. Original Rule Coverage

The new rule extraction algorithm was developed to completely capture the polygonal regions of the input space that represent the structure of the trained DCS. The previous rule format was non-deterministic and although understandable, could not be used as input to custom-off-the-shelf (COTS) tools or implemented. The new rule format is:

IF input $\in$ region 1 (input satisfies a set of constraints)

THEN output = multivariable linear expression   (8.6)

Below is an example of the new deterministic rules for a two-dimensional data set.

IF $(6 * x + 0 * y >= 48)$ AND $(2 * x + 2 * y >= 32)$
AND $(-1 * x + 4 * y >= 8.5)$ AND $(-3 * x + 2 * y >= -25.5)$
AND $(4 * x - 2 * y >= 16)$ AND $(-3 * x + 2 * y >= -23.5)$
AND $(-5 * x + 0 * y >= -57.5)$ (8.7)
THEN $z = 0.75 * x + 0.75 * y - 7.5$
ENDIF

These rules are specifically designed for the DCS structure implemented by the IFCS project. The first part of the rule (after the IF) gives a set of constraints that defines a region of the input space based on a possible BMU and second best matching unit (SEC) pair. The subsequent parts (after the THEN) give the DCS output based on this region. For the IFCS DCS implementation, the output is determined based on the BMU and SEC pair.

The algorithm for the deterministic rule extraction technique for the DCS is shown in Fig 8-6. This algorithm was developed because no such technique existed for self-organizing maps. However, a similar rule extraction technique does exist for the feed-forward neural network. Techniques developed by Setiono [2002] and outlined in his paper "Extraction of rules from artificial neural networks for regression" align with the technique created for the DCS.

```
Inputs:
        P = Set of all weights (centroids of the Voronoi regions)
        A = Adjacency Matrix

Output:
        R = Set of rules that describe a partition of the input
            space with associated outputs

Procedure:
        Use P to define a Voronoi diagram that partitions the
            input space.
        Use A to determine neighboring regions in the Voronoi
            diagram to find BMU and SEC pairs.

        For each p ∈ P (centroid of Voronoi region and BMU)
            Calculate Voronoi region boundaries.
            For each q ∈ P - {p} such that v is a neighbor of w
            (centroid of neighboring region and SEC)
                Determine boundaries that divide the region
                    with centroid w into subregions.
                Determine antecedent based on boundaries
                    defined by p and q.
                Determine consequent equation based on DCS
                    output determined by p and q.
                Write rule.
```

Figure 8-6. Deterministic Rule Extraction Algorithm

To test the accuracy, deterministic rules were generated for three different data sets. The rule output and the neural network output had 100% agreement. The rules are constructed to completely cover the input space and to use the DCS recall function as the output based on the region, therefore these rule have complete agreement with the neural network. Fig. 8-7 shows a two-dimensional example of how the rules partition the data based on BMU and SEC. The solid lines, in the figure, indicate the original Voronoi regions that divide the plane based on the BMU. The dotted lines show how the original regions are subdivided to account for the SEC. The lines that define the subregions form the rule antecedent. Note that the entire input space is covered, with each of the subregions representing one rule.

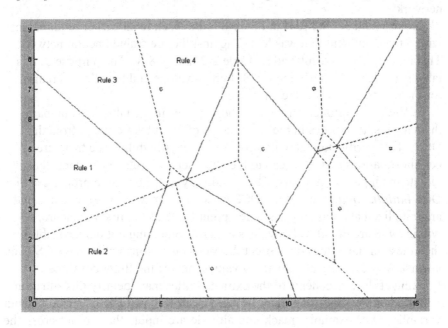

Figure 8-7. Deterministic Rule Coverage

2.2   Using Extracted Rules for V&V of DCS

One goal of this research was to demonstrate that the rules extracted from the DCS neural network could be used to assist in the V&V of the neural network used in a safety-critical application. The rules are viewed as a descriptive representation of how the DCS *handles* data. This representation provides the inner knowledge of the neural network that can be used to help understand whether the neural network is functioning as expected.

After extracting the rules from the IFCS neural networks, the rules were compared against the two documents provided by the IFCS project team, the Software and Interface Requirements Document (SIRS), IFC-SIRS-F004-UNCLASS-051501 [ISR 2001a] and the Interface Control Document (ICD), IFC-ICD-F008-UNCLASS-011501 [ISR 2001b]. The usefulness in requirements traceability and the overall usefulness of rule extraction to the IV&V practitioners understanding were assessed.

2.2.1   Comparison of Rules Against Requirements

The first way the extracted rules can be used is as an assessment against the expected ranges of the inputs and outputs of the DCS system. The SIRS for the IFCS project identifies the following requirements for the DCS network:

Requirement 3.2.4.3 [04] in Fig. 8-8 refers back to an earlier requirement within the document that was levied against the pre-trained neural network. This requirement is displayed as Table 2-2 in Fig. 8-8. The purpose of this table is to clearly identify the IFCS flight envelope and the allowed ranges for the inputs that define the envelope.

A V&V practitioner can look at these ranges in the table and compare them against the ranges in the antecedents of the rules extracted from the DCS. This verification activity proves to be worthwhile since there are certain situations that may lead to the DCS network rule antecedents that violate the input range limits. One possibility could be the improper use of a DCS *initialization* point. If the DCS networks start with no knowledge and are initialized at an improper starting point (such as the first two neurons within DCS are initialized to values of zero, something not unreasonable), then these initial values may affect the Voronoi regions within the DCS in an adverse way causing them to allow values outside the flight envelope. Looking at the antecedents of the extracted rules may identify this situation.

Another way the rules may be used is in the analysis of specific input variables. For example, mach and altitude are inputs that do not cross the zero value within their acceptable ranges. One may want to check to ensure that the extracted rules align with the expected ranges, and in situations where the zero value is within a rule, perhaps identify this as an area of special interest that requires additional analysis.

The rules may have an additional use in examining different modes of operation. The purpose of the IFCS is to induce *safe* failures and allow the system to adapt to accommodate these failures. Some of the failures may induce learning that extends beyond the expected ranges of the inputs. (This will be especially true for output ranges that will be discussed a little later.) Retaining prior learning, especially after a failure occurs, may be something the IFCS project team will want to investigate. The rules may identify Voronoi regions that violate the expected input ranges and point to an area of the input space that will require further simulation and understanding before the project proceeds.

3.2.4.3 [04] Inputs

The OLNN inputs **shall**[01] process the following 8 sensor inputs: mach, altitude, alpha, beta, stabilator deflection, rudder deflection, aileron deflection, and canard deflection.

The OLNN software **shall**[02] conform to the units as specified in the ICD. The inputs of beta and rudder deflection **shall**[03] be absolute magnitudes only.

The sensor inputs into the OLNN **shall**[04] undergo the same input pre-processing used for the BLNN as described in 3.2.2.1 and Table 2-2.

Additional OLNN inputs **shall**[05] include the derivative deltas, which are the differences between each stability and control derivative output from the PID and output from the BLNN. These derivative deltas are described in Section 3.2.3.4 PID Outputs.

The specific derivative deltas are as follows:

$$\Delta C_{z_\alpha} \quad \Delta C_{z_{\delta_c}} \quad \Delta C_{z_{\delta_s}} \quad \Delta C_{m_\alpha} \quad \Delta C_{m_{\delta_c}} \quad \Delta C_{m_{\delta_s}} \quad \Delta C_{m_q}$$

$$\Delta C_{y_\beta} \quad \Delta C_{y_{\delta_T}} \quad \Delta C_{y_{\delta_{DC}}} \quad \Delta C_{y_{\delta_r}} \quad \Delta C_{y_{\delta_a}} \quad \Delta C_{l_\beta} \quad \Delta C_{l_{\delta_T}} \quad \Delta C_{l_{\delta_{DC}}} \quad \Delta C_{l_{\delta_r}} \quad \Delta C_{l_{\delta_a}} \quad \Delta C_{l_p} \quad \Delta C_{l_r}$$

$$\Delta C_{n_\beta} \quad \Delta C_{n_{\delta_T}} \quad \Delta C_{n_{\delta_{DC}}} \quad \Delta C_{n_{\delta_r}} \quad \Delta C_{n_{\delta_a}} \quad \Delta C_{n_p} \quad \Delta C_{n_r}$$

Table 2-2. BLNN Input Range Limits

Input Signal (dimensions)	Minimum Value	Maximum Value	
Mach (Mach)	0.20	1.60	
Altitude (feet)	5000.00	50000.00	
Alpha (degrees)	-4.00	Function of Flight Envelope	
		20.00	14.00
		(if Mach <= 0.85 OR Altitude >= 25000.00)	(if Mach > 0.85 AND Altitude < 25000.00)
Beta (degrees)	-10.00	10.00	
Stabilator Deflection(degrees)	-30.00	15.00	
Rudder Deflection(degrees)	-30.00	30.00	
Aileron Deflection(degrees)	-40.00	40.00	
Canard Deflection(degrees)	-35.00	5.00	

Figure 8-8. Requirements for the OLNN Input

Just as with the inputs, the SIRS also identified a range of expected outputs. These requirements were spread across the Parameter Identification (PID) and on-line learning neural network (OLNN), the DCS, and sections of the SIRS and the ICD. Some of the requirements that are levied against the OLNN appear below in Fig. 8-9.

2.2.1.1 Output

The OLNN attempts to remember the derivative deltas between the PID and the BLNN. The OLNN then produces an output that is the learning of these derivative deltas. These outputs are called the derivative corrections and there is a derivative correction for each of the 26 stability and control derivatives. The specific "derivative corrections" are as follows:

$$\Delta C_{z_\alpha} \quad \Delta C_{z_{\delta_c}} \quad \Delta C_{z_{\delta_s}} \quad \Delta C_{m_\alpha} \quad \Delta C_{m_{\delta_c}} \quad \Delta C_{m_{\delta_s}} \quad \Delta C_{m_q}$$

$$\Delta C_{y_\beta} \quad \Delta C_{y_{\delta_r}} \quad \Delta C_{y_{\delta_{IX}}} \quad \Delta C_{y_{\delta_r}} \quad \Delta C_{y_{\delta_a}} \quad \Delta C_{l_\beta} \quad \Delta C_{l_{\delta_r}} \quad \Delta C_{l_{\delta_{IX}}} \quad \Delta C_{l_{\delta_r}} \quad \Delta C_{l_{\delta_a}} \quad \Delta C_{l_p} \quad \Delta C_{l_r}$$

$$\Delta C_{n_\beta} \quad \Delta C_{n_{\delta_T}} \quad \Delta C_{n_{\delta_{IX}}} \quad \Delta C_{n_{\delta_r}} \quad \Delta C_{n_{\delta_a}} \quad \Delta C_{n_p} \quad \Delta C_{n_r}$$

These derivative corrections **shall**[01] be computed to a minimum precision of six places after the decimal point.

The OLNNdoes not provide any outputs to the SOFFT controller when the PID and OLNN are executed in the passive open-loop mode. For this Build, the outputs are only used for internal recording and then for later study and analysis. The OLNN **shall**[02] provide outputs to the Instrumentation bus as described in IFC -ICD -FXXX -UNCLASS-011501.

The outputs generated by the OLNN will include the processed inputs that the OLNN makes use of in its computations.

Figure 8-9. Requirements for the OLNN Output

The ICD contains the output description for all 26 stability and control derivatives, which includes the expected minimum and maximum values. The extracted rules from the DCS can be compared against the description of these derivatives. This could identify if the Voronoi regions of the DCS allowed for outputs that can violate those expected ranges.

2.2.2   Comparison of Rules Against Design Considerations

One of the most important steps of V&V is the traceability of requirements throughout the lifecycle processes. Requirements traceability can be a difficult task with a neural network because of their adaptive capabilities. Another factor that can make traceablility difficult is the fact that neural network requirements are often not clearly or concisely written, even though the overall goal for the system is generally well understood. The extracted rules represent the learning of the neural network, thus the rules could be used to determine if the network is meeting specific implied requirements.

For example, one requirement for the network used in the IFCS that is hard to explicitly state is "the network will provide smooth transitions of derivatives between regions within the flight envelope." If the neural network has been pre-trained to learn the different regions within the flight envelope, then the network's knowledge near the boundaries should be examined. This can be achieved by examining the extracted rules. If system designers are not satisfied with the network performance, then it is possible the network may require further training or modification. Either way, the examination of the extracted rules can help to determine the integrity of the neural network.

Fig. 8-10 depicts the IFCS flight envelope used for GEN1. The flight envelope can be broken into regions (a process known as gain scheduling) where a set of linear equations is used to approximate the behavior of that region. Due to the non-linearities of the aerodynamics throughout the entire flight envelope, several regions are often used.

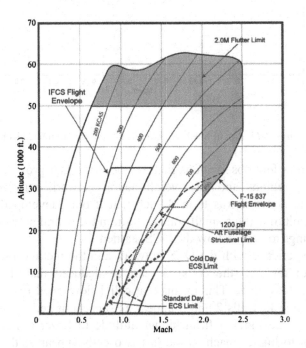

Figure 8-10. IFCS Flight Envelope

Fig. 8-11 is a graph that shows the mach-altitude components of the extracted rules for this same data set. Fig. 8-12 shows an example of the rules extracted from the DCS C1 network after training on a single set of flight data. The plot was constructed just using mach and altitude to see if the ranges of the rules may have any relationship to the use of gain scheduling or can visually tell us anything important.

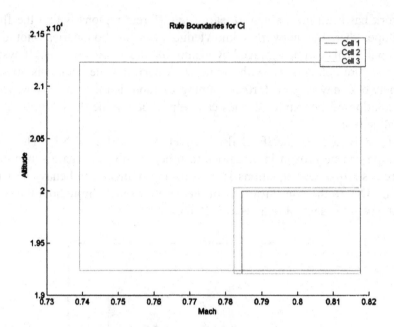

Figure 8-11. Plot of Mach vs. Altitude Cl Network Extracted Rules

There are a few observations that can be made that provide insight into the Voronoi regions and the overall neural network performance. For example, the network was trained such that it only developed three cells. This is a result of using a small data set to train the neural network and using certain settings to control how the DCS learned

From experience with the DCS network and the method used to extract the Voronoi regions (the cells), it can be deduced that the cells were developed across time. This means that cell 1 developed first, followed by cell 2 then cell 3. Cells 2 and 3 appear as subsets of cell 1. It also seems that the cells are moving from higher altitude to lower altitude and from lower mach to higher mach as the last two cells appear in the lower right hand side.

The V&V practitioner may be able to gain insights from these observations. With the limited data, he or she may be able to identify the type of flight maneuver used to train the DCS. For example, if the data is decreasing for altitude and increasing for mach, this may indicate the plane is diving. This might explain the placement of the cells representing the data extracted from the DCS after learning on this maneuver.

The practitioner may also be able to assess the size of the regions. For the problem at hand, the first cell may be too large and the other cells should

RULES FOR CELL1
IF (mach >=0.73926 AND <=0.8178) AND
(altitude >=19236.9846 AND <=21233.6014)AND
(alpha >=1.3343 AND <=2.4619) AND
(beta >=-0.079409 AND <=0.057813) AND
(dstbd >=-0.079409 AND <=0.057813) AND
(drudd >=-0.079409 AND <=0.057813) AND
(dalid >=-0.079409 AND <=0.057813)
THEN (clb >=2.7495 AND <=2.8781) AND
(cldt >=-0.052976 AND <=0.077512) AND
(clddc >=-4.8212 AND <=-3.3811) AND
(cldr >=-4.8212 AND <=-3.3811) AND
(clda >=-4.8212 AND <=-3.3811)
(clp >=-4.8212 AND <=-3.3811)
(clr >=-4.8212 AND <=-3.3811)

RULES FOR CELL2
IF (mach >=0.78455 AND <=0.81763) AND
(altitude >=19205.5546 AND <=19998.3911) AND
(alpha >=1.2545 AND <=1.6976) AND
(beta >=-0.20803 AND <=0.64913) AND
(dstbd >=-0.20803 AND <=0.64913) AND
(drudd >=-0.20803 AND <=0.64913) AND
(dalid >=-0.20803 AND <=0.64913)
THEN (clb >=2.8005 AND <=2.898) AND
(cldt >=-0.24914 AND <=0.65812) AND
(clddc >=-3.8321 AND <=-3.278) AND
(cldr >=-3.8321 AND <=-3.278) AND
(clda >=-3.8321 AND <=-3.278)
(clp >=-3.8321 AND <=-3.278)
(clr >=-3.8321 AND <=-3.278)

RULES FOR CELL3
IF (mach >=0.78235 AND <=0.8178) AND
(altitude >=19205.6047 AND <=20032.147) AND
(alpha >=1.4345 AND <=2.0295) AND
(beta >=-0.065293 AND <=0.2066) AND
(dstbd >=-0.065293 AND <=0.2066) AND
(drudd >=-0.065293 AND <=0.2066) AND
(dalid >=-0.065293 AND <=0.2066)
THEN (clb >=2.7964 AND <=2.8791) AND
(cldt >=-0.051466 AND <=0.19309) AND
(clddc >=-4.2774 AND <=-3.5067) AND
(cldr >=-4.2774 AND <=-3.5067) AND
(clda >=-4.2774 AND <=-3.5067)
(clp >=-4.2774 AND <=-3.5067)
(clr >=-4.2774 AND <=-3.5067)

Figure 8-12. Extract Rules: Cl Network Trained on dcs_in1

not be subset of the first. The fact that this figure is only drawn across two of the input dimensions can distort the analysis and perhaps a 3D drawing, or the data spread across multiple plots, may be better able to highlight differences in the cell.

Since the initial intent here is to look at the data with regards to the flight envelope, it is apparent that the flight envelope between .74 and .82 mach and 19250 and 21250 altitude will be able to generate outputs. If we were interested in this region within the IFCS flight envelope, the coverage might be satisfactory.

Fig. 8-13 is the plot of the combination of DCS extracted rules for the five networks on one graph. Such a plot can be used to visualize how the neural network Voronoi regions are spaced across the region. It can be determined if there is complete coverage of the flight envelope.

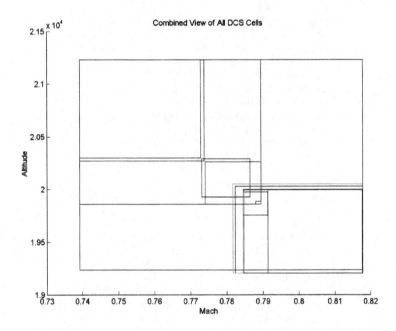

Figure 8-13. Plot of Mach vs. Altitude from All Extracted Rules

In the DCS flight application, the V&V practitioner may be interested in specific information related to input/output ranges, size and location of Voronoi regions across the entire input/output domain, or maybe chronological formation of the Voronoi regions. Also note that since the DCS is adapting during operation, the rules will only represent a particular instance in time. The network could be allowed to continue to train, stopped, and rules extracted to compare to the previous sets. This is an iterative process that can continue until a sufficient understanding of the neural network's adaptation is accomplished. This would allow the V&V practitioner to view the movement of the Voronoi regions across time as new data is presented to the neural network for training.

2.2.3 Using Extracted Rules to Uncover Coding Errors

The rule extraction algorithm, which generated human understandable rules, is based on how an input stimulus is matched to a centroid of the DCS or its best matching unit (BMU). The human understandable rules support verification inspection methods. Each input stimulus results in the selection of a BMU internal to the DCS network. The BMU is considered the centroid of a cell and each input that related to that BMU is considered to be a member of that cell. The human understandable rules were generated to describe each cell. The minimum and maximums of each input variable related to a specific BMU are used in the rule antecedents. The minimum and maximum of each output variable associated with this cell make up the rule consequent. Any BMU that did not have input stimulus matched to it did not generate a rule.

When the human understandable rule algorithm was applied to a DCS network that had been trained on the Iris data, a discrepancy was noted between the number of rules generated and the number of nodes within the DCS network. There were fewer rules than nodes. This implied that for the set of input data that was used to train the neural network, a node was established that never matched any of the other data, and thus these BMUs did not have corresponding rules. This led to investigation of the existence of these nodes by walking through the source code and looking for problems. Debugging and execution traces pointed to a problem in some of the DCS code that had been optimized to run within a MATLAB environment. The original IFCS DCS code was developed within the C programming language. For optimization purposes, when the code was moved into a MATLAB script for experimentation, all usage of 'for' loops were removed and replaced with vectorized math. One of the lines of code used for the optimization dealt with the identification of BMUs, and incorrectly referenced the BMU variable.

Instead of only looking across the existing set of nodes within the DCS network, it made use of the DCS maximum allowed number of nodes. In effect, when looking for the BMU, the DCS was allowed to consider nodes which had not yet been assigned, and by default were at zero value and can be thought of as existing at the origin. At times, these nodes were actually better at matching the input than any one of the existing nodes, and DCS manipulated these non-assigned nodes when it shouldn't have. The result was that nodes that had not been assigned learned and adapted. They showed up as having non-zero values and appeared to be nodes upon visual inspection of the DCS structure, but didn't actually exist. DCS was losing some potential learning within these nodes. The rules ignored these nodes since they weren't able to ever become BMUs that led to the discrepancy. The line of code was modified to ignore non-assigned nodes, and then DCS nodes correctly matched up with the human understandable rules.

Another example involves using the refined deterministic rules to uncover two coding errors. The deterministic rule extraction process is designed to have 100% agreement with the performance of the DCS network. However, testing of some of the first sets of deterministic rules showed that there was a large disagreement between the rules and DCS.

The rules were re-structured so that the antecedents were broken into a rule pertaining to each BMU, and then under the BMU rules, each neighboring SEC rule was present. This allowed comparison to see if the errors between the rules and DCS were based upon BMU selection, SEC selection, or within the consequent. By comparing the BMU output from DCS with the specific BMU rule that the input corresponded to, it was discovered that the BMU selection was consistent between the rules and the DCS. But the selection of the SEC was not matching between the two. Further investigation required analysis of the DCS recall function.

In the DCS recall function, two errors within the same line of code were discovered. One was related to substitution of the 'max' for 'min' commands within DCS. For the recall function to perform properly, the smallest distance is always used to identify the closest node to a stimulus. This is true also when selecting the second closest node from among a BMU's neighbors. But the code showed that the 'max' function was being used in place of the 'min' function. This would subsequently show up within the DCS recall function as the DCS always selected the node furthest away from the stimulus.

Further, this same line of code contained an incorrect reference to the strengths of the neighborhood for the BMU rather than the distances of the neighbors from the stimulus. This mistake is quite a large mistake, but due to the nature of the small DCS networks, and the small values on which the network was learning, the mistake was masked much of the time. Normal testing of the DCS showed that it could achieve accuracies above 90%, even with this error present. The robustness of the DCS network made discovery of this error difficult.

The line of code was changed to consider the distances rather than the connection strengths and to choose the min instead of max. The rules and

DCS were compared again. This gave the expected results of 100% agreement. The deterministic rules were deemed a success because they had allowed for the discovery of two coding errors, which were not readily apparent during normal testing.

3. SUMMARY

Along with the IFCS example mentioned in this chapter, neural networks are used in safety-related areas including advisory systems for healthcare, load forecasting for electrical power and gas, industrial process control and monitoring, and fire alarms. The commercial benefit for this technology is evident from the extent of industry-led research [Lisboa 2001]. There is no doubt that with the use of neural networks expanding to safety-related areas that rigorous V&V processes specific to neural networks are required. Traditional software V&V must be augmented to accommodate the opaqueness and the adaptive nature of the neural network.

Neural networks lack the ability to explain how they reached a specific output. This is one of the main reasons neural networks are not trusted: in most applications users want to know the reasoning behind the conclusion of the learning system or expert system. Rule extraction algorithms provide a means for either partially or completely *decompiling* a trained neural network. This is seen as a promising vehicle for at least indirectly achieving the required goal of enabling a comparison to be made between the extracted rules and the software specifications.

Rule extraction would satisfy several roles in the development and V&V of high assurance neural network systems.

1. The V&V practitioner could apply rule extraction to obtain a set of rules that mimics the functionality of the network and then use these rules for comparison against the original set of requirements.
2. Rule extraction can provide a tester with insight into what a fixed neural network has learned and assist in determining the acceptability of the network.
3. After a neural network has been trained and tested to satisfactory levels, a system developer could then apply rule extraction to refine requirements. The refined requirements would aid the system tester in the development of adequate testing procedures and test cases.
4. Additionally, these rules could be validated through the use of formal methods, such as a model checker.

At a minimum, extraction of these rules would provide some sense of confidence that the network will behave as it was intended. Extraction would be used as static analysis for adaptive systems. The rules would need to be extracted after each iteration of learning and then judged for correctness.

There is still much to discover about the use of rule extraction usefulness for the V&V of neural networks. Rule extraction offers the possibility of requirements traceability in a system that is not explicitly designed. The rules can also undergo design team review and analysis to detect improper network behaviors or missing knowledge. Through rule extraction, a system analyst might be able to ascertain novel learning behaviors that had not been previously recognized. By translating these features into a comprehensible English sentence, the analyst can gain a better understanding of the network's construction and perhaps the input domain as well.

The same techniques used to map rules from the network in rule extraction can also be used in two additional ways: rule initialization or rule insertion. Rule initialization is the process of giving the adaptive network some beginning knowledge. A system developer may have improved confidence if the starting condition of the network is known, which may lead to a constrained path of adaptation. Rule insertion is the method of moving symbolic rules back into a network, forcing the network's knowledge to incorporate some rule modifications or additional rules. An adaptive network could benefit from this scheme if the system developer wanted to exert a condition onto the network or reinforce conditions in the network. Examples of this might include restricting the network to a region of the input space or instructing it to deliberately forget some data.

These rule extraction techniques that are prevalent in the academic literature must be compiled into a usable form that will assist the developer or V&V team in certifying that the neural network is dependable, predictable, and ready for use in a system. Toward the goal of making rule extraction techniques readily available to assist in V&V, the authors of this document will further their research through a NASA ARC STTR project with the goal of developing a comprehensive and practical tool to transfer neural network rule extraction technology into neural network development practice.

REFERENCES

Andrews, Robert; J. Diederich; and A. B. Tickle. 1995a. A Survey and Critique Of Techniques For Extracting Rules From Trained Artificial Neural Networks. *Knowledge Based Systems* 8:373-389.

Andrews, R. and S.Geva. 1995b. RULEX & CEBP Networks as the Basis for a Rule Refinement System. Hybrid Problems, Hybrid Solutions, ed. John Hallam. IOS Press.1-12.

Andrews, R and S. Geva. 2002. Rule Extraction From Local Cluster Neural Nets. *Neurocomputing* 47:1-20.

Bruske, Jorg and Gerald Sommer. 1994. Dynamic Cell Structures. In *Proceedings of Neural Information Processing Systems (NIPS)*, 497-504.

Craven, Mark; and J.W. Shavlik. 1994. Using Sampling and Queries to Extract Rules from Trained Neural Networks. In *Proceedings of the 11th International Conference on Machine Learning* 37-45.

Fisher, A. 1936. Annals of Eugenics 7:179-188.

Fritzke, B. 1994. Growing Cell-Structures - a Self-Organizing Network for Unsupervised and Supervised Learning. *Neural Networks* 7(9): 1441-1460.

Fu, L. M. 1994. Rule Generation From Neural Networks. *IEEE Transactions on Systems, Man, and Cybernetics.* 28(8):1114-1124.

Institute for Scientific Research, Inc. (ISR). 2001a. Software and Interface Requirements Document (SIRS). IFC-SIRS-F004-UNCLASS-051501.

Institute for Scientific Research, Inc. (ISR). 2001b. Interface Control Document (ICD). IFC-ICD-F008-UNCLASS-011501.

Institute for Scientific Research, Inc. (ISR). 2002. Toward Reliable Neural Network Software for The Development of Methodologies for the Independent Verification of Neural Networks. IVVNN-LITREV-F001-UNCLASS-11120.

Jorgensen, Charles C. 1997. Direct Adaptive Aircraft Control Using Dynamic Cell Structure Neural Networks. NASA Technical Memorandum 112198, NASA Ames Research Center.

Lisboa, P. 2001. Industrial Use of Safety-Related Artificial Neural Networks. Health and Safety Executive Contract Research Report 327.

Martinetz, T. M. 1993. Competitive Hebbian Learning Rule Forms Perfectly Topology Preserving Maps. In *Proceedings of International Conference on Artificial Neural Networks (ICANN)* 427-434. Amsterdam:Springer.

McGarry, Kenneth, John Tait, Stefan Wermter, and John McIntyre. 1999. Rule-Extraction from Radial Basis Function Networks. In *Proceedings of International Conference on Artificial Neural Networks* 1:613-618. Edinburgh, Scotland.

McGarry, Kenneth, Stefan Wermter and John Macintyre. 2001. The Extraction and Comparison of Knowledge from Local Function Networks. *International Journal of Computational Intelligence and Applications* 1(3): 369-382.

Pecheur, Charles. 2000.Verification and Validation of Autonomy Software at NASA. NASA/TM 2000-209602.

Pecheur, Charles and Stacy Nelson. 2002. V&V of Advanced Systems at NASA.

Rodrigues, Pedro, José Félix Costa, and Hava T. Siegelmann. 2001. Verifying Properties of Neural Networks. IWANN (1) 2001: 158-165.

Setiono R., W. K. Leow, and J. M. Zurada. 2002. Extraction of Rules from Artificial Neural Networks for Nonlinear Regression. *IEEE Transactions on Neural Networks* 13(3): 564-577

Tickle, Alan B.; R. Andrews; M. Golea; and J. Diederich. 1998. The Truth is in There: Directions and Challenges in Extracting Rules from Trained Artificial Neural Networks.

Thrun, S. 1995. Extracting Rules from Artificial Neural Networks with Distributed Representations. In *Advances in Neural Information Processing Systems (NIPS)* 7, eds G. Tesauro, D. Touretzky, and T. Leen. Cambridge, MA: MIT Press.

Towell, G and J. Shavlik. 1993. The Extraction of Refined Rules from Knowledge Based Neural Networks. *Machine Learning* 13(1):71-101.

Chapter 9

AUTOMATED TEST GENERATION FOR TESTING NEURAL NETWORK SYSTEMS

Brian J. Taylor
Institute for Scientific Research, Inc.

1. INTRODUCTION

Neural networks in control systems present a difficult problem for testing: generation of sufficient sets of data for adequate test coverage. Commonly, the neural network developer has a set of data of which upward of 75% is used to train the network. This usually leaves less than 25% of the remaining dataset for neural network evaluation. Often, that is not enough to conduct an in-depth study of the network and certify it for safety- and mission-critical systems.

This chapter presents a test generation algorithm that will facilitate this need and improve upon the many different ways the neural network system is evaluated. From a system integration perspective, the algorithm can increase the size of the available data for testing, and at a reduced cost from other forms of generating data. Based on user settings, the algorithm could be used to find interesting pieces of new data to exercise the system in ways which normal data generation would not. Other forms of testing are possible with the algorithm including reliability assessment, stress testing, and sensitivity analysis. To facilitate evaluation of the tool itself, a MATLAB implementation was created called the Automated Test Trajectory Generator.

Test data generation is defined as a technique that assists in the generation of test data. These can include system simulations that allow recording of data for later usage, pieces of software that generate random sequences of data, or more sophisticated algorithms that are directed in specific ways to create test data.

Generation algorithms, and test data generation tools especially, have a purpose of reducing the testing time by aiding a system developer in generating a large volume of test data.

Several different types of test generators exist but three basic ones are: random test data generators, pathwise generators and data specification systems. Data specification systems generate test data from a language that describes the input data. Pathwise test data generators work to generate test data that follows an execution path throughout the program. Random test data generators perform exactly as they sound, generating data in a random fashion.

One technique that is lacking in data generation is the development of methods to create continuous sets of data. Continuous data (for this chapter, referred to as trajectories) can be time-dependent, previous value dependent, or some combination thereof. In the case of control systems, continuous data is necessary to fully test how the system performs.

When neural networks are placed within the control system, they require being tested with continuous data as well. That requirement was the primary thrust of the development of the Automated Test Trajectory Generation (ATTG) algorithm.

If the neural network was not in a control system, random data generation might work to assist in testing. Due to the nature of the data, the neural network should be exercised with trajectories rather than disjoint data points. The use of trajectories is even more critical if the neural network learns from data trajectories rather than single-point data.

Within the IVVNN methodology, the algorithm fits into the investigation of steps required for the testing of neural network systems. The traditional testing approach taken by many neural network developers is the brute-force method where the network undergoes testing, testing, and more testing. Based on prior experience, this level of testing may fail because of the likelihood that inadequate test data is available. This situation leads to the consideration of data generation techniques, and this algorithm seems like a good candidate. Evaluation of the technique will be done against the intelligent flight control system (IFCS).

In particular, three main questions will be evaluated for this work:

1. Can this test data generation technique be applied to the non-linear IFCS flight data to produce sets of new data that are meaningful?
2. Can the ATTG tool be improved to facilitate the investigation of question 1?
3. How would a verification and validation (V&V) practitioner make use of test data generation to apply to the testing of neural networks?

2. DETAILS OF THE AUTOMATED TEST TRAJECTORY GENERATION ALGORITHM

The test generation technique draws upon prior work conducted at the West Virginia University under the guidance of Dr. Bojan Cukic for completion of a Master's Thesis with the then Department of Computer Science and Electrical Engineering. During that time, the technique was programmed as a command-line interface (CLI) tool which was hard-coded to work on a special case: a sensor failure detection, identification, and accommodation flight control scheme [Taylor 1999; Napolitano 1999].

The possible improvements to test data generation, offered by the step-by-step process of the ATTG, were significant for purposes of providing improvement in the evaluation and analysis of control systems, especially in regards to neural network systems. The test case used throughout this chapter, the IFCS first generation (GEN1) flight control system, makes use of two neural network systems, each of which can benefit from usage of the test data generation technique.

For the pre-trained neural network (PTNN) system, a significant amount of training data is available from which the PTNN was developed. However, this data is collected as single-point data of generally disconnected points in the flight envelope. While the PTNN can be tested against each of these single points, the training-testing data is not set up to enable testing across a continuous range.

As the PTNN undergoes system integration testing, the data applied to it is continuous in nature, originating from aircraft states and measurements generated in real-time from either a hardware-in-the-loop simulation or another sophisticated high-fidelity simulation. A test data generation scheme, as described in this chapter, would aid in the integration level testing by providing an ability to generate additional continuous data, at a reduced cost by reducing the need for piloted simulations.

The dynamic cell structure (DCS) network experiences a similar need for integration testing and a different need in regards to studying its online adaptive learning. Since the DCS network will be adapting in real-time, researchers would like to feel comfortable that given different sets of test data, the network will adapt in an acceptable manner. The set of data generated from piloted simulations may not be enough to achieve that level of confidence. This algorithm can offer the DCS developers an option.

Because one of the IVVNN methodology goals is the creation of guidance to aid the V&V practitioner with neural network systems, the ATTG needed to undergo several improvements to prepare it for generating input into the methodology development. It needed to change to accommodate the different kinds of IFCS flight data so that the application of the technique to the PTNN and DCS can be documented and used to improve the IVVNN guidance. The following subsections detail the test generation algorithm and the modification made to the ATTG to facilitate its usage upon IFCS.

2.1   Description of the Algorithm

This algorithm works by expanding an existing set of test trajectories into a larger set. Here, a trajectory is defined as a sequence of continuous data across varying time. The test trajectories must have the characteristic of being separable into independent and dependent variables. The independent variables are clustered into coarse grain regions of the operational profile, and their corresponding dependent variables are placed into their own clusters based upon the results of the independent clustering.

Regressive models are then developed to describe these clustered regions and the relationships between the independent clusters and the dependent clusters. Each model in turn acts as a predictor for its particular region of the operational profile.

Note that in the use of regression to predict new trajectories, an assumption is made that the trajectories undergoing generation can be considered random variables that are describable by some function. A second assumption is that within the clustered sections of the operational profile, the mathematical independent variables can be fitted via regression to the random dependent variables that make up the corresponding test trajectories of the cluster implying a need for relatively strong correlation.

The algorithm can be thought of as a function that transforms one set of inputs that can be controlled into a set of trajectories that define the operational profile for the system that cannot be controlled. A mapping of the independent variables into regions of the system input space will occur. Once created, the models will be able to generate several new trajectories in the input space that are then used for testing.

2.1.1   Collect Data

Collection of the test data that undergoes this generation process can be done from various sources, such as data collected from actual system usage or from data retrieved via a system simulator.

Because the regressive models require independent-dependent variable relationships, the collected data should consist of the intended test trajectories to be expanded, along with additional variables that either help to create the trajectories or help to define them. The sample trajectories satisfy the dependent variable need and in some cases may contain several parameters, with each parameter consisting of a series of data. The additional variables will fulfill the role of the independent variables and must contain the same size of data as the trajectories.

Two requirements for proper operation of the regressive models are that the additional variables have some correlation to the test trajectories and that they be mathematical variables. For example, if the trajectories for a system define an airplane's flight path, pilot inputs would qualify as additional variables. If the trajectories described a chemical reaction, additional variables could be the amount of reactants used and temperature variation during the process. Since these variables will later be perturbed in the algorithm, it should make sense that they can be altered in a controllable manner. If the independent variables themselves depend upon the trajectories, no prediction of new trajectories will be possible.

2.1.2   Processing the Data

Depending upon the data collected, some processing of the data may be required before it can be used by the model generation routines. For the clustering algorithm to work correctly, all data sets should contain the same length of data points. This can be accomplished by truncating data sets to the size of the smallest data set. If truncation would lose too much data, other possibilities include eliminating shorter data sets or interpolation of the data to increase the size of the shorter sequences.

Conversion of the data may also be required if the test trajectories have been collected from sources using different units of measurement. This does not mean normalizing the different components of a trajectory, but normalizing any differences in measurement units between trajectories. This might occur if trajectories are recorded on different systems or perhaps even across different days.

If noise is part of the collected data, noise removal by filtering should be done as part of the data processing. Several well-known noise-filtering algorithms exist from the area of signal processing. These algorithms can consist of smoothing filters that will attempt to average out spikes in the data due to noise.

2.1.3   Clustering the Data

If testing of a system is directed by the operational profile, failures that are likely to occur during normal operation are detected based upon how often they are used. Lyu [1996] discusses two ways that the operational profile test selection can be done: coarse grain and fine grain. Coarse grain testing is the process of selecting a region or cluster of the operational profile while fine grain testing is the process of selecting tests from within the coarse cluster. While the coarse grain guides the test selection, fine grain testing requires several different elements from within the coarse grain region.

Since the goal of the entire approach is to develop test trajectories, it is useful to separate parts of the controllable variables into clusters that will allow the generation algorithm to predict new trajectories within a coarse input domain region. By applying clustering techniques to the independent variables, division of the test trajectories into the coarse grain regions of the operational profile is done simultaneously.

Once a cluster has been determined, the centroid for each group can be found and then used by the regressive models. The centroid is defined as the median value of all data contained within the cluster. The basic steps for a trajectory-clustering algorithm (dealing with the independent and dependent variables) would consist of the following:

1. Acquire a set of test trajectories
2. Identify the independent and dependent variables
3. Select, from amongst the independent variables, data that can be used to perform the clustering
4. Transform these variables, if necessary
5. Select a distance measure
6. Select a clustering technique and a desired number of clusters.
7. Perform clustering
8. Select a representative component from each cluster
9. Interpret results
10. Change variables, clustering technique, number of clusters, etc.
11. Repeat steps 3 to 9 until results are acceptable

2.1.4   Variable Selection

The independent variables that correlate to a trajectory will be the parameters that guide the clustering process. If several parameters exist, some may have a greater impact on the clustering process than others. Less important parameters should be ignored as they can increase the cost of the process.

The selection of parameters to use for clustering can be done with analysis techniques like principle component analysis (PCA) and multivariate analysis. These techniques can identify variables with higher statistical significance, which should be included in the clustering process. For example, characteristics of important parameters are their significance to the trajectory and their amount of variance. Low variance will not provide a distinguishing metric between trajectories and have little impact on clustering.

No limit is imposed on the number of variables used, but it is suggested that the clustering process uses fewer, as opposed to more, variables when possible. Larger number of variables can slow the clustering process down. The criteria, which designates an appropriate number, is influenced by the available processing power of the computer being used to generate the trajectories. Memory and processor limitations would have more of an impact for a desktop, but probably not for a high-end unit.

2.1.5   Transforming the Data

Data scaling may be applied if the parameters are linear in nature and have widely varying relative values or are spread across different dimensional units. Such a scenario may occur if multiple parameters are used in the clustering and one parameter uses measurements in feet while a second uses measurements in seconds. These two parameters have little relation to each other and scaling them to use non-dimensional units will help the clustering process. Scaling should not be applied to data with non-linear parameters as the scaling can remove this non-linearity. Three common techniques used to scale data are normalizing to zero mean and unit variance, range normalization, and percentile normalization.

Normalizing to zero mean and unit variance forces each value of the data sequence to fall within a uniform distribution centered around zero. Given a series of data $X \in \{x_1, x_2,..., x_k\}$, the ith value x_i' is scaled by

$$x_i' = \frac{x_i - \bar{x}}{\sigma}$$

(9.1)

where $\bar{x}$ is the measured mean and σ is the standard deviation.

Range normalization transforms a series of data from $[x_{min}, x_{max}]$ so that each data point falls in the range $[0, 1]$. The scaling formula is

$$x_i' = \frac{x_i - x_{min}}{x_{max} - x_{min}}$$

(9.2)

x_{min} and x_{max} are the minimum and maximum values that make up the series of data. A problem with the range normalization approach is that data outliers of extreme ranges will have a major influence on the min and max values causing poor normalization. The next scaling technique works better under those circumstances.

Percentile normalization performs very similarly to range normalization except that data is transformed so that 95% of the data points making up X fall between 0 and 1. With this technique, data outliers who will fall above 97.5% or below 2.5% of the average value will not affect the normalization process. The data is scaled by

$$x_i{}' = \frac{x_i - x_{2.5}}{x_{97.5} - x_{2.5}}$$

(9.3)

2.1.6   Distance Metrics

A standard way of expressing relationships of trajectories in a cluster is through a distance metric between those trajectories [Hartigan 1975]. The distance metric is calculated over an n-dimensional space where n represents the number of chosen parameters used to describe a trajectory. This metric is then used to identify which group a trajectory belongs to by determining how close it is to the group centroid. The distance metric selection is just as important as the selection of which variables are to be used to perform the clustering. One distance metric may perform well at distinguishing between trajectories in the cluster while another distance metric may include every single trajectory.

The most commonly used distance metric is Euclidean distance. Euclidean distance is simply the distance, d, between two trajectories across the entire sequence of data.

Assuming that a trajectory is defined as $X\{x_1, x_2, ..., x_k\}$, then the distance between two trajectories, x and y, is given by:

$$d = \left[\sum_{i=1}^{k} (x_i - y_i)^2 \right]^{\frac{1}{2}}$$

(9.4)

where the distance squared between each parameter of a trajectory is calculated. If the trajectories are n dimensional, the distance metric changes to:

$$d = \left\{ \sum_{i=1}^{k} \left[(x_{1_i} - y_{1_i})^2 + (x_{2_i} - y_{2_i})^2 + \cdots + (x_{n_i} - y_{n_i})^2 \right] \right\}^{\frac{1}{2}}$$

(9.5)

A variation on Euclidean Distance is the Weighted Euclidean Distance. This distance metric applies a weighted value a_i to each parameter based upon that parameters significance.

$$d = \left[\sum_{i=1}^{k} a_i (x_i - y_i)^2 \right]^{\frac{1}{2}} \qquad (9.6)$$

where a_i, $i = 1, 2, ..., n$, is the chosen weight for the respective parameter. The weighted distance metric can be used if the parameters have not been scaled yet or to give more control over how the clustering algorithm will perform based on a priori knowledge [Hartigan 1975].

Another suggested distance metric is the Chi-Square distance. This metric is primarily used in distribution fitting. Before this metric is used, each individual parameter, x_i, must be normalized in order to prevent parameters with lower values from having higher weights.

$$d = \sum_{i=1}^{k} \frac{(x_i - y_i)^2}{x_i} \qquad (9.7)$$

2.1.7   Clustering Techniques

Clustering techniques fall into one of two categories: hierarchical and non hierarchical. In non-hierarchical techniques, trajectories are assigned into k arbitrary clusters until the intragroup variances of each cluster reach a minimum. The value of k can be user specified.

In hierarchical techniques, the collection of trajectories is divided into n desired groups. Hierarchical techniques may be either agglomerative or divisive. With agglomerative techniques each trajectory is separated into its own cluster. Neighboring clusters are merged together based upon distance metrics until the desired n groups are attained. Divisive techniques start with all trajectories in one cluster. The cluster is then divided until it reaches the desired number of n clusters.

2.1.8   Interpreting the Results

The number of trajectories in each cluster will serve as a measure of coarseness of the regions of the operational profile. A typical cluster generally should have around 4 or 5 trajectories within it. If no trajectory was omitted from the cluster, the number of expected clusters could be increased or reduced. While it can happen that each cluster contains only one trajectory, having more than one per cluster will allow for better model fitting for that particular cluster. If there are obvious trajectories existing as outliers of the cluster, the clustering technique should probably be refined. Any outliers will skew the model development results.

2.1.9   Selecting a Representative Trajectory

After the clustering has been performed, a set of independent variables should be selected that serves as the average of the cluster. Since the clustering was performed upon independent variables, the component selected should be the sequence of data that lies closest to the centroid of the cluster based upon the chosen distance measure.

After the set of independent variables have been selected, the trajectory associated with this set becomes the representative trajectory. The purpose of the representative trajectory will be to give the regressive models the best selection that they can use to develop new trajectories within the cluster. The representative trajectory serves to define the cluster by labeling the coarse region of the input domain.

2.1.10   Developing a Model

Ideally, whatever model is chosen should be of much less complexity than the software component being tested. Use of various regressive models is suggested, including simple linear, multiple linear, autoregressive moving average (ARMA), and non-linear models. The linear models have shown to be a simplistic approach achieving short computational time. The important point to remember is that the success of the models will be determined by the acceptability rate determined by the acceptance testing of the data being generated.

In order to choose the best model, the algorithm should develop several different models and try different combinations of input data. For example, for each representative trajectory, a simple linear model could be developed for one of many different independent variables. The same can be done for combinations of independent variables for the multiple-linear regressive model. By exhaustively trying combinations of independent-dependent variables, the algorithm can vote to choose which model works the best for that particular cluster of trajectories. This also prevents the algorithm from being *locked* into any one type of regressive model across the entire domain. As regions of the operational profile change, the models are allowed to adapt to that part of the domain.

2.1.11 Discriminant Analysis

When attempting to determine which variables are the most significant for use in the regressive models, discriminant analysis may need to be considered. Many techniques for discriminant analysis exist, such as PCA and multivariate analysis. PCA looks at the correlations between the independent and dependent data. By using a correlation matrix, PCA assigns weights to variables that have a higher correlation to the dependent data. The higher the weight, the more significant the variable will be. The variables chosen for the models should represent the most significant parameters.

If multiple-linear regression is chosen, it is suggested that only models using two, three, or four variables be used. Additional variables will not increase prediction significantly and will decrease time efficiency and add unnecessary complexity.

2.1.12 Smoothing

Application of a smoothing function to the final results of the model may be applied to remove sharp edges in the model output. The easiest form of smoothing is averaging the trajectory. Under averaging, a point of data is added to neighbors on both sides of the data point and divided by n, the number of data points added together.

2.1.13 Cross Correlation Analysis

The advantage of using the trajectory closest to the centroid to represent the cluster becomes apparent when a decision has to be made about choosing the best regressive model. After a regressive model is constructed, the model can be applied to the remaining trajectories in the cluster. The regressive model's predicted output to these unused trajectories can then be directly compared to the actual trajectories themselves through the use of correlation analysis to determine the accuracy of the models.

Cross-correlation analysis looks at the relationship between two sequences of data through a correlation coefficient, r. The stronger the relationship, the higher the value of the coefficient. The equation for correlation is given by:

$$r = \frac{\sum XY - \frac{(\sum X)(\sum Y)}{n}}{\sqrt{\left[\sum X^2 - \frac{(\sum X)^2}{n}\right]\left[\sum Y^2 - \frac{(\sum Y)^2}{n}\right]}} \quad (9.8)$$

where X is the summation of all data points in X, XY is the summation of the product of all data points in X and Y, and n is the total number of data points.

The values of r can range from +1.00 to -1.00 with a perfect relationship occurring at 1.00 and a perfect inverse relationship occurring at -1.00. Values for r between 0.00 and 1.00 indicate that some relationship exists but that it is not perfect. As r approaches 1.00 the relationship between the two trajectories becomes stronger.

After a model has been developed, it is then applied to each of the remaining trajectories in the cluster. The model's predicted output is then compared against the actual recorded rates through cross-correlation. This will result in a table of correlation values for each model against each trajectory in the cluster.

2.1.14   Choosing the Best Model

The choice of the best model is dependent upon the results of the correlation analysis from each model and the total computation time per model. An equation describing the selection can be written as

$$P = \overline{T}_{model} + e^{(1.0 - \overline{cor}_{model}) \cdot 10} \quad (9.9)$$

where $\overline{T}_{model}$ represents the average time to build a particular regressive model, and $\overline{cor}_{model}$ represents the average correlation of that model. P is then a quantifiable measurement of the value of the particular regressive model approach towards the prediction within the cluster. This equation has smaller values for regressive models that can be built faster and for regressive models that have higher correlations between the predicted and recorded trajectories. Model selection is then made by choosing the regressive model with the smallest value of P.

2.1.15   Perturbing the Original Data

By perturbing the original parameters used as independent variables in the regressive models, the system is able to generate predictions from the new input. The amount of newly generated trajectories is then related to the amount of new independent variables that can be perturbed. Any trajectories within a cluster are available to undergo perturbation, even the representative component.

How the original data is perturbed is very important. It cannot be modified too much, lest the data becomes irrelevant to the models just developed. Provided that the time series data resembles multiple step functions, there are various ways to perturb the data.

One method is to multiply the original data by some value. This keeps a consistent rate of change but modifies the amplitudes of the time series data. The value by which the original data is multiplied should not be so large that the perturbed data would no longer correspond to trajectories inside the cluster. Perturbation via multiplication should probably keep the new data within ±5% of the original data.

A second method is to modify the duration of some value in the data sequence while keeping consistent values for the amplitudes.

2.1.16   Application of the Model

After a new set of data has been generated, this data is then given to the model for prediction of new test data. While this is the simplest module, care must be taken to ensure that all model descriptions, including coefficients, have been stored for later use. As was done with the model generation, a smoothing function can be applied here to the regressive model output.

2.1.17   Acceptability Rules

One of the more important parts of the algorithm is to determine if the newly created test data actually qualifies as acceptable data. A set of rules describing acceptable trajectories can be used against the predicted trajectories to determine valid tests. After each iteration of the algorithm, the rules are applied to both the output trajectories predicted by the models and the perturbed independent variables used for those models.

The acceptability rate of the generated trajectories can guide the generation process as well as give an indication to how successful the approach is. If a certain perturbation process produces higher acceptability rates, that process could be further used with minor modifications as needed during each iteration. Perturbations producing bad results, of course, would be avoided. This implies a relationship between the perturbation and acceptability modules.

One guide to developing acceptability rules upon the perturbed input can be the distance metric used for the clustering process. Since the clustering was performed upon the independent variables, the distance between the perturbed data and the cluster centroid can decide if the perturbed data falls within the cluster. Perturbations, which produce new values falling outside the cluster, are discarded.

Acceptability rules defined to analyze the regressive model outputs can be based upon the correlation of the output trajectories to the trajectory defined as the representative component for the cluster undergoing regression. Since this trajectory acts as the classification of the coarse grain input, predictive trajectories that fall outside of a 70% correlation could be rejected as falling outside of the coarse grain region.

Another possible area of regressive output rules are those that are system specific. These rules would identify any trajectories or perturbed independent variables that violate some definition of the input domain, perhaps by exceeding minimum or maximum values. These rules can look at anything from slope analysis of the trajectories to comparisons of global minimums and maximums.

2.2   Example Tool Usage Results

For testing the suitability of the algorithm, two different data sets were used. The first was an original set of data that had been used to create the first implementation of the test tool. The second was a set of data that was generated from a simulation used by the IFCS program.

2.2.1   Usage of the ATTG Algorithm on SFDIA Flight Data

The SFDIA data set comes from a project between ISR, WVU, and the NASA DFRC. This data set is a collection of independent variables (pilot inputs of pitch, yaw, and roll, and aircraft speed, Mach) and dependent variables (aircraft state measurements of P, Q, and R). The test data available was completely generated through the usage of the Aviator Visual Design Simulator flight simulation program.

Since the original version of the ATTG was written to produce extra sets of SFDIA test data, this data was used for tool testing purposes throughout the ATTG's re-design and development.

The SFDIA data was collected in a manner that lent itself to pre-clustering of the data sets. Each of these pre-clusters was a collection of roughly 15 sets of data from a reasonably consistent performance of an aircraft maneuver. Because of this, the ATTG was only able to perform minor improvements to the clusters by eliminating outliers.

This was one of the differences with the new ATTG. When a data set was read in, the ATTG performed clustering within this pre-cluster, often times separating the pre-cluster into three to four good clusters. This meant that the ATTG was differentiating the same consistent maneuvers into finer, more closely related maneuvers. This consequently led to better regressive model development over the prior implementation and better acceptability results.

Results from applying the CLI version of the ATTG to the SFDIA data can be found in "Regressive Model Approach to the Generation of Test Trajectories" [Taylor 1999]. Since the GUI ATTG matched the results from the CLI ATTG, no further results are presented here for brevity.

2.2.2 Usage of the ATTG Algorithm on IFCS Flight Data

The IFCS flight data is a collection of independent variables (eight sensor readings including mach, altitude, alpha, beta, stabilator deflection, aileron deflection, canard deflection, and rudder deflection) and dependent variables (26 stability and control derivatives). The NASA DFRC-developed F-15 flight simulator generated the available data.

There were several problems encountered in applying the ATTG to the IFCS flight data. Briefly, these included:

1. Handling of the IFCS validity flags and their consequences on generating data
2. Handling a single IFCS data set per cluster
3. Dealing with partially controllable independent variables
4. Dealing with different test data sets

Problem 1 - Handling of the IFCS Validity Flags

The IFCS data set is intended as a collection of data used to train the DCS neural network. For space consideration, details on the workings of the DCS neural network are not presented here, but additional information can be found in "Direct Adaptive Aircraft Control Using Dynamic Cell Structure Neural Networks" and the DC neural network report for the IFC program [Jorgensen 1997; ISR 2001].

The IFCS data set is composed of three classifications of data: sensor readings, stability and control derivative deltas, and stability and control derivative delta validity flags. The sensor values are the independent variables for the system. The DCS networks use these for training, but they are not the values that the DCS networks recall. The sensor values work well as the independent variables within the ATTG tool.

The stability and control derivative deltas (or just derivative deltas) are generated by another software component, the parameter identification (PID) system. The derivative deltas are the important dependent variables that are used by the DCS networks to train upon.

The derivative validity flags are an indication of the confidence the PID has in the values it is generating. In this way, the validity flags act as an initial check, or even run-time monitor, on the PID output. When the flag is a one, the derivative delta is considered valid and should be used by the DCS for training. When the flag is a zero, the derivative delta is considered non-confident and the DCS does not use the value for training.

This presents the first problem. The ATTG algorithm should not be used to estimate the validity flags. Statistical generation of the validity flags would have no meaning within newly created data sets. However, the ATTG should only generate data that the PID has considered valid - it would do V&V personnel no good to generate data that is considered invalid by the system.

This leads to one possible solution: pre-process the IFCS data by identifying slices within the dependent data which are considered valid, and only use these valid segments from which to generate models and new data.

The solution is complicated though by the nature of the usage of the dependent data by the DCS networks. Each DCS network takes in multiple dependent variables for training. For example, the Cz DCS network uses Cza, Czdc, and Czds as dependent variables. These variables have to be presented at the same time and synchronized for the same time because they utilize the same independent variables (the sensor data). So any slices that are created through the pre-processing need to be a slice across all of the dependent variables together.

This could lead to difficulty in model fitting because for any given dependent variable there may be sections within the slice that contain invalid data (because the corresponding dependent variables are valid during this section).

Problem 2 - Handling a Single IFCS Data Set Per Cluster

Problem 2 occurs because each IFCS data set is usually one maneuver across a time of 60+ seconds, with some maneuvers extending beyond several minutes. Obtaining consistent maneuvers over long periods of time is difficult because human pilots can be highly non-deterministic. This implies that each set of collected data for a maneuver will reside within its own cluster. If not, then the collected data within a cluster for a particular maneuver may be so different between each instance of that maneuver that good regressive models cannot be made to fit the entire cluster.

Problem 3 - Dealing with Partially Controllable Independent Variables

The third problem is a relatively minor problem, but is something that should be considered and addressed. For a proper perturbation of the independent variables, the variables are assumed to be controllable. By this it is meant that the variables are somehow specifically selected or chosen. For example, a pilot's inputs are a function of a pilot's desires; the motion of controlling an aircraft is repeatable and generally by design.

With the IFCS data, the independent variables are sensor readings describing the state of the aircraft. These include Mach, altitude, alpha (angle of attack) and beta (sideslip angle). While the pilot can influence each of these (Mach - throttle control, altitude, alpha, beta - stick inputs), it could be argued that these variables do not necessarily lend themselves to perturbation. They are not true controllable variables because they are not selected or chosen; they are measurements from the results of other selected or chosen variables.

For the purposes of this experiment they were chosen anyway. However, perturbations placed upon these variables should be well understood. Perturbations such as adding random noise would be acceptable, while modifying them to resemble a step function or application of a non-linear multiplication may not.

Problem 4 - Dealing with Different Test Data Sets

The fourth problem is less of a problem and more of an important consideration. As there are five DCS networks within the IFCS system, and each network requires a different set of independent-dependent inputs for training, the ATTG must be applied five different times to generate data for each network. It is not configured to automatically generate subsets of data - the ATTG user must do this manually.

2.2.3   Example from Applying ATTG to IFCS Flight Data

There was not enough time within the schedule for this subtask to complete an exhaustive application of the ATTG tool to the IFCS data. It is expected that during later tasks, the tool can be re-applied to IFCS data to garner better results.

There was enough time to use a single set of flight data that was generated by a NASA DFRC simulation with the ATTG tool. Since there are five DCS networks, the Cz network was chosen for data generation. The

Cz network has four independent variables (mach, altitude, alpha, and beta) and three dependent variables (Cza_delta, Czdc_delta, Czds_delta).

2.2.4   Cluster Results

As explained in the description of the problems encountered when applying the ATTG algorithm to the IFCS data, each cluster only includes a single member. Therefore no real clustering was performed on the IFCS data.

2.2.5   Regressive Model Results

Each dependent variable had 57 models created for the single cluster. Predictions for Cza_delta were very good with an average correlation usually around 90% with real data. The linear and ARMA models were able to achieve above 90% for some situations. Predictions for Czdc_delta had equally similar results with most of the models achieving between the upper 80% to lower 90% cross-correlation. As expected, Czds_delta was the worst because it never contained valid data, and therefore model fits were usually in the mid-30% to low 40% range.

2.2.6   Best Regressive Model Results

Since there was only one cluster, there were only three best models selected, one for C_{za}_delta, C_{zdc}_delta, and C_{zds}_delta.

Table 9-1. Selection of the Best Model for Each Dependent Variable

Dependent Variable	Best Model to Predict Variable
C_{za}_delta	ARMA {mach_avg_new}
C_{zdc}_delta	ARMA {alpha_avg_new}
C_{zds}_delta	ARMA {alpha_avg_new}

New Generated Flight Data

New independent variables were created by applying a randomly distributed white noise of 2% to the original set of independent variables. This new data was then fed into the regressive models and new dependent variables were generated as indicated in the following examples.

Cza, as shown in Fig. 9-1 had the best visual and acceptability results.

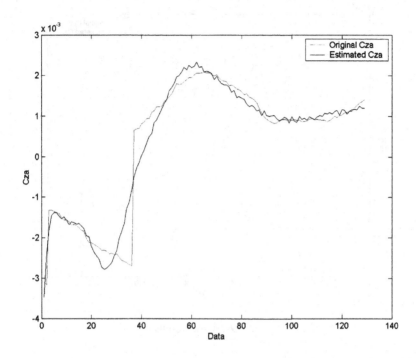

Figure 9-1. Cza Results

Czdc, as shown in Fig. 9-2, while having high correlations (around 90% for the regressive models) did not produce as acceptable a visual result. As expected, the Czdc acceptability was quite low.

The results for Czds, as shown in Fig. 9-3, are at first disappointing visually, but they are explained by the fact that Czds is never considered *valid* within the IFCS system, and so building a model to predict the Czds data would not be beneficial in the first place. The amount of variance seen within Czds is a reason for it being considered invalid by the IFCS system and a reason why the regressive models were not able to fit the data very well.

2.3   How the Algorithm is Useful to V&V Practitioners

The algorithm has many potential uses, some of which are briefly discussed here. It can create new data for general testing purposes, can assist in the specific creation of larges sets of similar data for sensitivity analysis or

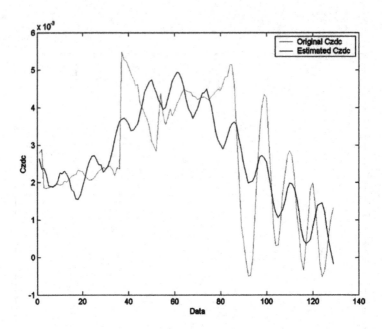

Figure 9-2. Czdc Results

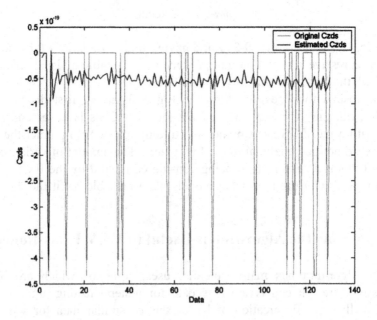

Figure 9-3. Czds Results

large sets of widely different data for anomalous testing, and is an overall aid in brute force testing or reliability assessment.

2.3.1 Creation of New Data

One of the expected problems facing V&V practitioners is the lack of available test data to test a system with neural networks. In fact, the V&V practitioner may be presented with only the exact same data used to train/test the neural network. The test generator will offer the ability to take those data sets and create additional data sets.

In some situations, the generation algorithm can fit the original data well and thus be able to produce very similar sets of new data. But from experience, what is more common is slightly poor fitting due to nonlinearities within the data. In those situations, the model can share similar trajectory characteristics like spiking trends and general shape, but it is not a perfect fit. Yet this might be the strength of the algorithm.

Because of the difficulty in matching nonlinear data, the model is close, but not exact. This imprecision offers the ability to create new data that is different and perhaps entirely new to the existing neural network knowledge.

The created data sets can have any number of different characteristics. The V&V practitioner can choose to create good approximations with the regressive models and allow for small perturbations of the independent variables to perform a sensitivity analysis on the neural network system.

Consider Fig. 9-4. These are the results of building a predictive model describing the stability and control derivative Cma. The model was composed of the independent variables alpha, beta, altitude, and Mach number. This derivative is highly influenced by the independent variable *alpha*, or the angle of attack of the aircraft. In the figure, the original Cma value is represented in red. The predictive model, applied with no perturbation on any of the independent variables, is represented in blue. To evaluate the change in the output of the predictive model given small changes to alpha, three perturbations were applied to alpha. These were merely multiplication by constant values of 1.1, 1.3, and 1.5.

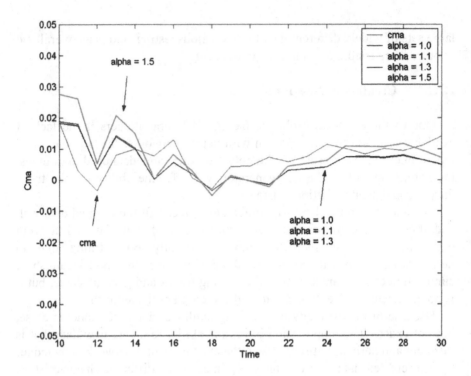

Figure 9-4. Example of Sensitivity Test Generation

The small constants applied to alpha produced similar trajectories. It wasn't until alpha was modified by a 50% change that the generated trajectory started to change. This gives the ability to create data that is very similar, yet have a small enough difference to examine how the network will perform. It is possible that small changes between test trajectories can show interesting behavior patterns of the neural network. This may lead to more direct testing efforts or re-evaluation of the network's learning and to a better understanding of how it will handle data within the system.

2.3.2   Anomalous Data Evaluation

Another approach a V&V practitioner may desire is to create imperfect regressive models or to widely perturb the independent data so as to create significantly different test sets with lower statistical relationship to the original data. This technique may introduce the neural network to entirely new sets of test data, even test data that may not totally exist within the operational profile of the system. Such data could allow the V&V practitioner to examine how the system will react to anomalous data. Does the neural network system handle anomalous data and can it operate correctly given such data?

Fig. 9-5 depicts the test generation algorithm modeling of the Cnda derivative. In this instance, the best model chosen was a 4-variable multiple-linear regression built using the independent variables of alpha, beta, altitude, and mach. The model lacks some of the spiking characteristics of the original signal and is perhaps a suitable candidate for creating drastically different data sets for testing.

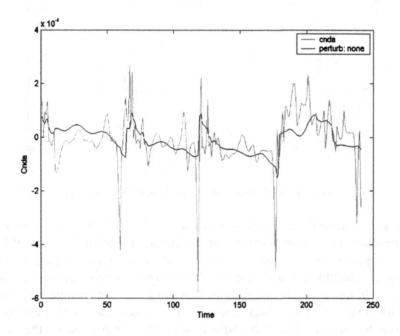

Figure 9-5. Predictive Model for the Cnda Derivative

Figs. 9-6 through 9-9 show some of the possible combinations that can be selected with the perturbations on the independent variables to give different data sets.

In Fig. 9-6, alpha has been augmented with a 2% random noise across its entire trajectory. None of the other independent variables were modified. Combining this alpha with the unmodified beta, altitude, and Mach, the multiple-linear regressive model generated a slightly noisy signal. Some of the spiking characteristics of the original Cnda begin to appear with this augmented data.

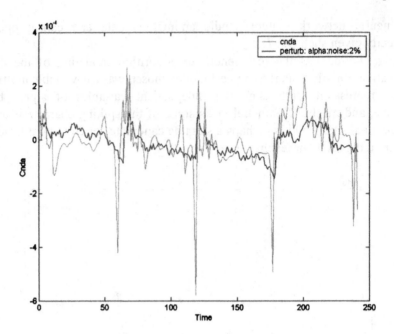

Figure 9-6. Results from Introducing Random Noise on Alpha

Fig. 9-7 (note the different y-axis scale from other figures) shows what happens when the independent variable, altitude, is modified to account for a 0.05% random noise. The high amount of variance now apparent in the newly generated trajectory indicates the close reliance the regressive model has on altitude and demonstrates how much Cnda can change with small perturbations. But this high amount of variance may be something of interest to the practitioner because it will allow inspection of the neural network should it receive such a signal during operation. The practitioner may want to investigate how an adaptive neural network would respond to this high amount of variance, or he/she may want to see how a non-adaptive network will behave.

Changes in beta did not affect the newly generated data as much as shown in Fig. 9-8. Like the perturbations on alpha, changes in beta show up as spikes within the generated trajectory. Again, this shape of the signal may be useful during testing and analysis.

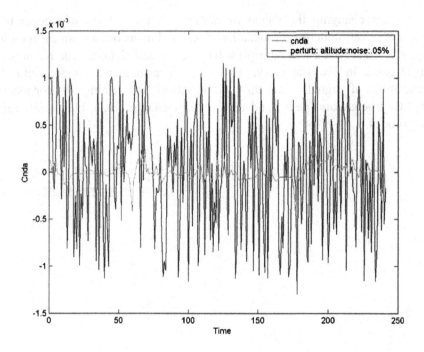

Figure 9-7. Results from Introducing Random Noise on Altitude

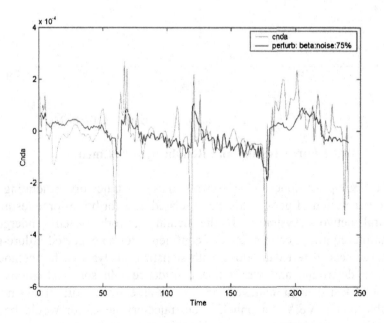

Figure 9-8. Results from Introducing Random Noise on Beta

Besides changing the signal by adding variance, the newly generated trajectories can undergo a translation along a dimension, as can be seen in Fig. 9-9. Here Mach was multiplied by a very small change. The result was an increase in the trajectory, almost as if a bias was added into it. Generation of signals like this would allow for testing of consistent trajectory behaviors (peaks and dips, rate of change, etc.), but at different magnitudes.

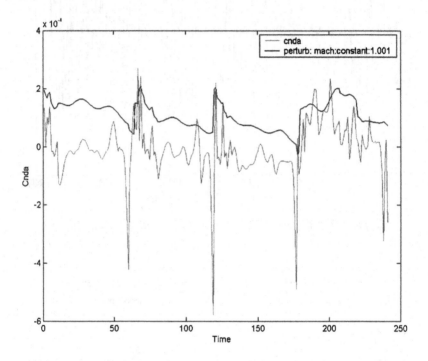

Figure 9-9. Results from Introducing a Constant Multiplier on Mach

2.3.3   Brute Force Testing and Reliability Assessment

The V&V practitioner may also want to use the trajectory-generating tool for the generation of good statistically related data for brute-force testing of a neural network system.   If the neural network system undergoing evaluation requires a certain level of confidence for an expected failure-rate, then large sets of test data along with statistical analysis is the method by which to determine and verify that confidence.   In some situations, the amount of test data to achieve that level of assessment will simply not be available to the V&V personnel.   The trajectory generator would be one option they would have to try to increase the number of test sets.

3.   SUMMARY

Three questions were investigated for this work.

1. Can this test data generation technique be applied to the non-linear IFCS flight data to produce sets of new data that are meaningful?

As the results within Section 2.3.2 show, the algorithm is applicable to the non-linear IFCS flight data and, with the usage of the ARMA models, can produce acceptable new data. The technique still requires several more iterations upon the IFCS flight data to produce better acceptable statistics. Other answers may be needed in regards to the four problems that were experienced in applying the algorithm to the data, and perhaps some of these solutions can be folded back into the algorithm itself.

2. Can the ATTG tool be improved to facilitate the investigation of Question 1?

The ATTG tool was improved and is now flexible enough to allow the generation of data from different sources, with different dimensionality, and with different sizes. This was necessary because the algorithm needs to be tested and the tool should not interfere with that process. Now that it exists as a generally easy to use GUI within MATLAB and provides improved user feedback including visual displays, it allows the algorithm to be applied and studied much more easily than it had before.

3. How would a V&V practitioner make use of test data generation to apply to the testing of neural networks?

Section 2.3 provides some discussion on the usefulness of the technique, but there are probably even more possibilities. Essentially, though, the algorithm will facilitate the application of testing and testing preparation because it provides a way to create additional test sets. These test sets can be controlled during development to allow a V&V practitioner to decide how the test sets can be used and possibly what to expect from them. The algorithm allows for the creation of very similar trajectories from original trajectories (facilitating sensitivity analysis, reliability assessment, or brute force), for creation of widely varying not-too-similar trajectories (for sensitivity analysis or stress testing), and for the creation of combinations of the two types, which may allow for discoveries within the testing process through an automated means.

REFERENCES

Hartigan, J. A. 1975. Clustering Algorithms. Yale University. Wiley & Sons.

ISR 2001. Dynamic Cell Structure Neural Network Report for the Intelligent Flight Control Program. Internal Deliverable written by the Institute for Scientific Research, Inc. for NASA Dryden Flight Research Center, Co-Op Agreement NCC4-125, January 4, 2001.

Jorgensen, Charles C. 1997. Direct Adaptive Aircraft Control Using Dynamic Cell Structure Neural Networks. NASA Technical Memorandum 112198, NASA Ames Research Center, Moffett Field, California, May.

Lyu, Michael. R. 1996. Handbook of Software Reliability Engineering. IEEE Computer Society Press. New York: McGraw-Hill.

Napolitano, M.R., Molinaro, G., Innocenti, M., Martinelli, D. 1999. A Complete Hardware Package for a Fault Tolerant Flight Control System Using On-Line Learning Neural Networks. In *Proceedings of the 1999 American Control Conference*. San Diego, CA. 4:2615-2619.

Taylor, Brian J. 1999. Regressive Model Approach to the Generation of Test Trajectories. Master's thesis, West Virginia University. Available at http://etd.wvu.edu/templates/showETD.cfm?recnum=1077.

Chapter 10

RUN-TIME ASSESSMENT OF NEURAL NETWORK CONTROL SYSTEMS

Bojan Cukic[1], Edgar Fuller[2], Martin Mladenovski[1], and Sampath Yerramalla[1]

[1]*Lane Department of Computer Science and Electrical Engineering, West Virginia University,*
[2]*Department of Mathematics, West Virginia University*

1. INTRODUCTION

Since online self-adaptive systems are characterized by continual adaptation to changing environmental conditions, the safe behavior of such systems cannot be guaranteed using traditional software validation methods. This chapter presents *run-time risk assessment methodology*, a novel methodology for validating self-adaptive software systems based on online operational monitoring and data fusion techniques.

Online operational monitoring is a multiple-monitor based validation methodology that inherits its theoretical underpinnings from the generic stability and convergence analysis of Lyapunov's theory. The output data from various monitors are fused together using *Murphy's rule based on Dempster-Shafer framework* [Murphy 1998, Murphy 1996] and *Fuzzy Inference System* to form a single measure of confidence. The confidence measure indicates whether or not the output from the self-adaptive system's learning can be trusted over time.

The presented validation technique is applied to a neural network based online self-adaptive system, the intelligent flight control system (IFCS). In this application, environmental changes include system failure modes, such as a stuck stabilator, broken aileron and/or rudder, sensor failures, etc. Even though this case study is very specific, sound theoretical foundation of the presented validation technique makes it generally applicable to assure a wide range of autonomous online self-adaptive systems with embedded soft-computing learning paradigms.

Self-organizing neural networks, introduced by Kohonen [1988] and modified by several others over the last twenty years, offer topology-preserving adaptive learning capabilities. These learning capabilities can, in theory, respond to abstractions from a much wider variety of complex data-manifolds. The significance of this is that the type of data encountered in an adaptive flight control system in general consists of complex data-manifolds.

A provably self-stabilizing neural network ensures that while the adaptive system tries to achieve its central goal, the embedded neural network may not deviate the system in an unpredictable manner towards instability due to a dramatic change in its learning state (possibly due to a system-failure). It is not known at this point whether a neural network of such capabilities exists, let alone the complicated and challenging task of proving that it is self-stabilizing in some manner for all conditions of input data [Yerramalla 2004a, Yerramalla 2004c].

This leads us to the following set of questions:

1. Is the online neural network learning algorithm self-stabilizing in some manner for certain data representations?
2. Is there a means to detect if the neural network is not stabilizing but deviating towards instability (abnormal behavior)?

Online stability monitoring is employed using multiple monitors to provide an answer to the above questions. The construction of an online stability monitor is based on rigorous mathematical stability analysis methodology - Lyapunov's direct method [Yerramalla 2004b]. The output data from various monitors are fused together using Murphy's rule based on Dempster-Shafer framework [Smets 1990] and Fuzzy Inference Engine to form a single measure of confidence. The confidence measure indicates whether or not the output from the neural network's learning can be trusted over time. The complete validation scheme is shown in Fig. 10-1 on the next page.

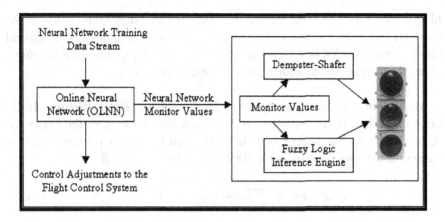

Figure 10-1. Neural Network Validation Scheme

The NASA Dryden Flight Center IFCS first generation (GEN1) contains an online learning neural network, the Dynamic Cell Structure (DCS) neural network. The purpose of the DCS network is to learn stability and control derivatives in real-time to augment the fault-tolerant flight control system onboard an F-15. The DCS network, its structure, and its learning algorithms are explained in several publications [Jorgensen 1997, Bruske 1994]. This chapter assumes the reader has an understanding of DCS operation and a basic understanding of self-organizing neural networks.

2.   RUN-TIME MONITORING AND DATA FUSION

The online learning neural network, although close to representing the input data pattern, may fail to mirror the topology of the training data, especially if the neurons representing topological and non-topological data patterns are equidistant from each other. For the software validation purpose, a single monitor may not provide sufficiently thorough understanding of the adaptation dynamics [Yerramalla 2004a]. Any online self-adaptive system is likely to encounter multi-dimensional datasets.

For most flight profiles in the IFCS, input datasets contain 32 dimensions. It is not practical to plot all 32 dimensions of the data over time and manually detect network faults. Hence, a monitoring approach is needed that can observe different aspects of the adaptation and indicate if and when the network generates faulty representations of the presented training data. This will be a way to detect whether the states of the adaptive system deviate towards instability. Consequently, multiple Lyapunov-like functions are needed to observe various aspects of the neural network to adequately monitor its the behavior during online adaptation. This is the role that run-time monitors play in the validation methodology discussed here [Yerramalla 2004a - Yerramalla 2004c]. The Lyapunov-like functions selected for run-time monitoring will be briefly described.

Definition 2.1 (Monitor #1, Best Matching Unit (BMU) Error). BMU Error is the Euclidean distance between each data element of the presented input (training) data pattern $m \in M \subset R^D$ and its closest neuron (node) of the neural network, known as the BMU $w_{BMU}(m) \in W \subset R^D$.

$$Monitor\#1 = \sum_{m \in M} \|m - w_{BMU}(m)\| \qquad (10.1)$$

Definition 2.2 (Monitor #2, Second Best Matching Unit (SBU) Error). SBU Error is the Euclidean distance between each data element of the presented input (training) data pattern $m \in M \subset R^D$ and its second closest neuron (node) of the neural network, known as the SBU $w_{SBU}(m) \in W \subset R^D$.

$$Monitor\#2 = \sum_{m \in M} \|m - w_{SBU}(m)\| \qquad (10.2)$$

Definition 2.3 (Monitor #3, Neighborhood (NBR) Error). NBR Error is the mean Euclidean distance between each data element of the presented input (training) data pattern $m \in M \subset R^D$ and the set of neighborhood neurons (connected nodes) of the BMU of the neural network, known as the NBR-set $w_{\{NBR\}}(m, BMU) \in W \subset R^D$.

$$Monitor\#3 = \sum_{m \in M} mean\left\{\|m - w_{\{NBR\}}(m)\|\right\} \qquad (10.3)$$

Definition 2.4 (Monitor #4, Non-Neighborhood (Non-NBR) Error). Non-NBR Error is the mean Euclidean distance between each data element of the presented input (training) data pattern $m \in M \subset R^D$ and the set of laterally connected, non-neighboring neurons of the BMU of the neural network, known as the Non- NBR-set $w_{\{Non=NBR\}}(m, BMU) \in W \subset R^D$.

$$Monitor\#4 = \sum_{m \in M} mean\left\{\|m - w_{\{Non-NBR\}}(m)\|\right\} \qquad (10.4)$$

These monitors provide an estimate of how well a set of associated weights or nodes of the adaptive network are being overlaid on corresponding relative elements of the presented training data set. In other words, the monitors indicate how well the network represents the training data. However, when these monitors are deployed into the IFCS, it will be complicated to infer a reasonable measure of confidence by looking at all four monitors. Thereby, there needs to be a single confidence measure of the DCS network. To achieve this, the monitor values from the previously mentioned four monitors are combined using *Murphy's rule based on Dempster-Shafer framework* [Murphy 1998, Murphy 1996] and *Fuzzy Inference System* to form a single measure of confidence. The confidence measure indicates whether or not the output from the neural network's learning can be trusted over time.

2.1 Murphy's Rule of Combination

Dempster-Shafer theory [Smets 1990] is a general form of Bayesian theory. Bayesian theory requires knowing all of the probability laws in order to combine evidence and make a prediction. In spite of Bayesian theory, which has only propositions that are known as possible and propositions known as impossible, Dempster-Shafer theory adds propositions that are unknown. There are many rules of combination that are based on the Dempster-Shafer framework. In order to explain the Murphy's rule, some basic definitions and axioms from the Dempster-Shafer theory are needed.

Propositions of an event are called *elementary propositions* $\{\theta_1, \theta_2, ..., \theta_n\}$. These events must be exclusive. The finite set of the elementary propositions $\Theta = \{\theta_i\}$ is called the frame of discernment. The power set 2^Θ includes all possible propositions of interest. The belief in propositions is expressed with a *basic probability assignment* function: $m : 2^\Theta \rightarrow [0,1]$. The number $m(\theta_i)$ represents the total belief assigned to proposition θ_i. The basic probability assignment function must satisfy the following axioms: $m(A) \geq 0, \forall \in 2^\Theta$, $m(\varnothing) = 0$ and $\sum_{A \in 2^\Theta} m(A) = 1$.

Dempster proposed a rule of combination, assuming that all sources of evidence are independent:

$$m(C) = \frac{\sum_{A_i \cap B_j = C; C \neq \varnothing} m(A_i) m(B_j)}{\sum_{A_i \cap B_j \neq \varnothing} m(A_i) m(B_j)} \qquad (10.5)$$

Since the monitors from the DCS network that are used as sources of evidence are not independent, Dempster's rule cannot be applied. For such cases Murphy [1996] provides a rule that solves this problem:

$$m(C) = \frac{\sum_{A_i \cap B_j = C; C \neq \varnothing} f(m(A_i)m(B_j))}{\sum_{A_i \cap B_j \neq \varnothing} f(m(A_i)m(B_j))} \tag{10.6}$$

where $f(m(A_i)m(B_j)) = [m(A_i)m(B_j)]^n$ $(0.0 \leq n \leq 1.0)$. Function f is referred to as the *belief revision function*. When $n=1$, this rule becomes Dempster's rule.

In the monitors discussed here, each monitor tells a different error. These errors are normalized to values between zero and one (see Section 2.3 for details), which is used as beliefs that carry the information of how bad the learning process is of the DCS network. Therefore, from each monitor there are two propositions E and C with their beliefs: $m(E)$ (which is the normalized error value) and $m(C) = 1 - m(E)$ (which is the belief of how confident one is or how much one should trust the learning process of the DCS network). The final form of Murphy's rule is:

$$m(x, y) = \frac{(x \cdot y)^n}{(x \cdot y)^n + (1 - x)^n (1 - y)^n},$$

$$x, y \in (0,1); \ n \in [0,1]; \ n = const \tag{10.7}$$

$$m(x, y) \in (0,1)$$

where x and y are values of $m(E)$ from two monitors.

There are many ways of combining the sources of evidence. The following way is chosen, assuming there are k sources of evidence (with assigned beliefs $a_1, a_2, ..., a_k \in (0,1)$):

$$comb(1) = a_1$$
$$comb(i) = m(comb(i-1), a_i), \ i = 2, ..., k \tag{10.8}$$

where $comb(k)$ will give the final result expressed as a combined error belief. Fig. 10-2 is a graphical representation of this combination. The result that is of interest is one - $comb(k)$, which is a measure of confidence.

If there are more than two beliefs, different orders of combining them give different results (since associativity does not hold for the belief revision function f). The minimum and the maximum values of $comb(k)$ should be obtained, i.e., to find what ordering of the beliefs will give these values. The simplest approach to do this is to calculate $comb(k)$ on all permutations and determine the minimum and the maximum. However, this approach is not efficient with running time $O(k!)$.

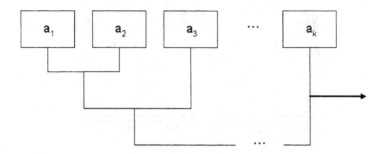

Figure 10-2. Combination Method

A claim is made here that if the beliefs are ordered in increasing order, $comb(k)$ will give the maximum value, and if they are in decreasing order it will give the minimum value. This reduces the running time to $O(k \cdot \log(k))$.

2.2 Fuzzy Inference System

Another approach for data fusion on the DCS monitors is based on fuzzy logic. For the system discussed here, the Mamdani model [Mamdani 1975] is used, which is one of the most widely used fuzzy models in practice. It is a Fuzzy Rule-based model. The rules are very simple and are based on linguistic variables, for example: IF x is *Small* AND y is *High* THEN z is *Medium*. Each input in the system is partitioned into regions. A region corresponds to a membership function (e.g., *Small*, *Medium*, etc.). The same is applied to the output variables.

In our system the monitors are normalized to values between zero and one (see Section 2.3 for details). Since the monitors are error functions, small errors (closer to zero) mean that the DCS network state is good and large errors (closer to one) mean that the DCS network state is bad. The first try was with simple triangular membership functions. Later, the system was improved with smooth functions that resulted in smoother transitions in the output. Three regions were used to partition (Fig. 10-3) the input space into *good* (with *Z-shaped curve* membership function), *normal* (with *Gaussian curve* membership function), and *bad* (with *S-shaped curve* membership function).

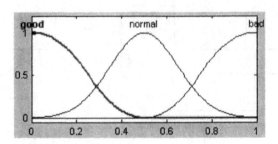

Figure 10-3. Input Variable

The output, which is a fusion of all inputs, means how much confidence or belief there is that the network has learned well. Fig. 10-4 shows the partitioning of the output into five regions: *very-low* (with *Z-shaped curve* membership function), *low, medium, high* (the last three regions with *Gaussian curve* membership function) and *very-high* (with *S-shaped curve* membership function). The lowest value, *very-low*, tells us that something is going wrong with learning process of the DCS network. Similarly, the highest value *very-high* means that the DCS network learning process is very well. The defuzzification method used to obtain a numerical value is centroid, and one example of the fuzzy rules that can result is shown in Fig. 10-5.

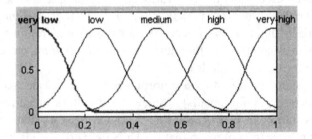

Figure 10-4. Output Variable

4. If (QE is bad) and (Q-NBR-E is bad) and (Q-NON-NBR-E is normal) and (Q-SBU-E is bad) then (confidence is very_low) (1)
5. If (QE is bad) and (Q-NBR-E is bad) and (Q-NON-NBR-E is normal) and (Q-SBU-E is normal) then (confidence is low) (1)
6. If (QE is bad) and (Q-NBR-E is bad) and (Q-NON-NBR-E is normal) and (Q-SBU-E is good) then (confidence is medium) (1)
7. If (QE is bad) and (Q-NBR-E is bad) and (Q-NON-NBR-E is good) and (Q-SBU-E is bad) then (confidence is low) (1)
8. If (QE is bad) and (Q-NBR-E is bad) and (Q-NON-NBR-E is good) and (Q-SBU-E is normal) then (confidence is medium) (1)
9. If (QE is bad) and (Q-NBR-E is bad) and (Q-NON-NBR-E is good) and (Q-SBU-E is good) then (confidence is medium) (1)

Figure 10-5. A Set of Fuzzy Rules Used in the Fuzzy Inference System

As can be seen from Fig. 10-6 on the next page, the mesh plot of the control surface of the fuzzy inference system is not a flat surface. For the inputs that are used to plot this surface, when the error values (x and y axes) are close to zero, there is a high confidence measure (z axis). This is followed by a smooth decrease in the confidence measure as the error values get closer to one.

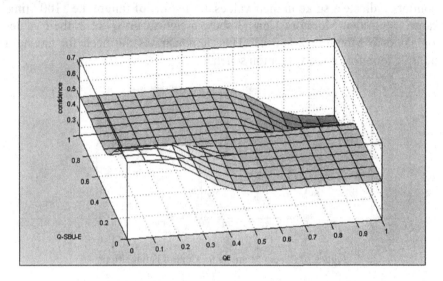

Figure 10-6. Mesh Plot of the Control Surface of the Fuzzy Inference Engine

2.3 Experimental Studies

The experimental data consists of data sets collected from an F-15 flight simulator. The tested flight-modes consisted of seven failure modes (five control failure modes and two surface failure modes) and two no-failure, or nominal, modes. The studies presented in this section consist of the result from the C_z DCS network. This network learns the stability and control derivatives associated with pitching moments due to normal force. Four independent variables, in addition to the three dependent C_z derivatives, are used as inputs into the C_z DCS network.

Neural network independent variable inputs are: mach, altitude, alpha (angle of attack), beta. The neural network dependent variable inputs are: $\Delta C_{z\alpha}$, $\Delta C_{z\dot{\alpha}}$ and $\Delta C_{z\delta}$. The outputs used for data fusion are the four monitor values. In each time step these values are normalized to values between zero and one using the current maximum from each monitor as the normalizing base. Usually this maximum is at the beginning of the learning process.

2.3.1   Learning During Flight-failure Mode

Fig. 10-7 shows the four monitor values as obtained in a real-time manner for the control failure mode - *locked left stabilator stuck at +3 degrees*. The failure was induced into the simulator at the 600th time frame (corresponds to the 100th time frame for the monitor values). All of these monitors indicate a spike in their values at the time of failure, i.e., 100th time frame. Note that Monitors 1 and 3 show a significant spike in their values compared to Monitors 2 and 4. This demonstrates the need for having a multiple monitor-based validation scheme.

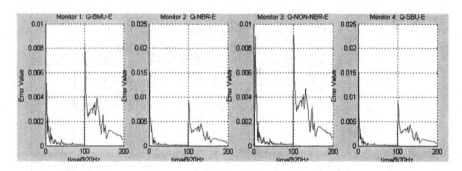

Figure 10-7. Four Monitors for Control Failure Mode

The corresponding confidence measures are obtained using the previously described methods of data fusion and are shown in Fig. 10-8. Fig. 10-8 on the next page shows the minimum and maximum values of the confidence measure acquired from the method based on Murphy's rule. Fig. 10-8 also shows the difference between the maximum and minimum values. At the time of failure (100th monitor time frame) the minimum and maximum values decrease, which indicates that the neural network cannot be trusted at that instant in time. Other useful information is indicated from the difference between the maximum and the minimum, which is increasing rapidly at the 100th time frame. In Fig. 10-8 the confidence measure obtained from the developed fuzzy inference system is shown. The confidence measure provided by the fuzzy inference system shows similar behavior, decreasing significantly at the 100th time frame and meaning that the network cannot be trusted during this time.

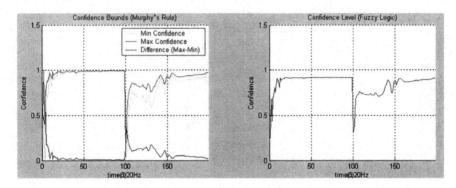

Figure 10-8. a) Confidence Measure from Murphy's Rule; b) Confidence Measure from Fuzzy Inference System

2.3.2 Learning During Flight No-failure Mode

The results from the four monitors during the neural network's learning under no-failure flight-mode are shown in Fig. 10-9. All monitors during the learning process show a steady descent with no spikes, indicating no abnormal neural network behavior.

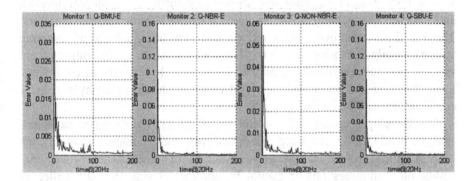

Figure 10-9. Four Monitors for No-failure Mode

Fig. 10-10 shows the confidence measure obtained from fusing these monitor values from both methods: fuzzy logic and Dempster-Shafer. From the method based on Murphy's rule, the minimum and the maximum values of the confidence measure are high and stay around the same value. Their difference is very small during the entire learning process. The fuzzy inference system shows similar results by providing a high confidence measure.

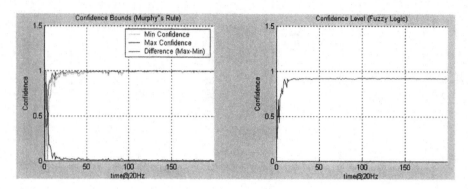

Figure 10-10. a) Confidence Measure from Murphy's Rule; b) Confidence Measure from
Fuzzy Inference System

3.   SUMMARY

A novel approach for validation of soft computing systems (neural
network) embedded in safety-critical online self-adaptive systems is
presented in the form of run-time risk assessment methodology.   The
approach is based on run-time operational monitoring of the neural network
and data fusion techniques for combining outputs from various monitors.
The run-time monitoring is based on the stability analysis of dynamic
systems similar, in principle, to the Lyapunov analysis.   The outputs from
various monitors are fused together to form a single measure of confidence
from the data fusion techniques of Dempster-Shafer (Murphy's rule of
combination) and Fuzzy Inference System.

The developed concept of run-time monitoring and data fusion can serve
as a powerful tool for assessing risk in real-time and a complementary means
of validating on-line self-adaptive systems in cases where traditional
validation techniques fail or cannot be applied.   Using the data collected
from an F-15 flight simulator, heuristic evidence is provided that supports
the prospects of using run-time monitoring and data fusion techniques to
form a run-time risk assessment methodology. This work can be viewed as a
step towards a solution to the V&V of online self-adaptive systems. This is
a complex yet very important problem facing the dependability research
community. It is believed that the application boundaries for adaptive and
intelligent systems will widen as the underlying software/system verification
and validation theory becomes better understood and derived techniques
achieve a higher level of maturity. Current work on this approach consists
of fine-tuning the fuzzy inference system (modifying rules, membership
functions) and providing a signaling system, similar to traffic control system

that can warn the pilot/aircraft validation engineers of an imminent threat due to neural network misbehavior.

REFERENCES

Bruske, Jorg and Gerald Sommer. 1994. Dynamic Cell Structures. In *Proceedings of Neural Information Processing Systems (NIPS)*, 497-504.

Jorgensen, Charles C. 1997. Direct Adaptive Aircraft Control Using Dynamic Cell Structure Neural Networks. NASA Technical Memorandum 112198, NASA Ames Research Center.

Kohonen, T. 1988. Self-Organization and Associative Memory, Second Edition, Springer-Verlag, New York.

Mamdani, E.H. and S. Assilian. 1975. An Experiment in Linguistic Synthesis with a Fuzzy Logic Controller. *International Journal of Man-Machine Studies*. Vol. 7, No. 1, pp. 1-13.

Murphy, Robin R. 1998. Dempster-Shafer Theory for Sensor Fusion in Autonomous Mobile Robots. *IEEE Trans. Robotics and Automation*. vol. 14, no. 2, pp. 97206.

Murphy, Robin R. 1996. Adaptive Rule of Combination for Observations Over Time. Multisensor Fusion and Integration for Intelligent Systems (MFI96), Dec. 8-11, 1996, pp.125-131.

Smets, Phillipe. 1990. The Combination of Evidence in the Transferable Belief Model. *IEEE Transactions on Pattern Analysis and Machine Intelligence*. Vol. 12, No. 5, May 1990.

Yerramalla, Sampath; Yan Liu; Edgar Fuller; Bojan Cukic; and Srikanth Gururajan. 2004. An Approach to V&V of Embedded Adaptive Systems. III NASA-Goddard /IEEE Workshop on Formal Approaches to Agent Based Systems.

Yerramalla, Sampath; Edgar Fuller; and Bojan Cukic. 2004. A Validation Approach for Neural Network Based Online Self-adaptive Systems. Submitted for publication at the Special Issue of Software, Practice and Experience Journal on Experiences with Auto-Adaptive and Reconfigurable Systems.

Yerramalla, Sampath; Yan Liu; Edgar Fuller; Bojan Cukic; and Srikanth Gururajan. 2004. Adaptive Control Software: Can We Guarantee Safety? Submitted for publication at the First International Workshop on Software Cybernetics.

About the Authors

Brian J. Taylor

Brian J. Taylor, a Principal Member of Research at the Institute for Scientific Research, Inc., has been working in the area of verification and validation of neural networks for over seven years. His work includes the development, analysis, and verification and validation of neural network components for F-15 adaptive flight control systems within the NASA Dryden Flight Research Center Intelligent Flight Control System project. He is also the Co-Principal Investigator (PI) on the NASA IV&V Facility-funded effort for the "Development of Methodologies for the IV&V of Neural Networks" and a technical expert on a NASA Ames Research Center STTR-funded "A Formal Method for the Verification and Validation of Neural Network High Assurance Systems." Mr. Taylor holds a B.S. in Electrical Engineering, a B.S. in Computer Engineering, and a M.S. in Electrical Engineering.

Dr. Marjorie A. Darrah

Dr. Darrah is a Principal Scientist and Visualization and Informatics Branch Supervisor at the Institute for Scientific Research, Inc., Fairmont, WV. She holds the position of Co-Principal Investigator (PI) on a NASA funded effort on "Development of Methodologies for IV&V of Neural Networks." She is Principal Investigator of the NASA Ames STTR effort, "A Formal Method for the Verification and Validation of Neural Network High Assurance Systems." Her responsibilities at ISR include research and development in the areas of Neural Networks, Data Mining, Virtual Reality, and Education. She was also a researcher for the Goddard Institute for

Systems, Software and Technology Research project where she focused on implementing innovative human machine interfaces. Before joining ISR in 2002, she was the chairperson of the Division of Natural Sciences and a Mathematics professor at Alderson-Broaddus College, Philippi, WV. Dr. Darrah holds a BS, MS, and PhD in Mathematics.

Dr. Laura L. Pullum

Dr. Laura Pullum, a Principal Scientist and Vice-President of Research and Advanced Concepts at the Institute for Scientific Research, Inc., has over 20 years of experience in system and software dependability research and development. Dr. Pullum is the author of Software Fault Tolerance - Techniques and Implementation and has written over 350 papers and reports. She has performed research and development in software fault tolerance and system integrity for NASA, the U.S. Air Force, the Naval Surface Warfare Center, the National Science Foundation, the U.S. Army, industry, and universities. In addition, Dr. Pullum holds a patent in this field. Her research has ranged from invention of new techniques and approaches, to analysis of system performance and cost, to selection of appropriate techniques and other design assistance. Dr. Pullum holds a B.S. in Math, a Masters in Operations Research, an MBA, and a Doctorate of Science in Systems Engineering and Operations Research.

James T. Smith

James T. Smith, a Principal Member Research Staff at the Institute for Scientific Research, has over 20 years experience in the development and fielding of advanced technical systems. Currently, he is involved in a NASA IV&V-funded effort for the development of certification guidance of neural network-based real-time control systems. He continues to actively monitor the pulse of emerging technologies for ISR, and has a newsletter that he distributes. He has over twenty years of artificial intelligence-related work experience. His prior work included design and development of expert systems for the DARPA Pilot's Associate program, and an Artificial Intelligence toolkit successfully used in the implementation of real-time expert systems. Mr. Smith holds a B.S. in Mathematics/Physics, a M.Ed. in Mathematics/Education, and a M.S. in Applied Mathematics/Computer Science.

Spiro T. Skias

Spiro T. Skias is a Senior Project Manager at the Institute for Scientific Research, Inc. Mr. Skias is the project manager of three neural network-related projects: Development of Methodologies for the IV&V of Neural Networks for the NASA IV&V Facility, the Intelligent Flight Control

System for the NASA Dryden Flight Research center, and A Formal Method for the Verification and Validation of Neural Network High Assurance Systems, an STTR with ProLogic for the NASA Ames Research Center. Prior to his role as a project manager, Mr. Skias worked as a software engineer and computer science researcher with focus on data mining, power plant control systems, and software architecture and engineering. He has also honorably completed four years of military service with the United States Navy as an Operations Specialist. Mr. Skias holds a B.S. in Computer Science.

Dr. Bojan Cukic

Dr. Bojan Cukic is an associate professor of Computer Science and Engineering at West Virginia University. His research interests include software engineering for high assurance systems, fault-tolerant system architectures, computer security and biometrics. He is a Principal Investigator on several research projects related to verification and validation of adaptive systems. NASA Office of Safety and Mission Assurance awarded him the Tycho Brahe Research Excellence Award in 2004 for the research on real-time neural network monitoring techniques. Dr. Cukic is the author of more than 100 refereed publications. He received a B.S. in Computer Engineering from the University of Ljubljana, Slovenia, and M.S. and Ph.D. degrees in Computer Science from the University of Houston, TX.

Dr. Edgar J. Fuller

Dr. Edgar Fuller is an Assistant Professor in the Department of Mathematics at West Virginia University. He received his Ph.D. from the University of Georgia in the area of differential geometry and topology. He currently works on applications of topology and geometry to the study of autonomous learners, especially those in mission critical applications. His other interests include applications of computational geometry to knot theory, the analysis of non-deterministic systems, bioinformatics, and mathematics education.

Sampath K. Yerramalla

Sampath Yerramalla is a Doctoral Candidate in Electrical Engineering in the Lane Department of Computer Science and Electrical Engineering at the West Virginia University. Yerramalla has been working in the area of neural networks based adaptive control systems for over 5 years. His work focuses on the development, analysis, and applications of Lyapunov based stability techniques for verification and validation of neural networks in adaptive systems. Yerramalla's work has been sponsored by the West Virginia research interests include control systems, artificial neural networks, fuzzy logic, and adaptive systems. He holds a M.S. in Control Systems Engineering.

Index